PAT CHAPMAN'S
NOODLE BOOK

PAT CHAPMAN'S
NOODLE BOOK

PHOTOGRAPHY

BY

Gerrit Buntrock

Hodder & Stoughton

Copyright © 1998 by Pat Chapman

The right of Pat Chapman to be identified as the Author of the
Work has been asserted by him in accordance with the Copyright,
Designs and Patents Act 1988.

First published in 1998 by Hodder & Stoughton
A division of Hodder Headline PLC

1 3 5 7 9 8 6 4 2

British Library Cataloguing in Publication Data

ISBN 0 340 71539 1

Designed by Peter Ward
Printed and bound in Great Britain by
Butler & Tanner Limited

HODDER & STOUGHTON
A division of Hodder Headline PLC
338 Euston Road
London NW1 3BH

CONTENTS

PROLOGUE

It is always a pleasure to write a book, the more so when one is invited to do so. I am certain that it would never have occurred to me write about noodles. Indeed, when the invitation came, two years ago, I did not know much about them. Like most people, I just took them for granted.

In fact I owe the concept of this book to two very good friends of mine.

It was Robin Weir's idea. Robin is a remarkable man. He's one of the few people I've met who run two totally different careers in tandem and he is at the top of both of them. He directs a product development and marketing company, which takes him on long sales trips around the world. At the time of writing he has been to Japan fifty-six times, and there is no continent he does not visit regularly.

His other career is in the food business. He has been an active and energetic member of the Guild of Food Writers, that thriving body to which most British food and drink journalists and authors, including myself, belong. Robin is a successful food writer, with such co-authored titles as the best-selling *The Compleat Mustard* published by Constable, and *Ices, The Definitive Guide*, published by Grub Street Press under his belt.

As if that is not enough, Robin is a food consultant to multiples, such as Sainsbury, where he has pioneered and operated training and seminar sessions for buyers, and is also a consultant to G. Costa, owner and manufacturer of the Blue Dragon brand, more of which appears on page 233.

Tim Barlow is the energetic, ambitious Managing Director of G. Costa Ltd. Established in 1879, G. Costa was for a over century based in London's Peckham, an unfashionable suburb of south-east London. During that time, it built up a reputation as the exclusive importer and UK distributor of a huge list of fine, specialist, quality foods. At Peckham it began to produce its own brands, of which Blue Dragon is one. Since 1988, Tim, a former salesman, has been in charge of the operation, and under his guidance Blue Dragon has grown ten fold and entered areas other than Chinese products, namely Thai, Korean and Japanese ranges. Not satisfied with that, Tim has acquired two manufacturing plants in Wales, and has been a major force in getting noodles established as a serious product in Britain and beyond. He also closed the Peckham head-quarters, and boldly moved the entire operation to the company's warehouse base in Aylesford, Kent. Tim is an intense and relentless worker, but one whose infectious laugh punctuates his conversation and no doubt seals the deal of the moment.

When Robin put the idea of this book to Tim, he enthusiastically and wholeheartedly embraced it. I am thrilled that they entrusted the project to me (in fact it is a double thrill, because it was at my house that they both first met); I hope they both like the result.

FOREWORD

If you thought noodles were simply something encountered in a minor role at the Chinese takeaway in the form of Chow Mein, I've got news for you! Noodles are, according to the supermarkets, set to take the millennium by storm. They are predicted to become as popular in the West as the mighty pasta, but with a lot more to offer. Like pasta, they are made of wheat, but, being made of softer flour, even dried noodles are three times quicker to cook than pasta. Noodles are probably the world's oldest fast food, and they are undoubtedly the world's easiest ingredient to cook. As such, they are great for people in a hurry – just immerse them in boiling water, wait three to five minutes, strain and eat! It's that simple.

But noodles are so versatile too. They can be made from buckwheat, rice and mung beans, they may be steamed, pan-fried, stir-fried and deep-fried, giving a range of tastes and textures unlike any other staples. Noodles are cheap to buy, and they store indefinitely. They are nutritionally healthy, satisfyingly filling, and above all, they are perceived to be exotic. Though of minimal flavour themselves, they take on and absorb everything around them, and are thus perfect companions for any other non-staple ingredient you care to name. Noodles are delicious hot or cold, in stews and stir-fries, spicy or mild. In this book, all types of noodle are described, along with all their cooking methods. And as the hundred recipes in the book show, they can make appearances at every course – as crispy nibbles, starters and snacks, soups, salads, and main courses, which I have divided into chapters containing meat, poultry, fish and seafood, and vegetables, and there are even noodle desserts.

I first encountered spaghetti at school, and on a youthful trip to Florence, but I had no idea how to cook it. In the early 1960s, when I was a student, a female I fancied, but did not dare to woo, cooked it for me and the bloke *she* fancied, at her bedsit. I never got the girl, nor did I get much of a recipe, though she did say 'just cook it for ten minutes'. But I did get hold of some spaghetti, which I gave to my mum along with those terse instructions. Unfortunately, she cooked it in her beloved pressure cooker, and the result was something resembling hot wallpaper paste. She did not try it again, and it was many years before I learned how easy it was to cook myself.

As for noodles, I first encountered them in the Cantonese restaurants which were springing up all over Britain in the early 1960s. A little later I went on a business trip to Singapore, where some good friends took me on a gastronomic tour. We naturally visited the amazing open-air food stalls, where we watched Chinese food being prepared in front of us. I marvelled at the freshness of the ingredients, and the dexterity of the cooks, who tossed the contents of their woks high into the air, then deftly caught them again, whilst, at the same time, flambéeing them in a spectacular whoosh of fire. Noodles had never tasted so good.

When it was suggested I write this book, I realised that although many of my previous books contain noodle recipes, I did not know much about them. I had always taken noodles for granted, and I knew there was a great deal more waiting to be explored, and a lot of research waiting to be done. For a start, I needed to define all the different types of noodles, and find out how they were made. I wanted to know about the history of both noodles and pasta; which came first is one of the great food debates. I also wanted to understand the differences and similarities between the two. Why do we compartmentalise them? Surely noodles, with their versatility, could be used, not just as an oriental speciality, but with any sauce or flavouring from anywhere in the world. Until I started work on this book, this thought had not occurred to me.

I decided to find out all I could about noodles. Before doing anything else, I needed the professional perspective. First, I interviewed Paul Ugo, MD of London's oldest fresh noodle makers, The Oriental Noodle Company, a three-generation team in Holloway. I also talked to Europe's largest noodle-producing factory, situated in, of all places, Belgium, and to Liam Mackam, Sainsbury's chief noodle and pasta buyer, to bring as much up-to-date background information to the book as possible.

Then it was time for my wife Dominique and me to pack our bags and sally forth to the noodle lands to collect stories, facts, anecdotes, and new recipe ideas. Of course, no noodle book would be complete without traditional noodle dishes. To start, we went east, to the home of the noodle, where we visited factories, chefs, kitchens and households in China, Japan, and south-east Asia. Whilst in Japan, we visited a Japanese noodle factory, and the world's fourth largest soy sauce producer, Shoda in Tokyo.

The result of the trip is a varied and exciting collection of recipes, with their age-old traditional, familiar and increasingly popular flavours of garlic and ginger, with lashings of soy sauce. Many such noodle dishes have remained unaltered since they were devised two thousand years ago. In their classic and traditional form these dishes contained no New World ingredients, such as tomato, bell pepper and sweetcorn, although there is no reason why we, like modern Asian chefs, should not add them.

The book contains many old favourites, such as Chinese Chow Mein, Black Bean Egg Noodles, Malaccan Laksa or Thai Green Curry Noodles. And lovers of hot food will die for Szechuan Chilli Rice Noodles, or Penang Paradise Curry Crispy Noodles. The adventurous can learn the secrets of Noodle Bird's Nest, Noodle Spring rolls, and how to tie noodles into bows or wrap them around Thai Golden Thread Pork Balls. And the innovative can try Japanese Noodle Sushi and Tokyo Fish Soba.

Naturally, as a curryholic, I took my quest for noodles to the curry lands. In all the years since noodles were invented, they never really caught on in India, but there are a few noodle dishes from curry lands, and some of these are presented here – delightful spicy dishes from India, Burma, Indonesia, Malaysia and Singapore. The Middle East is another zone where noodles hardly took off, but I managed to locate one recipe, Tutmaj, from Armenia and Turkey.

Wanting still more, I ventured further afield, to such cosmopolitan cities as Sydney, San Francisco and New York. In all three cities, there are fresh, innovative chefs and restaurants, where old and new, East and West happily mix, evolving great new taste combinations, fashionably called fusion dishes. And why not? There need be no rules, and this inspired me to create such wonderful new noodle dishes as Darling Harbour Crab Claws, Golden Gate Lime and Honey Sweet and Sour, Texan Chilli Bean Noodle, and Bronx Pastrami Glass Noodle. From closer to home come Noodles with Butter and Black Pepper, the aromatic Fresh Herbs Noodles, and a variation on my signature dish, Chilli-baked, Honey-glazed Boned Quail, stuffed, not with its normal spicy rice, but with noodles! Stealing pasta's ground, there's Noodles Napoletano, with an Italian tomato and garlic sauce, or a traditional mince and celery

Bolognaise Noodle, and the chicken variant, both indistinguishable from spaghetti, and twice as quick to cook. And I hope you'll agree, my Paella Noodles are a fascinating innovation, and Canelloni Noodle Pancakes are just wicked.

As explained in the prologue, I have teamed up for this exciting new book with Blue Dragon, whose legendary, brand-leading range of oriental products is sold worldwide, so even for the more exotic recipes, you will be able to get your ingredients easily from your favourite deli or supermarket, assisted by the Store Cupboard List in Appendix 2.

I certainly know a lot more about noodles now than when I began my research, and I hope you will too by reading and cooking the fruits of my labour. Noodles *are* charismatic. All the professionals I have met are passionate about them, and I share their view that the day of the noodle is very nearly upon us.

I hope that my efforts will in some small way help bring that day a little closer. But of course, for that to happen, we need you to become a serious noodler.

Please enjoy my book.

Pat Chapman

Haslemere
December 1997

INTRODUCTION

Noodles versus Pasta

I have to confess that, until I started the research for this book, I was not totally clear about the differences between noodles and pasta. To tell the truth, I had never even thought about it. At most, it seemed to me that dried noodles were a little quicker to cook than dried pasta. But was this the case with fresh pasta and noodles? Pasta came in a greater variety of shapes, such as straight rods and tubes, bow ties, shells and ribbons. Noodles only seemed to come in strips and rods, which were sometimes straight, sometimes irregular, and they could be made of a variety of different ingredients such as wheat and rice (but what had egg to do with it?), whereas the strictly European pasta appeared to be made from only wheat. But was it the same wheat, since wheat noodles and wheat spaghetti seemed to have different cooking properties? I had also firmly believed that noodles should only be eaten with oriental flavourings, preferably with chopsticks, while the pasta family must be confined to Mediterranean flavours, such as tomato, basil, cheese, olive oil and black pepper. But why should this be? Who made such rules? The time had come to get to the bottom of it all.

Following the fashion on trendy television programmes, I decided to start by seeking the *vox populi* on the subject, on the streets of London outside a branch of Spaghetti House, the celebrated restaurant chain. I then did the same outside a Pasta House in New York, and a noodle shop in Tokyo. In both London and New York, the respondents were, at first, quite clear in their beliefs: to some pasta meant just spaghetti, to others it meant Italian food. Pressed to explain further, they became less sure of themselves. If pasta is Italian food, what, then, is antipasto? And if pasta is just spaghetti, what are tagliatelle and fettuccine, or macaroni and penne, to mention a few?

As for noodles, they were just a dish encountered at a Chinese restaurant weren't they? In Tokyo, where there is a Noodle House around every corner, the question, posed through an interpreter, evoked a somewhat incredulous response, with a withering smile reserved for ignorant foreigners, along the lines of, 'if you don't know what noodles are, sonny, you haven't lived'. As to pasta, not one Japanese person questioned knew what it, or Italian food was. And although I didn't carry out a survey on the streets of Naples or Rome, I suspect that many Italians would have little idea about oriental noodles. So it was time to get out the reference books.

Noodles and Pasta defined

The word 'noodle' does not appear in the Latin dictionary, nor do 'spaghetti', 'macaroni', 'tagliatelle' or any other such contemporary Italian pasta terms. Moving along, the only reference to 'noodle' in my 1932 Oxford dictionary is 'a simpleton, hence noodledom'! Sixty years on, and this use has almost passed into obscurity. In the USA and Canada, 'noodle', along with 'noddle', means a (person's) head. But for the most common contemporary use of the word, Oxford describes noodles as 'pasta made from flour and water cut into thin flat strips, ribbons or strands; the word deriving from 18th century German, Nudel'. Does this mean noodles and pasta are one and the same thing? More clues required! The classic food encyclopedia, *Larousse Gastronomique* says, 'noodles can be used fresh or dried. Famous Italian noodles are tagliatelle and the slightly broader fettuccine. Noodles can be served as a main dish with butter, cheese au gratin, with tomato or meat sauce, etc., as the classic accompaniment to rich game stews, coq au vin and white meat. They are also used as a garnish for soups and consommés, often in the form of small short noodles.'

So, it was becoming clear that the words noodle and pasta were interchangeable, at least with regards to the Italian version.

Next, I thought I had better define the word 'pasta'. Again the word does not appear in the 1932 Oxford dictionary, so its entrance into English usage had to be quite recent. Nor does it appear in Latin, though *pastus* means 'pasture' or 'food'. The English word 'paste' translates into Latin as *gluten*, and 'pastry' as *crustum*. That takes us into the realms of baking, where 'baker' translates as *pistor*, and a 'bake-house' as *pistrina*. All close, but not the answer. Where else might the word be used? Since noodle is of German derivation, I thought I'd see what the Germans have to say about pasta: in German it is *Teigwaren*, where *teig* means 'dough', and *knödel* means 'dumpling'. Back to Larousse for a definition of 'pasta': 'a dough made from durum wheat semolina, water and often eggs. Pasta is shaped in various ways and is sometimes flavoured. It is sold fresh or dried, ready to cook in boiling salted water (to serve with a sauce).'

So, if pasta is a dough, does antipasti refer to any Italian food without dough? Clearly not, since bread is popular in Italy, and it is not called pasta. And, why in the English-speaking world, have we recently replaced the correct word (Italian) 'noodles' with 'pasta'? Next stop, the Italian dictionary. Yes, Larousse is correct, pasta means, simply 'dough'. *Impasto per dolce* means pastry and *pasticcini* (pastries) *in brodo* (broth) is a noodle soup. *Impasto* means 'to knead'. Look up 'noodles' in the Italian dictionary, and we find it translates to *taglierini*. *Tagliare* in Italian means 'to cut', and *taglio* 'cutting'. This leads us to *taglietellie*. *Telle* is little, so *tagliatelle* means 'little cuts'. Incidentally, *verme* means 'worm', so *vermicelli* means 'little worms'!

But we aren't through yet. Remember that Larousse definition for 'pasta' two paragraphs back? It mentions two other words we have not previously encountered: 'durum' and 'semolina'. Back to the dictionaries. *Durus/durum* in Latin means 'hard, harsh, rough, hardy, tough, rude, uncultured, severe, unfeeling, impudent, miserly, hard, cruel'. Collins dictionary told me that 'durum' or 'durum wheat' is: 'a variety of wheat with a high gluten content, used chiefly to make pastas, from the Latin *triticum durum*.' Pastas? So it's now in the plural! Better look 'pasta' up in Collins: 'any of several variously-shaped edible preparations made from a flour and water dough, such as spaghetti.' As for *triticum*, it means 'wheat' in Latin. As for 'semolina', it comes from the Latin *simila* (fine flour). The most common semolina is obtained by grinding hard wheat (durum) into granules by the milling process, which will be examined in the next chapter. Best grade semolina is made by grinding the wheat kernel. Lesser grades contain more of the grain. Fine semolinas are used to make pasta. Any grain can be used to make semolina. White semolina, for example, is ground from rice, semolina for polenta from maize, and that for the Russian dish, *kasha,* from buckwheat. Just one more word to define: 'gluten'. This is a protein present in wheat, and to a lesser extent, oats and rye, whose concentration determines the 'strength' of the flour. The more gluten present, the more cohesive the dough becomes.

So, noodles are made from a particular grain, which must be milled into flour to make a dough, then processed by hand or machine, to create strands or strings. Whilst the German word 'noodles' can be used for both the Italian and Oriental versions, the word 'pasta' refers only to Italian noodles. The oriental dough can be made from a number of grain types, including soft wheat, all of which we meet in the next chapter, while the dough for Italian noodles, or pasta, confines itself to hard wheat flour. Fresh pasta (including noodles, spaghetti, ravioli, cannelloni and lasagne) is made with flour, not semolina, and always contains eggs. Pasta, fresh or dried, comes in a greater variety of shapes than its oriental counterpart. Both can be pre-coloured or flavoured, and Italy prides itself on using only natural flavourings such as purées of spinach, tomato, mushroom, and prawn.

Both noodles and pasta are easy to make by hand. Mostly, though, both are machine-made by passing the dough between rollers to form thin sheets which are then cut into strips. Fancy cutters may be used to produce wavy edges, squares, rectangles, circles and triangles. For pasta only, other cutters can shape shells, bow ties and ribbons. Cylindrical pasta is made by forcing the dough through a pierced plate. The hole through which the dough is forced may be straight, curved, notched or fluted to produce hollow tubes of various sizes and shapes. Drying takes place in hot cabinets, and the best pasta has a translucent almost amber appearance. Classic pastas are categorised into soup pastas, long pastas and short pastas.

The Great Debate

There seems to be an obsession with some pasta food writers to establish which came first – the noodle or pasta. Some attribute the noodle's arrival in China to the great medieval explorer, Marco Polo. Others say he found it there and brought it back to Italy. Neither version, however, is correct. Let's examine the facts.

About twelve thousand years ago, when mankind first began to cultivate the land of the fertile crescent, in the area now called Iraq, Jordan and Lebanon, one of the first major crops was wheat. It was eaten in a fairly unrefined form, but before long, a process was developed to make it more palatable. The wheat grain was cracked, partly cooked, dried in the sun and then ground. It was stored until required, when it was reconstituted with water in a porridge-like form. It was probably mankind's first processed food. Known as *burghul*, it is still enjoyed today in the Middle East. Some time after that, the complex process of milling fine flour, and with it, dough-making was slowly developed. Simple unleavened flat breads were dry-fried. By 2000 BC the ancient Egyptians had mastered the art of fermentation, to make wine and beer. They also discovered how to ferment dough (leavening), designed a complex oven, and prefected the baking of bread. By 1500 BC they were baking round risen loaves. Unfortunately, although there is ample archeological evidence of the evolution of the grinding wheel and the oven, no evidence remains showing whether or not the unleavened dough was ever made into noodles by the Egyptians. But the very absence of pictorial evidence in wall paintings and the like, means that, in all probability, they were not.

The secrets and skills of the milling process slowly spread from Egypt, eastwards along the trading routes. Earliest records of it's reaching China indicate that the ancient Chinese had learned to mill flour by the time of the Han dynasty (206 BC to AD 221). What did they do with it? Bread, as such, has never figured largely in the Chinese culinary repertoire, although in some regions, steamed dumplings (*jiaozi*) are a favourite staple. Noodles are popular all over China, and since Chinese food has remained largely unaltered over the years, it is reasonable to conclude that the ancients made noodles from their dough. The first firm date is set by Chinese historian Shu Hsi, who states that noodles were an invention of the common people. He believes that by about AD 200 even the Han emperors had discovered the noodle. We know for certain from other early writings, that by the Tang dynasty (AD 618–907) noodles and wonton had become popular at court, although only the former were available for the ordinary people. By the twelfth century, restaurants, including the renowned Noodle Shops had opened all over China. To this day in northern China, wheat and buckwheat noodles are more common than rice as the staple, being cheaper and, so say their supporters, more satisfying because they take longer to digest. In south China, where rice noodles predominate, the view is different.

During the twelfth century, the secrets of noodle-making were introduced by the Chinese into Japan, and Japanese noodles at once evolved in their own style. A Japanese Buddhist monk named Genkei wrote in the fifteenth century about *udon* and *somen* noodles, and the first written mention of *soba* was in the diary of a priest named Jisho in 1614. The first Japanese noodle shop opened at around this time. Remarkably *ramen*, or Chinese-style noodles did not appear in Japan until Chinese traders introduced them at the end of the nineteenth century.

The peoples of Thailand, Korea, Laos and Vietnam, are all of Chinese ancestry, and all took the art and skills of noodle-cooking with them when they left China many centuries ago. This has resulted in some interesting national dishes, some of which appear in my recipes.

Just as milling skills spread eastwards from ancient Europe, so they did westwards. We know that the Greeks made dough and bread, yet in all the plentiful Greek writings, nowhere do we read of noodles, nor do we see them depicted on the famous Greek urn decorations. Yet both these sources portay the most intimate details about Greek food, and the people's way of life. The same can be said of the equally prolific Roman writings and art, in which nothing leads us to pasta-type food. In his culinary study of Ancient Greece, *Siren Feasts*, Andrew Dalby makes no mention of pasta or noodles. One school of thought attributes noodle-making to the ancient country of central Europe, Etruria. The Etruscans were contemporary to the ancient Greeks and pre-dated the Romans, but, although they did make noodles, there is no tangible evidence that they passed such skills to the Romans. The great Roman food writer Apicius, writing in the first century AD, would undoubtedly have recorded such a significant food, had it existed then.

The Spice Route had been established by 100 BC linking China with the Mediterranean, and for over 1700 years, it became a hive of active two-directional trading, involving Chinese, Central Asian, Persian, Indian, Arab, and Italian merchants. Indeed, from its inception in Roman times, fortunes had been made by many middlemen, trading spices, silk and slaves for gold. It was the relentless lust for oriental luxuries that ultimately drained Rome of its wealth, and by AD 400, made inevitable the decline of the Roman Empire.

Noodles first appeared in Persian recipe books in pre-medieval times. Called *Reshteh*, meaning 'thread', these thin wheat noodles were eaten in a soup called *Ash-e-Reshteh* as early as pre-Islamic times. Today Moslem pilgrims still eat it on the eve of their departure to Mecca. Its variation, called *Aush*, is found in Afghanistan.

Tutmaj (see page 106) is the Turkish variation of this dish. Other occasional noodle dishes are to be found all over the Middle East. The Spice Route continued to operate well beyond the time of the great European spice explorations of the fifteenth century. The final part of the Route took the cargoes over the inhospitable deserts of the Middle East. The trading monopoly here was in the hands of Arab nomads, whose camel caravans were perfectly adapted to onerous travelling. Upon arrival at the Mediterranean ports, the Arabs traded with Europeans, amongst whom the merchants of Venice, immortalised by Shakespeare, predominated. Their armed Venetian galleons commanded the Mediterranean seas, and with a near monopoly on trade with inland Europe, they could simply name their price.

The Arabs also became very wealthy, and with that came their thirst for power. In the name of their new-found religion, Islam, they used their wealth and power to become empire builders. Mohammed was forty when he founded the Islamic religion in AD 630, which led the Arabs to extend their territory in the name of Allah. His followers took Damascus. During the late seventh century, they captured Sind (Pakistan), went on into India, and later entered China, where their descendants became the Mongols. At the same time, the Arabs, with little opposition, captured all the north African territories of the southern Mediterranean, and known as the Moors, easily took Spain, and even went into France, occupying the southern half of that country, until they were driven out by resolute Christian opposition in 732.

It was not just luxuries that travelled up and down the Spice Route. Dried fruit, nuts, pottery, carpets, fabrics, weapons, indeed anything which could be bought and sold, were carried. It is quite conceivable that dried noodles from China were one such commodity. It is equally conceivable that noodles would have been distributed further westwards by Venetians and Arabs. This could validate the first European reference to noodles in Sicily in the Middle Ages. The island came under Arab domination in 827, and, according to food writer Claudia Roden, they brought durum wheat flour there, having acquired it from Persian traders, and the Sicilians made it into pasta. We do know that the Arabs did not bring wheat itself into Italy, because as we saw earlier, the Romans made bread. Whether they used durum wheat flour for this is not clear. And even if the Arabs did bring it to Sicily, it does not prove that the Sicilians made noodles from it, nor is there any evidence of noodle-making in any Arab territory. Semolina, a by-product of durum wheat flour, was then, as now, used in Italy as an ingredient in bread-making, puddings and, slightly further afield, in the age-old north African dish couscous.

What is certain is that noodles did not catch on in mainland Italy at that time. So could that early reference to noodles in Sicily have concerned imported Chinese noodles? If it did, they would undoubtedly have been an expensive and rare luxury, available only to the rich and princely. But it was equally obvious that the secrets of their manufacture were not difficult to learn. By the 1400s, noodles were being made in Italy, first in Naples and Genoa, and a little later in Rome.

We do know that noodles were adored by one well-heeled royal. Catherine de' Medici was a daughter of the great dynastic trading family who owned Florence and Tuscany. Following her marriage to Henry II of France, she introduced noodles into the French court in the mid-sixteenth century, after which they spread into other fashionable homes in Europe.

As I mentioned earlier, the classic noodle recipes from China and the orient contained no New World ingredients, because, quite simply, they were devised hundreds of years before Columbus discovered such delights as tomatoes and capsicum peppers. Even now oriental recipes manage perfectly well without them. Yet, it is almost impossible to imagine an Italian pasta sauce without the wonderful flavour, aroma and colour of the Italian plum tomato. It is indispensable surely. Yet, unlike the lightning spread of the chilli to the East, the tomato took centuries to become an important ingredient in Italian pasta. So what did the medieval cooks use? The answer is, amongst other things, olive oil, garlic, onion, herbs, wine, mushrooms, and peas. Black pepper, meat and poultry were options too, but these were luxuries, and not on offer to commoners. This fully explains why the original and traditional Napoletana recipe for pasta contains no tomatoes. It appears on page 207 as a testament to history.

In Britain, by late Tudor times, we find that a food called 'macrows' (from the Greek *makros*, meaning long) was made in long tubes from a 'wheaten paste'. By the eighteenth century, it had become known as 'macaroni', indeed the word was used to describe all varieties of pasta at that time. Macaroni and vermicelli became essential pantry requirements in the homes of Georgian nobility, and were used in recipes by such established cookery writers as Hanna Glasse as early as 1747. It was not long before they were in demand all over the British Empire. They had reached India by the height of Empire. Wyvern (a Colonel Kenney-Herbert), one of the most respected food writers of the time, says in 1880: 'Macaroni is the best known of the numerous Italian paste (sic) family'. He warns 'remember, it is a much handled comestible, and washing it in water is not enough'. Various pastas were available by the beginning of the twentieth century. One Anglo-Indian cookbook gives a recipe for making the dough, using eggs and flour, and no water. 'Roll it out to a sheet the thickness of an eight anna piece,' (a low value Indian coin) 'then cut it into small squares, or into any shape or design you please. If pipe macaroni be required, cut the sheet into ribbons of the required width, put longways over glass pipes, and draw the pipes out as the pastry hardens'.

In India proper, although noodles have never featured largely in the diet, they have been enjoyed in savoury dishes, and even more importantly in sweet dishes, for as long as anyone can remember, though we do not know exactly when that was. By 2500 BC, the world's third literate civilisation, in what is now called the Indus Valley in Pakistan, was using grinding stones, not unlike those in Egypt, to make flour. Plentiful well-preserved remains have recently been unearthed. Sadly, though, as elsewhere, it is not possible to deduce what they made with their dough. Since Indian food has slowly evolved from that time, clearly, bread, similar to that made in India today, was made, with flour milled on those very stones. Judging by the fact that vermicelli recipes exist in various Indian regions, and the word 'vermicelli' has an equivalent in most of India's languages, we can assume that vermicelli came from early times. In Hindi, for example, the word is *Siwain*; in Tamil, *Semiya*; in Marathi, *Shevaya*; in Bengali, *Sewai*; in Kannada, *Shavige*; and in Kashmiri, *Ku'nu*. One early pre-Moghul southern Indian royal described his *semiya payasa* as a pudding, 'with cream, butter, molasses and sandalwood, flavoured as the eye of the moon'. We may never know whether Indian noodle-making predated Chinese. In neighbouring Nepal and Tibet, the ancestry is almost certainly Chinese. Wheat noodles are routinely and predominantly made there, though rice, maize and millet doughs are also used.

As for Marco Polo, he was born in 1254, into a family of Venetian traders. His father and uncle decided to venture along the Spice Route as far as it would take them, to see what trading opportunities might exist It took a minimum of two years to traverse the Spice Route from the Mediterranean to Peking (then under the control of Kublai Khan, hence its name at that time: Khanbalik) in just one direction. Few people ever did it. In the event, the Polos only went half way down the route, and it took them five years to return home. Their tales so inspired the young Marco, however, that he joined them on their next trip in 1271. But instead of returning home after a few years, he stayed for twenty-four, reaching not only Peking, but Khan's court itself. Polo was to become one of the world's best-known explorers and adventurers. He was wealthy, and accompanied by numerous servants. He himself was certainly no cook, though one or more would certainly have been in his party. Noodles were still new to Italy in 1271. (As we have seen, they had scarcely arrived in Naples at this time and Venice had probably not even heard of them, particularly as there was no love lost between the two states.) In the unlikely event that Marco Polo had even seen them, it is inconceivable that he would have transported packets of dried pasta from Venice to Peking, and kept them in one piece. In any case it would have been fruitless, given that noodles had become hugely popular with the Chinese masses hundreds of years earlier.

Polo must have eaten noodles – he certainly ate in many Chinese restaurants and the newly conceived noodle shops, during his long stay in the country. Furthermore, Polo was not the first European to visit Peking. Italian monks had been doing it for centuries. What made Polo unique, however, was that he happened to write at length about his travels and his experiences in his huge work *Il Milione*. Polo told the world of coal, fireworks, asbestos and paper currency. His work, dictated while he was a prisoner of war, was at once discredited by some as totally inconceivable, although it survived as *the* authority on the orient for 200 years. No less an explorer than Christopher Columbus used *Il Milione* to convince his doubters and potential investors that he could reach China by sailing westwards. Yet in such an observant and vast dissertation Polo fails to mention some of the most common things to be found in the China of the time: foot-binding, the Great Wall, printing, tea, noodles, and, of great concern to Robin Weir (*see page* 7), ice cream. Certainly, if he was there, how could Polo not have eaten ice cream, tea and noodles? During his alleged long stay in the country, he certainly must have eaten in the many Chinese restaurants and noodle shops yet he makes no mention of them. Indeed, there is scant mention of meals at all in his journals. Furthermore, Polo was not the first European to visit Peking. Arab explorers and Italian monks had been doing so for centuries.

Robin's concern was so great that he inspired Chinese authority Dr Frances Wood to write her book *Did Marco Polo go to China?*, published by Secker and Warburg in 1995. She speculates that Polo recounted his story from second-hand accounts. Perhaps the argument is as academic as the existence of Robin Hood and who wrote the plays attributed to Shakespeare. *Il Milione* exists. Polo is a legendary figure who, like Hood and Shakespeare, will survive until Doomsday. But one thing is for sure – Marco Polo taught neither the Chinese nor the Italians about noodles!

The Contemporary Noodle

In countries where noodles are the main staple, instead of bread or rice grain, they are taken seriously. Noodles are usually eaten three times a day, at breakfast, lunch and dinner, and they are served at auspicious occasions such as weddings, anniversaries and other celebrations. The average person's daily cooked noodle consumption is 450–500g (16–18oz) of cooked noodles per day. That's up to 183 kg per person per annum, or a fifth of a ton a year! That's a lot of noodles, and it adds up to a vast and profitable industry in the Far East. The total number of people in the noodle lands, including China, Japan, Indonesia, plus the other nations of south-east Asia, is some 1.8 billion, about one third of the world's population. Given that they eat a fifth of a ton a year each, that makes a colossal one million tons of noodle a day consumed.

And these are not just any old noodles. The appearance of a noodle matters greatly. They must look lustrous and appetising; fresh ones must not be cracked, and dried sticks must not be broken. There is no room for innovation in noodle-making, and the finished product must be precisely the shape and size of its age-old predecessor. Recipes are almost rigid in their inflexibility, with disputes and disagreements between cooks about the detail of this or that dish sometimes becoming heated. To the traditionalists, the longer the noodles the better – they are symbols of longevity of life; indeed, rice sticks are known as long rice in Hawaii.

Noodles in The West

In the 'non-noodle-lands', consumption is, of course, infinitely much smaller. Noodles are a speciality food. They are not a staple. East of Suez, bread has always held that position, since pre-Biblical times, and it still does. Wheat, the 'staff of life', has always been indigenous there, even though rice grain, and noodles themselves had made their way over from the East even in those early days. Rice was cultivated and still is in Italy and Spain, but it never became flour for noodle making. The situation is now changing rapidly. Noodles are not only becoming a significant product in their own right, they are actually being manufactured in Britain.

The Noodle Market

Market statistics are of great interest to all those who trade. Food businesses are no exception. The big supermarkets, called multiples by the professionals, may be accused of doing away with the small grocer and delicatessen, but love them or hate them, they are always busy, and they certainly turn over more than 80 per cent of the food business in every developed country. And they are the arbiter of trends. What the supermarkets do today, the nation does tomorrow.

I decided to get the view of one of the most experienced professional noodle and pasta people, Liam Mackam, who for over two years, has been Sainsbury's specialist noodle and pasta buyer. 'The British pasta market was worth some £82 million in 1997', he states. 'Excluding the not-insignificant volume of trade done by Chinese wholesalers and retailers, (who mainly cater for the Chinese restaurant sector and ethnic population), noodles were £30 million worth in the same year. In terms of volume, though, pasta, being a much cheaper product, outsells noodles some tenfold. But noodles are 'new' to Britain, and at Sainsbury's it is a growth market.'

Mackam views noodles in positive terms. 'We allocate 2 to 3 metres of shelf space per store to a variety of noodle types. And we introduce new noodle products on a regular basis.' Mackam is proud of the fact that Sainsbury's achieved around one quarter of all British noodle sales in 1997. 'Noodles are so much more versatile than pasta. They are particularly popular with A, B and C1 "foodies", who are seeking a fitter lifestyle, and perceive noodles as healthy food. The future of noodles is dynamic and ever-changing.'

A British Noodle-maker

Noodles, until relatively recently, were nearly all imported from the Orient. Currently there are noodle factories in Belgium, northern France, Manchester, Bradford and Swansea. But these are all new-comers. Britain has been making noodles since 1929, when they were made, in fact, by Italian pasta-maker Luigi Ugo. He spotted an opportunity to make pasta (or noodles) for the then large East London community of Chinese dockers and seamen. After the war the business steadily grew, with taxi deliveries of fresh noodles being made daily to the newly forming Chinatown. Paul Ugo, Luigi's grandson, carries on the noodle-making tradition in his new north London factory, the Oriental Noodle Company. Now the output has outgrown taxi-size deliveries! Seven tons of fresh and dried noodles are made there daily. Paul describes the skills and qualities needed to make good noodles. 'You need protein in the flour and calcium in the water,' he states 'and the speed of the mixing, the heat of the steam and its flow all matter crucially. It can turn into a biscuit if done wrong. It must not dry out on the outside. In cook-ing, the noodle must have enough elasticity to prevent it breaking up in the wok, but not so much that it turns sticky.' Ugo is not a believer in additives. 'Some manufacturers add potassium to remove bacteria,' he states dismissively, 'but this shortens the dough, so they must then add gluten. Insufficient gluten causes the noodles to crack. Japanese udon is soft flour, i.e. it is less glutinous and similar to Italian double zero flour. It has zero ash content - ash makes the flour grey. Bran makes it cause brown spots, so both must be removed, from noodle flour. The best flour comes from Canada, though others are blended into the dough.'

Paul Ugo's patter is rapid and animated, his enthusiasm bound-less. 'There are lots of happenings with noodles,' he proclaims 'they are exciting. We have just started supplying high-protein egg noodles to the Manchester United football team. What could be healthier than that?' Asked about the future, Paul mentions that his son, aged four at the time of writing, would, if he joins the business, be the fourth generation at it. 'It's too early to tell yet,' says Paul, 'though his first words were "Ugo noodles"!'

Making Noodles

I know of two different ways that hand noodles are made. There is the Chinese way, which requires no tools. The Japanese way requires a board, rolling pin and special knife. Like so many age-old crafts, these skills take years to learn and are rapidly disappearing, having become replaced by automated factories. However there are still exponents of both Chinese and Japanese methods, whose skills are much required for public appearances.

In both cases an elastic dough is made, as described on page 70. In the case of the Chinese method, the noodle-maker takes a lump of dough, then, pulling his hands apart, makes the dough become a sausage shape. His hands come together again, and the dough sausage is now double. The two sausages are now pulled apart becoming thinner, and as the hands return there are four sausages. This action is rapid, and is repeated many times, each time the sausage becomes thinner, and is doubled to eight, sixteen, thirty-two and so on. The action is like playing an accordion. Within a couple of minutes the noodle-maker has produced hundreds of identically dimensioned strings of fresh noodles, which are ready to cook.

The Japanese method is quite different. Again a dough is made, and formed into a large ball. This is then hand-patted into a thick disc, on a very large wooden work surface. Keeping the disc well floured, the noodle-maker takes a special rolling pin, which is traditionally 90cm long x 3cm in diameter, and he rolls the disc out until it is huge but very thin. Then the sheet is cut into smaller ones, and, using a special noodle-cutting knife, rapidly cut into identically dimensioned noodle strings.

The Modern Noodle Factory

The factory process for making dried noodles is much the same anywhere. With the help of Monica Chia of distributors Tomen UK, I was met in Tokyo by her Japanese counterparts, Susumu

Yoshikawa and Mieko Furusho, noodle exporters from Yokohama's Yokishawa Corporation. They escorted Dominique and I on a visit to a typical Japanese noodle factory, Miyakoichi, in Chiba near Tokyo. There in the company of President Kazuhiko Murata, we donned protective white clothing, hair nets, hats and boots and were given the guided tour. First we climbed up to a first-floor gantry where the dough is made.

Wheat flour, neither too hard (glutinous) nor too soft, is sucked up from storage kilns, and mechanically mixed with water in a large funnel, until a sticky dough of marzipan consistency is formed. It then rests for 45 minutes, an important timing which allows the dough to become fully cohesive. Then it is mechanically crumbled and forced into the first of a series of seven enclosed heated roller presses, over 7 metres in length. Once it begins this journey, the process continues in a non-stop slow journey. At the first roller press, the dough is shaped into a strip about 45cm wide and 10cm thick. It takes about 10 minutes to reach the seventh press, by which time it is very thin (2.75mm) and resembles puff pastry. At this point, the sheet moves into a final roller which divides it into four, and then cuts the familiar noodle strings as the sheets advance. The strings can be cut to various lengths as required, and the four lots slide down on a chute to the floor below.

Mr Murata said that to make spiralled, rather than straight noodles, a special secret device is used after press seven. He did not elaborate on this mystery, except to say that his grandfather invented spirallings in 1954.

From press seven, each lot of noodles drops into separate trays which are immersed in boiling water for 40 minutes. After that they are removed, drained and at once lowered into ice-cold water. After a few minutes this is repeated to obtain the correct pH level and emulsification. After a final straining, the noodles are dried at 90°C/190°F for 30 minutes then they are air-cooled at 35°C/95°F for 30 minutes, after which they weigh 250g (9oz), and are packed into their familiar decorative cellophane bags. The whole process is fully automated, requiring just four personnel, to make 8,000 packs of noodles an hour, and, said Mr Murata, mine is just a small factory, one of many thousands of similar factories dotted around Japan.

Making Soy Sauce

From noodles we went on to see the making of Japanese shoyu sauce at Shoda Shoyu Co. Ltd in Tatebayashi City. Noodles and soy sauce go together like a horse and carriage in the Orient. Shoda is a four-generation family business started on the same site in 1877. Managing Director Takashi Shoda took pride in showing us around. Shoda is the fourth largest soy sauce manufacturer in Japan, bottling an astonishing 5,000 litre bottles an hour, of which 2 per cent are exported, some of which is branded Blue Dragon. In Japan alone consumption is 1.2 million kilolitres a year, or 1 litre per month per head of the Japanese population. In China the figures are much the same.

Our guided tour at Shoda was conducted by two lively young men, Masao Yoshikawa and Kazuhito Shoji from the Business Development Office. Roasted crushed wheat and steamed soya bean flakes are mixed together with salt and water, to which is added a culture or mould called *koji*. Donning another set of protective white clothing, hair nets, hats and boots, we climbed to the top of a giant warehouse. Inside are thirty or forty gigantic vats, 3.5 metres deep, containing a frothily fermenting brown mixture, called the *Moromi* mash. The smell is yeasty, reminding one of a beer brewery. After six months the mixture is piped off to a pressing machine on the ground floor. There, between silk sheets, the sediment waste, resembling cardboard in colour and appearance, is separated from the liquid, but not wasted. It is used for animal feed. The liquid is filtered and piped to the bottling room, where in stainless steel vats, it is heated to 80°C/176°F for pasteurisation, after which it is bottled.

Our hosts told us this 'old' plant employed just 150 staff. We were impressed. But they advised us to wait until we saw their new plant, which we did after lunch. Here, in a vast, multi-million dollar unit resembling mission-control Houston, everything was fully automated and state-of-the-art. The places of 150 personnel are taken by just a handful of engineers, who, after several years of build-up, had just achieved their target of turning out the same output of shoyu sauce in half the time, and one-third of the space. Soon the old town-centre plant would be closed, and demolished for housing. Over time, the new plant will expand to four times its current size. We did not doubt Takashi Shoda that that time would soon be coming.

Noodle Shops

Noodle Shops are the invention of the Chinese and they date back some two thousand years, or more. They are, quite literally, the world's first, and most enduring fast food cafés. Noodle dishes are all they sell. Nothing else. No nonsense, no frills, just plain and simple, tasty, inexpensive noodle dishes, served fast. They are the people's eating places; cheap and cheerful with no airs and no graces – the equivalent of the American diner or Britain's fast dying-out transport café. But far from becoming extinct in China, they are as popular now as they were all those centuries ago.

Noodle shops are literally everywhere in China. In every city, in every town, in every village, on every street. No one has counted how many there are in China, but someone has done so in Japan, where they are just as ubiquitous. In Tokyo alone, it seems there are some 7,000 noodle shops within a 20-mile radius of the city centre. And Japan not only has its noodle shops, it has Sushi and Sukiyaki Shops too, the former specialising in those highly decorative cold fishy specialities (*see page* 95) the latter in one-pot cooked dishes (*see page* 143).

On our last trip to Japan, Dominique and I were picked up at Narita airport by our friends Mr Susumu Yoshikawa and Mrs Mieko Furusho, noodle exporters from Yokohama's Yokishawa Corporation, to be driven to Miyakoichi, a noodle factory on the other side of Tokyo. Suburbs are suburbs, but Tokyo's seemed over-endowed with used-car lots. Every other site seemed to have one, with what appeared to be real bargain prices for relatively new second-hand, right-hand drive, Japanese cars. (As in Britain, they drive on the left there, but we only saw one Mini and one Jaguar in all our visit there!) In between car lots were flats and houses aplenty, and numerous undistinguished, one-storey grey sheds which might have been factories or warehouses. After driving for about 45 minutes, Mr Yoshikawa seemed to be taking undue interest in such sheds, and for mile after mile, he kept slowing down to peer at them. Eventually, he drew up in front of one, and grunted 'come' to us. We had no idea what he was getting at. He hadn't told us he was looking for our lunch venue. It was only when we stepped inside the somewhat shabby shed that we realised it, but what a transformation.

We passed through some small white banners. These, it turned out are a traditional symbol for welcome. Inside was a bustling busy eatery. It turned out to be the Sobaya Noodle House. All they sell is noodle dishes, in fact all they sell is Soba noodle dishes, to be precise. The decor was very plain, but very Japanese. At one end was an open sizzling, steaming, wok-clattering kitchen. The smells were very fresh and very appetising. The four kimono-dressed women, who were cooking and serving, immediately had a shy fit of giggles at the sight of the only Westerners they had probably ever seen in there. To the right and left was seating for perhaps eighty. It was half full, only with men, presumably local workers. Without exception they all stared at us, their chopsticks frozen in mid-air. The silence, punctuated by the female giggles, lasted for just a second, though it felt longer.

The seating in a Tokyo Noodle House is largely Japanese-style. You remove your shoes, and sit on matting floor on a cushion in front of tables for two, each with a lacquer black box containing chopsticks. In the centre were a few Western-style tables and chairs, at which we sat. The menu, was a blackboard, its offerings chalked in Japanese. By then we were seated, the conversation was buzzing again and the staff's giggles had changed to welcoming smiles. We looked at the blackboard, perplexed. 'Leave it to us,' said our hosts, and within minutes, bowls of steaming soba noodles were in front of us, and delicious they were too. We were bowed out, feeling full and contented, and just a little bit less alien than we had on our arrival.

The noodle shop is an institution yet to happen in Britain. Although there are some 6,000 Chinese restaurants in the UK, they all serve more or less the same formula Cantonese or Pekingese food. Noodles are on the menu, to be sure, but the restaurants do not specialise in them. There is no doubt a market for a high-street chain of noodle bars, along the lines of burger bars, and more than one entrepreneur is studying the notion of placing outlets in discos and cinemas. But these will bear no relationship to the real thing. There is but a relative handful of Japanese restaurants in London (under forty), with an equal number elsewhere in the country. Only two or three are noodle shops, in that they specialise in noodle dishes, but they are nothing like their Japanese counterparts, although, run by trendies for trendies, they are an interesting, and evidently very popular dining experience.

Wagamama, near the British Museum, is one of these. Its basement setting is more Oliver Twist than Bloomsbury, though the decor is chic minimalist, and not oppressive. On the gleaming wooden floor, a series of long, matching clerestory-style tables, with none-too-comfortable benches fills the room. An open stainless steel kitchen runs down the entire length of one wall. The menu is short, the service equally so, though it is not uncourteous. Such is its lunchtime popularity, that if you turn up much after midday, you are sure to queue around the block. It's the same in the evenings. But you do not queue for too long – turnover is fast. Soon you are crammed into your assigned seat, wedged between chopsticking, chattering diners. Then it's your turn. You quickly slurp up your huge bowl of ramen or somen, and almost before you have time to realise it, are making way for the next slurper!

Getting to grips with chopsticks

Neither noodles nor pasta is the easiest of foods to consume elegantly and neatly. Indeed 'slurping', or eating noodles with a great deal of sucking noises, is considered good form in Japan. In Italy too, miscreant strands are sucked up with gusto in many a provincial eating place.

In China, Korea, Vietnam and Japan, noodles are eaten with chopsticks made either from bamboo, wood, bone or metal. In Japan, they are more delicate, and often lacquered and highly decorated. In Thailand, it is the norm to eat most food with a spoon and fork. However, noodles are the exception; being of Chinese origin, they are eaten with chopsticks. Chopsticks have been around for as long as as the noodle. Cutlery i.e. spoons and forks, were around the kitchen from medieval times, but took rather longer than knives (or to be exact, daggers) to find their way on to the table. Pasta is eaten with cutlery. The fork in one hand is used to get hold of a strand of pasta. The fork is then put against the spoon, held in the other hand, and this is used to allow the pasta to be wound around the fork, and neatly popped into the mouth.

Nutrition in noodles

Noodles are high in starch, or carbohydrates, and they provide some protein, especially the varieties made from hard wheat and beans. The addition of egg gives further protein but vegetable dyes do not significantly change the nutritional value of noodles. Needless to say, it is the ingredients of the sauces with which they are served that add significantly to the calorific value of noodles. The calorific value of 100g dried noodles varies from type to type but averages are given below.

100g dried	Calories	Carbohydrate	Protein	Fat	Sodium (salt)
Rice sticks	380	88%	6%	0	
Rice vermicelli	363	85.5%	7.3%	0	
Egg noodles	341	70%	11%	1.9%	0.8%
Wheat noodles	308	60% + fibre 10%	12.5%	2%	0.8%
Bean thread	320	65%	20%	0	
Pasta	350	75%	11.5%	0.3%	

PLATE ONE

The number of noodles available is bewildering: there are so many different makes and packets, many of which are written in Japanese or Chinese. As you can see, they make a fascinating study. In this collection of noodles, there are many which are readily available, such as the Blue Dragon items. Some aren't so easy to find, such as the long strands of fresh brown and white Udon noodles, also appearing behind them and left, coiled in baskets. These were purchased in a Japanese filling station convenience shop, and they are a remarkable 70cm in length. To get an idea of their real size, compare them with the standard-sized drinks (middle shelf, left) which contains not cola, but Japanese green tea . . . The knife in the centre foreground is used to cut the rolled dough into Japanese noodles.

Overleaf, and in the next two pictures, various noodles are shown full-size, out of their packets.

CHAPTER ONE

THE NOODLE WORKSHOP

As seasoned readers of my books will know, it is a tradition of mine to call the first chapter 'The Workshop', in this case, the 'Noodle Workshop'. The reason for this is that, like any workshop, it's the depository of a number of unrelated items which are vital to noodle cooking and which appear throughout the rest of the book. This time the workshop is divided into four parts.

First I deal with the equipment needed for cooking noodles, freezing and keeping them, preparing ingredients, weights and measures, and portions.

Next I describe the various grains noodles are made from, as well as discussing flour, and the milling process, and better and lesser-known noodle types.

PLATE TWO

WHEAT NOODLES All noodles are shown full-size. See Noodle Directory (page 219) for more information.

Clockwise from top left: Dried: egg nest, chilli nest, wheat nest, longevity noodle (which stretches from the top right to the bottom left of the picture, and if unravelled fully, measures 50cm or more), thin tangle (top right). Below it, thicker tangle, large curly, tiny curly, green Hor-fun, flat white Hor-fun, cream noodle, thin ribbon, Shanghai, and Baifa at bottom right. Follow the longevity noodle to bottom left of page, where above it there is (going upwards, left of page): spinach flat, spinach round, egg noodles, whole wheat noodles, Persian white Reshteh and brown roasted.

In the centre, clockwise from top left: All fresh: black (squid ink) angel hair noodles, wheat noodles, flat wheat noodles, egg noodles and thread noodles.

Noodles themselves are pretty boring. They have substance and texture, they are filling, and have certain nutritional value, and indeed they have *some* flavour. But on their own, noodles do not have enough flavour to provide a satisfying meal. As with rice and bread, it is the sauces and ingredients we add to noodles, which makes them an outstanding staple.

Given that noodles and pasta are interchangeable, as we have seen in the Introduction, we need have no preconceived ideas about confining noodles to oriental flavourings as typified by soy sauce and five spice. We can choose all manner of flavours to accompany noodles. Indeed, the world is literally our food basket. However, a good number of the recipes in this book do require traditional oriental flavourings, which brings me to the third part of the workshop, devoted to defining some of those important ingredients. It includes brief notes about main ingredients including oils, herbs, spices, coconut, fish sauce, noodles, rice and wonton wrappers, amongst others.

The fourth and final part of the workshop comprises twenty-one key recipes including making and cooking home-made noodles, stocks, spice mixes, chilli oil, pickled items and sauces.

Kitchen implements and utensils

The Wok

Many of the dishes in this book require you to boil the noodles, others are stir-fried, and a few require deep-frying. Boiled noodles are easy to cook, needing just a saucepan full of boiling water. Their accompanying sauces can also be cooked in a saucepan or frying pan, although I prefer using a wok. Stir-fried noodles need boiling first if dried, after which they are wok-fried. Fresh noodles need only reheating, and may be stir-fried only.

If you don't already own a wok, I recommend that you purchase at least one, if not two good-quality steel woks. They are invaluable for all types of cooking, not just oriental. I prefer the one-handled wok to the two handled version as it is less likely to burn the fingers. The best sizes to buy are 30cm (12 in) in diameter and a smaller one of about 20cm (8 inches). Woks need 'seasoning' when new. Firstly, you must scrub off the machine oil which protects them. Next you must burn them in, dry, on the stove. Next oil them and burn the oil in (a smoky business, better done outside, when the barbecue is going perhaps). Repeat with a second oiling. It is said that when cleaning a wok, you should never scour the patina off. Often this is acceptable but if you have burnt in some food, it is hygienic to scour it off in which case you may need to season it again. Either way, every time you wash a steel wok, put it back on to the stove to heat it up. This prevents rust from forming. Keep it in a dry place for the same reason. If rust does form, wash it off, then re-oil the wok, as described above. Woks work well on gas, and electric, and Aga-type hobs, especially if you have a wok ring. Woks do not work well on ceramic and halogen stoves; they tend to cut off automatically because the wok base is smaller than the ring diameter. Always use non-metalic spoons in non-stick woks.

Deep-fryers

Deep-frying is best done in a thermostatically controlled electrical unit. It has to be said, though, that if the thermostat is inaccurate, the results will be poor. The deep-fry recipes in this book require a temperature of 190°C (chip-frying temperature, often the highest setting on the unit). If the temperature is below that your food may be soggy not crisp. One sure way to check is to buy a purpose-made cooking thermometer. If you must deep-fry using a saucepan on the stove, take great care. More home fires are caused by deep-frier accidents, than from any other cause. Never overfill the pan with oil; one third full is ample. Do not leave it unattended, and remember that if the oil overheats, it vapourises, and explodes.

Utensils

Here is a list of the items you will need to prepare and cook the items in this book. It is a mercifully short list, and most cooks will already have everything listed:

knives
chopping board
mixing bowls – large, medium and small
sieves
large, slotted spoon for use in a deep-fryer
deep-fryer

casserole dish(es) – 2.25–2.75 litres (4–5 pints)
saucepans with lids – 3.5 litres, 2.25 litres, 1.4 litres (6¼, 4, 2½ pints)
steel wok(s) 30cm (12in) and 20cm (8in) diameter
wok ring(s)

Keeping noodle dishes

Noodles themselves are best eaten fresh. However with refrigeration, many of the recipes in this book will be none the worse for keeping overnight, or even longer. Provided that the raw ingredients are absolutely fresh, not frozen, and are cooked immediately, and provided that the dish is cooled rapidly after cooking, then covered and placed in the fridge at once, the food should be safe for up to 48 hours.

As a general rule, any meat or poultry dish may be served immediately after cooking, a few hours later, or even a day or two later. The taste and texture of the dish will change as marination takes place. This usually means the flavours will become blander and the principal ingredient softer. Vegetables, in my opinion, like noodles, taste better served straight after cooking, but some of these will keep too.

Common sense must prevail when keeping any food, but I would recommend that you observe the following points:

1 Do not keep fish or shellfish dishes.
2 If you intend to keep a meat dish for a day or two, undercook it slightly by simply cutting back the timings by a few minutes. You will obtain a better texture when reheating – simply simmer until ready.
3 Use common sense about which vegetables will keep.
4 Keep dishes away from warmth, and preferably in a fridge.
5 Use a cover or film.
6 Inspect meat or chicken after 24 hours. Smell and taste it. It should look firm and good.
7 Heat must be applied relatively quickly when reheating. Simmer and stir for at least 10 minutes (especially for meat or poultry) and before serving check that the food is hot right through.
8 During reheating, taste, and if a little more flavouring is needed, add this early so that it cooks in well.
9 Do not use anything you suspect may be going off. Forty-eight hours is a long time for any dish to sit around, and freezing is a much safer method of storing.

Freezing

To the Western householder, the freezer is a mandatory item, though in the noodle lands, it is still a relatively rare piece of equipment. Like the fridge, it too has its uses and drawbacks.

One of the main advantages of home freezing is being able to preserve seasonal items for use out of season. I like to do this with some things and not with others. I prefer to freeze my own sweetcorn – it tastes so much better than the commercial versions. On the other hand I think bought frozen peas are in many cases better than home-frozen ones. You can freeze fruit and vegetables raw, exactly as they are when pickled or purchased (cleaning them and discarding any unwanted parts first). I often do this, but the textbooks advise that you should cook them first, or at least blanch them, to remove bacteria and gases. It's up to you. Freezing comes into its own with the preservation of cooked foods. Freezing can change the taste of a dish – it's like a long marination. It will soften noodles, meats and vegetables and tends to intensify certain flavours, though the overall taste will become blander.

Here are a few common sense freezer observations:

1   Use only fresh ingredients, not items that have already come from the freezer and been thawed.
2   Choose your subject carefully. Some ingredients are not suitable for freezing. Items with a high water content change markedly in structure when they thaw, their texture becoming unpleasant. Meat and poultry are excellent for freezing. Some vegetables work well – aubergines, peas, beans, carrots and mashed potatoes for example. Most soft fruit and vegetables and whole potatoes are not as successful. Fish and seafood work well. Boiled or stir-fried noodles (but not crispy deep-fried noodles) are satisfactory, but I can never see the point – it takes so little time to cook noodles and when fresh, they have a better taste and texture.
3   Always undercook a dish destined for the freezer by a few minutes to allow for 'tenderising' in the freezing process and reheating.
4   Take out any large whole spices before freezing, especially cassia, cardamoms and cloves as they tend to become a bit astringent.
5   Get the dish into the freezer as soon as it is cold. Do not freeze any food that has been kept warm for a long time or reheated, especially chicken. There is a risk of bacterial contamination.

6   Be aware that spicy, garlicky food can 'taint' other foods, so pack in a plastic container with an airtight lid.
7   Label contents with description and date of freezing.
8   Use within three months.
9   Before reheating ensure that the dish is thoroughly thawed, and that it is hot and cooked through after reheating.
10   You may find the flavouring has gone a little bland, so taste and cook in more flavourers as needed.
11   Finally, never ever freeze, thaw and refreeze a cooked item.

Ice cube mould

Certain highly flavoured items, such as garlic, ginger and onion can be made in 'bulk' and frozen in small portions (*see page* 51). I keep an ice cube mould specifically for this purpose. Freeze for 24 hours then transfer cubes to a suitable tub or double bag to contain the aromas.

Weights and measures

European legislation dictates that it is now illegal in the UK to serve a pint of beer in a pub, or a pound of peas at the supermarket. Although I have no wish to transfer my office to Wormwood Scrubs, I have given all weights and measures in metric and imperial or spoon meaures. Most ingredients and food products in the UK and Australasia only display metric weights. For those who still use only imperial measures (as in the USA), the conversion is best made by examining your measuring jug, scales, or tape measures as these generally carry both sets of measurements. Talking about daft laws, did you know that it is illegal to eat mince pies on Christmas Day? A set of laws were passed in Cromwell's time preventing 'having fun' on religious days. It was never repealed. See you inside!

Preparing ingredients

As with most oriental foods, noodles are quick to cook. It is stating the obvious, but do prepare all your ingredients before you start cooking: assemble any bottled or tinned items (open the tin), wash, trim and chop fresh items as required by the recipe; weigh and measure as necessary, and always have everything to hand. Once the cooking begins, one's concentration should be on timings and stirrings, not locating lost items.

Portions

Most of the recipes in this book serve four people with average appetites unless otherwise stated. I normally allow about 175g (6 oz) of raw principal ingredients (meat, chicken, fish, seafood or vegetables) in a main course, for four servings. Usually there is about 60g (2 oz) of various extra items in a dish, to give about 225g (8 oz) per person in total. For an accompanying main-course dish allow about 80g (3 oz) per person. As for the noodles themselves, when using dried noodles, allow 50–75g (2–3oz) uncooked noodles per person. Double this for fresh noodles, i.e. 450g (1 lb) fresh noodles is the equivalent of 225g (8 oz) dried noodles.

These quantities are given for guidance only. Appetites vary enormously. One person may eat two or even three times as much as another. So, as with all aspects of cooking, common sense should prevail.

Having said all that, rather than weigh things, it is often easier to visualise exactly what you expect each diner will eat. Think of potatoes, for example. You'll eat two, she'll eat three, Uncle Fred six, Aunty Mary one, and so on. If you are cooking for one person, either scale down the quantities or use the freezer for any surplus. If you are cooking for more than four, scale up. Taste and adjust as you go – if you feel a particular dish needs more flavouring, add some. Flexibility is, as always, the key.

Grain used to make noodles

Grain is a grass, whose edible fruit or seed is called cereal. This can be dried and used at once to make starchy staples, such as bread, or it can be stored for very long periods, and processed when required. The most common grain types used for noodle-making are buckwheat, mung bean, rice and wheat. Other grain types which can be used include barley, corn, gram, maize, oats, rye, sorghum and the soya bean. Here is a list of the main grain types of the world in alphabetical order.

Barley

Barley, one of the world's earliest-known cereals, is low in gluten, and therefore difficult to use for cohesive dough-making. However, it is possible to make barley noodles by adding wheat flour to the dough. Barley is widely used in brewing.

Buckwheat

Buckwheat is a cereal plant originating in the Orient. Despite its name, it is unrelated to wheat, and is an important ingredient for soba noodle-making in Japan. It is also used as a minor ingredient in some Italian 'pasta'. The buckwheat plant has fragrant white flowers, and is especially cultivated for its seeds, which, when ground become an attractive silvery-grey, fine powder, punctuated with black flecks. From the fourteenth century, until the end of the nineteenth, when its production diminished, it was a popular staple in Eastern Europe, and western France, where it was used to make gruel. It is unsuitable for making bread, but is used in France for traditional buckwheat pancakes (gallettes), and porridge. When husked, crushed and cooked, buckwheat forms the basis of the Russian dish *kasha*. It was also especially used for horse, cattle and poultry fodder. In the USA you will find the ever popular buckwheat breakfast cakes.

The word buckwheat derives from the Dutch, *boekweit*, from *boeke* meaning beech, and *weite*, meaning wheat, because the three-cornered, pyramid-shaped seeds resemble beechnuts. It is also known as Saracen corn, because of the dark colour of the grain, and in French as *blénoir*, *beaucuit* or *bucail*.

Buckwheat is rich in minerals and vitamin B, and is lower in calories than other cereal (290 cal. per 100g).

Corn

There is no such seed as corn. The word can be substituted for grain in general, although it refers to the predominant crop of a region. For example in England it refers to wheat, in Scotland to oats and in America to maize. It can either mean the seeds which are grain, or more specifically, it means wheat, oats and maize.

Fava bean

A so-called broad bean (*vicia faba*), the fava bean, with its large 3cm (1.2in) pods has been cultivated in China and Japan for millennia. Though more commonly used as a nutritious vegetable, or pickle, its flour is sometimes used for noodle-making.

Gram flour

Gram or *besan* is unique to India, and is popular all over the country. Bengalis, in the north-east of India adore gram flour, so much so, that one of its names is 'Bengal Gram'. It is made from *chana dhal*, which give the flour its gorgeous, blond colour, and its unique flavour. Its common use is for pakoras or onion bhajis, and breads, but it is also used for noodles in the form of crunchy crispy sev (*see Bhel Puri, page* 103) and Bolobi Besan Noodles (*page* 200).

Millet

Millet is grown in certain countries, such as north and west India, for flour, and it can be used to make noodles. Long, thin, delicate corn-like ears contain thousands of tiny seeds, the millet itself. The seeds are smooth spheres, their colour a stone-grey with a warm hint of yellow. Millet is finely ground into a silvery-grey flour, which is available from specialist shops. It can be substituted for all the wheat flour noodle recipes in this book. The recipe for Gujarati Bajra Talipeeth Curry Noodles (*page* 199) incorporates spinach, coriander leaves and chilli into the dough.

Rice

Rice was domesticated in south India 9,000 years ago, in heavily irrigated 'paddy' fields. The plant is a slender grass, whose grain forms thin 'ears'. The Tamils called this grain *arisi*, derived from their word to 'separate', referring to the process of splitting the grain from the husk, to produce brown rice. This must be further hulled to remove its brown bran, thus producing the familiar white polished grain. The Tamil word became the derivation for the ancient Persian *w'rijza'h*, the Latin *oryza*, and the modern Italian word, *riso*.

Today, there are over 7,000 varieties of rice, and it is the staple of over two-thirds of the world's population.

Sorghum

Sorghum (*jowar*), also called *durra*, Indian millet or guinea corn, is used for breads in central India.

Soya bean

A pulse originated in ancient times in Manchuria, China, and introduced into Japan by the sixth century, where is it called the 'meat vegetable'. Its plant bears brown pods each of which contains three small pea-sized seeds or beans. They are used ubiquitously as beans (fresh or dried) and to produce flour (which can be used to make noodles) and other foodstuffs from cheese and milk to soy sauce, soya oil and dough.

Wheat

Wheat is a grass plant, which grows in temperate areas. Its grain seeds grow in clusters, or 'ears'. It has been milled since ancient times (see milling), and by 2000 BC the Egyptians had invented baking and brewing, both of which involved wheat. The grain contains a husk (bran) and a kernel, which is composed of starch and proteins called gluten. Inside the kernel is the seed or embryo called the wheat germ. The exterior of the grain contains minerals such as calcium and vitamins.

Milling

Grain *per se* has little nutritional use, and is generally processed by 'milling' to create a fine powder called flour.

Milling is an ancient and complex process, where grain or seeds have their husks removed and discarded, and their inner seeds ground into flour. It has evolved over the millennia from crudely crushing wheat to make burghul, and a simple gruel to a more sophisticated process from 4000 BC in which purpose-made grinding stones were in evidence in the Middle East and Egypt. The Romans introduced the rotary mill (often a water mill) where one circular stone was turned around a stationary one. Windmills appeared at the beginning of the thirteenth century. It was not until the Industrial Revolution that steel roller mills first appeared, producing the fine flour we know today.

Modern-day wheat milling

When the wheat grain becomes ripe, the ears are harvested, and the grain is separated from the chaff by threshing. The all-important wheat grain, or kernel is composed of starch and proteins, called gluten. The harder the grain, the more gluten it contains. Eighty-three per cent of the grain is endosperm, which makes white flour, 14 per cent is bran (also called husk or small scales), 2 per cent is the wheatgerm (also called the germ, seed or embryo). The remaining 1 per cent is the exterior of the grain, consisting of minerals and vitamins.

The job of the miller is to separate these components and make different types of flour. The process is complex. Grain is first sorted to remove unwanted items. It is then soaked and dried, to harden it. Then it is 'winnowed', or cracked open, between grooved rollers. Sieving separates the endosperm. Larger pieces are air-blasted to separate remaining bran, then re-winnowed. Now called semolina, the endosperm is ground again, this time through various stages of fine rolling. It is now plain white flour. The number of stages depends on the grade and fineness of flour required. It is often bleached by the millers to make it whiter and the addition of a raising agent creates self-raising flour. Strong white flour is milled from one of the hard varieties of wheat grain, which has more gluten, and thus creates a more elastic dough, good for Italian pasta and Indian bread.

The separated bran is ground separately, and is blended into white flour, producing a coarser, browner wholemeal flour. Wheatgerm can be added to wholemeal flour, making a high-protein wheatmeal flour, or it is sold as a product in its own right.

As mentioned earlier, Italian noodles (pastas) and many types of bread are produced from high protein flour with good gluten content, known as hard (or durum) flour. Durum wheat flour is produced in the Mediterranean, the Middle East, Russia and the Americas. It is a hard wheat, high in gluten, which is ground into semolina. Oriental noodles (and cakes and biscuits) are mainly made from soft wheats with low protein and gluten content. It is for this reason that dried noodles cook much faster than an equivalent quantity of Italian pasta.

Dough

Flour and water are combined with optional salt, and after careful mixing, or kneading, the resulting elastic cohesive lump is known as unleavened dough or pasta. This can be made to make unleavened bread, such as chupattis, or noodles. (It is only when a raising agent such as yeast is added, that the dough rises and becomes leavened, when it is used to make standard bread loaves.) Other additives, such as egg, and flavourings and colourings can be added to the mixture before kneading.

Noodle types

Here, alphabetically listed, are the better- and lesser-known noodle types.

Arrowroot noodles

These noodles from China's western province of Szechuan where they like things chilli-hot, are not easy to find. They are made from arrowroot flour, and when dried are thread-like and yellow to amber in colour.

Beanthread, vermicelli, or cellophane noodles

Also known as transparent, pea-starch, bean-starch or glass noodles. Chinese: *fun-see, fen-szu, mee-hoon, sai fun* (falling rain); Japanese: *harusame* (spring rain); Thai: *wun-sen*; Indonesian *so-un lak-sa*.

The best quality come from China and are made from the flour of the mung bean (green lentil), though green soya beans (qv), fava broad beans (qv) or any bean flour can be used. They come in large, or one-portion bundles of semi-opaque or translucent, often buff-coloured, thin threads of very small diameter. Though they look fragile, they are almost impossible to break. Use kitchen shears for this job! Usually they are used in soups and wet stews, though their slimy texture makes them a little less popular in the West than other types of noodle. They can also be stir-fried following a soaking to reconstitute them. They work well in salads.

One Chinese variety of cellophane noodle is made from seaweed, and is longer and thinner in appearance. Certain Japanese cellophane noodles are wider and more ribbon-like, and some are made from potato flour or sweet potato flour. All types can be used in soups, stir-fries, stews and salads. They can also be deep-fried, when they puff up and become delightfully crispy, and are especially good as a garnish. *See also* Rice Vermicelli.

Broad bean noodles

Made from fava broad beans, they can be thin and thread-like (see arrowroot noodles, above). Alternatively they are cut to about one-eighth of an inch in width. They are good in soups and stews.

Buckwheat noodles

See Japanese Wheat Noodles, Soba

Cellophane noodles

See Beanthread Noodles

Egg noodles

Chinese: *Dan Mien*, (Cantonese): *Hokkein Mee*, Thai and Indonesian: *ba-mee*, and Malaysian: *mee*.

A Chinese noodle, made from wheat flour to which eggs (usually duck eggs) are added. The threads vary considerably in width from very thin, round strands, to ribbons about 8mm (⅓ in) wide. The thin ones are known as *ee-fu*, and the thick ones, *hokkien mee*. They also vary in colour from pale cream to deep yellowy-orange, depending on how many eggs are used. Factories use egg powder and, in some cases, food colouring to achieve the effect. Blue Dragon's dried egg noodles are their most popular noodle, resembling spaghetti in many ways, except that they are folded over in their packet into tangled flat bundles, and they cook three times faster. They may be cooked by simply immersing them into boiling hot water, then turning the heat off, and leaving them to soak for 5 minutes before straining and serving. They may also be par boiled and stir-fried or, completely dry, they can be deep-fried to make 'crispy noodles'. Some fresh egg noodles are 'oiled', ready to be stir-fried.

Refrigerated fresh egg noodles are available at Chinese or Asian supermarkets, or they can be made using the recipe on page 70. *See also* Japanese Wheat Noodles – Ramen.

Fun sie

See Beanthread or Cellophane Noodles

Glass noodles

See Beanthread or Cellophane Noodles

Hor-fun

See Rice Noodles

Japanese Wheat noodles

HIYAMUGI Japanese dried noodle from wheat flour dough, and a cross between somen (qv) and udon (qv) in appearance. As with somen, serve chilled, with a chilli hot, ice cold soup.

KISHIMEN A type of udon wheat noodles (see below), but broader and flatter.

RAMEN These Japanese noodles are a variation on the Chinese-style egg or wheat noodles, and they come in many dried forms, as crinkly tangles, bunches or packs. Called *chuka soba* in western Japan, they are served in a variety of ways, but usually in a bowl with a soya-based soup or broth, with slices of roast pork, pickled bamboo, fish paste and seven spice mixture.

SHIRATAKI Its Japanese translation, 'white waterfall', gives the clue that this very thin noodle is delicate in appearance, and translucent. It is made from *konnyaku*, or elephant's foot or devil's tongue. When cut, the root of the plant gives off a gelatinous resin. One way this is processed is to form it into strings, or noodles, which traditionally accompany *sukiyaki* (a one-pot dish of beef and vegetables). These noodles can be obtained dried, or vacuum-packed with water in sachets.

SOBA Soba, meaning 'nearness', is a very popular type of flat stick noodle in Japan. The best quality, and most expensive, is made either entirely from buckwheat (qv) – *sobako* – and its sweetish taste and texture is unique, and much respected in Japan. It is rich in protein and in lecithin. Soba is also available with up to 60 per cent wheat flour added. The standard soba length is 17.5–25cm (7–10 inches). Soba's natural colours range from grey to pale buff. Green soba (*Cha-soba*) has green powdered tea added for flavouring, and other colours, such as brown are common.

SOMEN Only sold dried, somen are a Japanese speciality. They are very small diameter round hard-wheat noodles, sold in round or flat pretty cellophane or paper packages often tied with a ribbon. They are normally a bright white, though recently a range of colours ranging from pink to bright green (dyed with food colouring, rather than natural flavourings) has become popular. They are normally served cold with a chilled soup, or salads. In order to remain al dente after cooking, they should be chilled in icy water.

UDON Another Japanese favourite also popular in Korea, udon noodles, made from soft wheat, are available fresh and dried in varying sizes. Fresh, *nama* (or raw) udon are long, thick or thin, round or square, narrow, noodles. Dried udon come as shorter, long, flat, brittle, white sticks and are often sold in boxes. Usually udon accompany a soup, which itself may accompany tempura fritters.

Nest noodles

Not to be confused with the bird's nest (*see page* 100), these are simply shaped into round, one-portion, nest-like clumps. They come in various flavours – egg, spinach, chilli, prawn – and they can be used attractively in presentation by carefully placing food on top of the nest.

Pasta – Three main Italian noodle types

MACARONI The dough is extruded into tubes of various diameters.
SPAGHETTI Still the most popular form of pasta, spaghetti is cut into long straight round thin sticks (*spago* meaning string). Spaghetti was invented in Naples during medieval times, from whence it spread around other parts of Italy.

VERMICELLI *Vermi* means worms and *celli*, little, so this pasta means small worms! The diameter of each strand is very fine, and the finest of all is called Angel's Hair, and is used in consommés or clear soups. *See also* Beanthread Noodles.

Rice noodles, dried

CHINESE DRIED – *Hor-fun*. Made from a rice-flour dough, and are always opaque and bright white in colour. They come in various basic forms.

Rice noodles, fresh

Chinese: *look-fun*; Thai: *kuaytiaw* or *gwaytio*; Malaysian: *laksa*.
These are sold in sheets, allowing you to cut them to the shape and size you need, or ready-cut into strips of varying sizes. They are made from glutinous rice flour dough, often with a little white wheat flour added to act as a stabiliser.

Rice Stick noodles, dried

Chinese: *mee-fun, ngunsi-fun, lai-fun*. Thai: *sen-mee*. Indonesian: *bee hun*. Vietnamese: *banh-pho*. Malay: *chee-cheong-fun*

Straight flat ribbons ranging from 1mm (1/24 in) to 4mm (1/6 in) in thickness are called rice sticks. Thicker, wider rice sticks are called *kway tew*.

Curly rice noodles, known as rice vermicelli (*mee-fun or mee-hoon*) are good to deep-fry. A fourth variety is wider than rice sticks and often flat. After reconstituting for an hour, they can be cut to shape.

Rice Vermicelli

Very thin irregular bright white strings made by extruding rice flour dough. Great for deep-frying.

Soba

See Buckwheat Noodle

Vermicelli (*oriental type*)

See Beanthread Noodles and Pasta.

Wheat Flour noodles

Chinese: *lo-mein, yee-mein* (brown)
As egg noodles, but without the egg. They can be white or brown depending on whether plain or wholemeal flour is used (*see* Wheat, *page* 42).

Flavouring and colouring noodles

The colour of the finished noodle is determined by the type of grain used in the flour. Rice noodles turn out white, wheat noodles brown or pale buff, egg noodles yellow, buckwheat noodles grey and so on. Recently, like pasta, noodles have had flavourings and colourings added. Japanese somen is coloured pale green and 'ice-cream' pink, using food colouring. Spinach for green and chilli and tomato for red are three flavourings and colourings added to egg noodles. These are readily identified by their colour in their transparent packets. A look around your noodle stockist's shelves reveals that there is a further range of flavoured noodles. Blue Dragon, for example have no fewer than ten in their range called 'Flavour Rice Noodles'. The flavours for these popular sellers include beef, chicken, crab, shrimp, won-ton, duck, mushroom, Singapore, Aromatic Thai and Tom Yum flavours. The flavouring in these varieties is not actually impregnated into the dough, as with the coloured noodles. The noodles themselves are, in fact, plain and unflavoured, but in their packets is a sachet of dry flavouring which is reconstituted in hot water to create a 'quick-and-easy-ready-to-eat' sauce, to accompany noodles which are separately immersed in boiling water. Simply combine sauce and noodles, and the dish is ready to eat

Instant noodles

The fact that noodles are very rapid to cook has not escaped the attention of the manufacturers and marketing people. Recent innovations have included a variety of 'instant' products, aimed largely at the under-thirty age group. One, called the 'Lunchbox', is a variation on the Flavour Noodle theme above, and is ready to eat in under three minutes. Pot Noodles take the concept further. They are sold in plastic tubs, ready-flavoured – just add hot water, which the sponge-like batter immediately absorbs and they are ready to eat! Such products are doubtless here to stay, selling in enormous quantities, and indicating just how popular 'convenience food' is. Of course, their flavourings can never be as good as home-cooked sauces or flavourings, using one's own choice of fresh ingredients, as I hope my selection of recipes will indicate.

Before we get to those though, let's look in detail at some of the more important flavourers needed to make tasty noodles.

Important noodle-flavouring ingredients

Here are some notes about certain flavouring ingredients which are used in this book. They are cross-referenced in the index, should you need to find them again.

Bulbs, Rhizomes and Roots

GALANGAL

Galangal is pale creamy buff with tinges of flamingo pink, and regular thin dark stripes around it. It has a more pointed appearance than ginger. Its flesh is white and its flavour is quite distinctive. Available from Thai and Chinese shops, it should be used in Thai cooking whenever you can get it. It is kept and used like ginger.

GARLIC

FRESH GARLIC Garlic, the most ancient of flavourings, was used as a form of pay for the Israelite slave labourers who built the

Egyptian pyramids. So important to them was it, that they went on strike – a truly courageous thing for any slave to do – following the withdrawal of their garlic ration by an over-pompous site fore-man, as a punishment for their not working hard enough. Amazingly, and probably because there were no replacement labourers available at the time, they won their battle, and their garlic ration was reinstated

At the same time garlic was the mainstay of both Indian and Chinese cooking, and as the other south Asian nations emerged, they too took to garlic. In Europe, the Greeks and Romans loved it, as did the Moors, and so it became widely used in all but north Europe. Indeed, much to the disdain of the French, it took the English and the rest of the English-speaking world until the latter part of this century to get to love garlic. I remember when I was young, back in the early 1950s, my grandmother having to place special orders with the greengrocer for garlic, which could take weeks to fulfil.

Mind you, current surveys reveal that 8 per cent of the British public say they have still never eaten and never will eat garlic! Fortunately, such uncompromising attitudes are on the decline, and as the recipes in this book testify, Britain's range of dishes and ingredients, leaves contemporary culinary France with much to envy.

As to the garlic products on offer, fresh is now universally avail-able. Buy big fat bulbs, yielding big fat cloves, if you can. Asian stores always have the best garlic.

I'm afraid, I cannot suggest any short-cuts for peeling garlic. All the gismos I have tried fail to work properly. Chopping garlic is easy enough with a small sharp knife. I am not a fan of the garlic press. It alters the flavour of garlic, in my view, probably because it squeezes the all-important juices out of it. Also, cleaning it always seems to create more work than simple chopping. If you must do it the labour-saving way, invest in a baby electric food processor.

It is a good idea to make up a large batch of chopped garlic (this minimises smells and washing up) and freeze it in an ice cube mould and tray, dedicated to the job of freezing spicy items. When frozen, break out of the mould and transfer to bags within a seal-able plastic box – again to minimise smells.

BOTTLED MINCED GARLIC This is the lazy person's answer to the above. It is a really good product, and will keep outside the fridge for several weeks. It does save time and effort, but the down side is that it simply does not taste as good as fresh.

GARLIC POWDER This powder or dried garlic granules is another labour-saving device for the lazy or time-starved cook. It is a fine powder, and should be kept, like any spice, in an airtight jar.

GINGER

FRESH GINGER Ginger is a rhizome or root which grows underground, and is native to Asia and other similar climates. Although it comes in various forms, it is used fresh and it stays fresh for many months after being cropped. As with garlic, I remember my grandmother attempting to order fresh ginger back in the Fifties. She met with far less success even than garlic, but every now and again, a nice big chunk of ginger would arrive, which formed the mainstay of her home-made ginger beer, and her curries.

Even in the beginning of the 1990s ginger was not available at most supermarkets. Nowadays, it is, although the best quality is always still to be found at specialist Asian shops. Size is not always a guide to quality. It should look plump, not withered, and have a pinky beige skin and a slight sheen. When cut the ginger should be a primrose-cream colour with no sign at all of blue or staleness. It is not possible to tell if it is stale until you cut it, so if you know your greengrocer well, ask him to cut it before you buy it. It should not be stringy or very dry and tough.

A tip to save you work: ginger does not need peeling. Cut away any dry scars or bad marks, but leave the skin intact. The skin is only a mimimal part of the whole ginger, and it becomes unnoticeable once the ginger is chopped. Contrary to some opinions, I do not find that the skin causes the ginger to taste bitter. Excess ginger can be frozen as garlic (*see above*).

Ginger is quite hot and pungent so do not overdo the amount used in a recipe unless you are a ginger freak.

DRIED GINGER This is bone hard and needs a 24-hour soak in ample water to reconstitute it, after which it can be cut and minced, though it has to be said that it is not as effective in flavour and texture as the fresh version.

GROUND GINGER Factory ground ginger is a useful spice in Indian curry spice mixtures. As a last resort, in the absence of fresh ginger, ground ginger can be substituted.

Bottled Minced Ginger As with bottled minced garlic, this too is a really good product, with the same up and down sides.

Pickled Whole Ginger This is a delicate and useful product, which can be a substitute for the real thing, but is better, in my view, as an accompanying pickle in its own right.

Young Ginger Also called stem ginger, this is paler and juicier than regular ginger, for which it can be substituted.

Lesser Ginger Lesser ginger has a cluster of yellowy brown fingers, each averaging between 6cm and 15cm (2½–6 in) in length and 1cm (⅓ in) in diameter, which drop down from a central stem. It has pale yellow flesh, milder, sweeter and more aromatic than ginger and it is particularly favoured in Thai dishes. Available from Thai and oriental shops, lesser ginger keeps well and is used like ginger.

ONION

The onion type I like to use is the large English or Spanish onion. Its size makes for minimal peeling (little onions require more work!) although I have no remedy for tears while chopping! Spring onions are a great boon for many dishes, and I generally use the bulbs and the best of the leaves.

TURMERIC

Turmeric is also a rhyzome, and a relative of ginger. The fresh root is available in various varieties and shapes from the Thai or Indian shop. The skin is browner than ginger. The flesh is bright orange. It is used in some Thai recipes, as is the more familiar turmeric powder.

WASABI

Wasabi is a Japanese member of the horseradish family. The root is black and knobbly, and grows in water. It even resembles a king prawn in appearance, however there is nothing fishy about it. Cut a slice off it and a moist pale green, rooty flesh appears. It smells like horseradish, and tastes like it, if a bit milder. Commercially wasabi is available as a powder and, from the tube, as a paste. Both these usually have food colouring, flour and mustard added, but if you can get the real thing from a Japanese grocer (sometimes Chinese or Thai grocers supply it) there is no comparison. *See page* 88 for wasabi soy.

WASABI POWDER This is finely ground dried wasabi root. It is pale green in colour, and is made up exactly like English mustard powder.

WASABI PASTE This is available in tubes, though, as with ready-made mustard, it is rather less pungent than the powder.

Chilli

The major spice, chilli is the seed-carrying, fleshy pod, or fruit, of a perennial shrub, whose botanical name is *capsicum*. The principal attribute of chilli is its piquancy or 'hot' taste. The level of 'heat' varies from zero in the Capsicum sweet pepper (also called bell pepper, as I have done in this book) to ten out of ten in a few species. Chilli pods are available fresh, or dried, in which form they can be powdered. Once the taste for chilli is acquired, and a tolerance level for heat is built up, it becomes an indispensable flavouring to certain people, especially in the East.

Yet, it was not until the sixteenth century, in the years just after Columbus that chillies were 'discovered' in the Americas, and were brought to India and the Orient by the Portuguese. Until then the heat agent had been peppercorns, but, of course certain chillies were hotter by far. The peoples of these spicy lands took to the chilli as if it had been native, and within a generation, it had become as much a part of their ancient cuisine, as if it had always been there. The chilli's conquest of the English-speaking world was not to come until much later. But come it has, and now our supermarkets offer increasing numbers of fresh chilli varieties. Here are the principal ones scored in descending order of 'heat' level:

MEXICAN HABAÑERO, 2–3cm, pointed heart-shaped,
    pale green, yellow, orange, scarlet   10
CARIBBEAN SCOTCH BONNET, 2 –3cm, more
    rounded, same colours   9 to 10
THAI MINIATURE, 1–2cm, red and green   8 to 9

INDIAN CAYENNE, 3–5cm, red or green	7 to 8
DUTCH RED, 10–15cm, needs de-seeding, and de-pithing	4 to 5
AFRICAN SNUB or JALAPEÑO GREEN, 5–7cm, ditto	3 to 5
ANAHEIM, 12–20cm or more, green, ditto	2 to 4
HUNGARIAN WAX, 10 to 15cm, canary yellow, ditto	2 to 4
BELL PEPPER, red, yellow, green, orange, white, black, ditto	0

Red dried chilli pods for these and many more varieties, are also readily available. Chilli powder is available in various heat strengths, the hottest of which is 'extra hot' (about 9 on the heat scale).

Coconut

The coconut is the largest edible nut in the the world. It grows pro-lifically in the eastern tropics, and is widely used in Indian, Thai and Malaysian cooking, though not in Chinese. This vast seed, growing atop a palm tree, is enclosed with a thick fibrous circular casing, green in colour. It is de-husked with a cleaver to reveal the more familiar brown hairy ovate coconut, with three small depressions, or 'eyes'. Inside it is coconut water – a pleasant-tasting transparent liquid.

When buying a fresh coconut, shake it to ensure it is full of liquid. The more liquid it has, the fresher it is. The liquid can be drunk or used in stock. A coconut without liquid, or with mouldy or wet 'eyes', should not be used. The all-important part of the coconut in culinary terms is its 'flesh'. This is a bright white layer, coating the inside husk of the sphere. To reach it, we must 'open' the coconut.

TO OPEN A COCONUT

1   Make a hole in two of the three 'eyes' with a clean screwdriver or nail. Drain off and keep the liquid (coconut water) for stock.
2   Try to split the coconut in half by tapping briskly with a cleaver or hammer.
3   Scrape out the flesh using a small knife, potato peeler or if you can get one from the oriental shop, a purpose-made coconut scraper.

4   Pare off the dark inner husk or skin (except on a younger coconut when it is soft and inoffensive, and always for desserts, when you need whiter flesh).

The flesh can be eaten in chunks or scrapings. It is also used to make coconut milk (not to be confused with coconut water, see above, which incidentally was charmingly named 'coconut pee' by Mai, the manageress of Bangkok's Oriental Hotel cookery school).

TO MAKE COCONUT MILK

1   Put the scraped flesh into a bowl with warm water. Squeeze it for a few minutes. Strain it. Thais use a purpose-made two handled close-weave basket for this job. This is called the 'first pressing' and it creates thick coconut milk (also called coconut cream).
2   Repeat stage one twice more for the 'second' and 'third' pressing.

Each pressing yields a thinner result. Medium coconut milk is a mixture of the second and third pressings. Thin is the third only.

COOKING WITH COCONUT MILK

Coconut milk sometimes appears to curdle when heat is applied. Don't worry; this is normal. It can't curdle, so just keep stirring.

READY-TO-USE COCONUT PRODUCTS

Dealing with a fresh coconut is very easy and they are quite inexpensive too. And nothing compares with the real thing, of course. However it is time consuming, and it is a good idea to keep some factory-made coconut products in stock.

CANNED COCONUT MILK Available in 400ml (13 fl oz) cans from various manufacturers. But not all supply thick coconut milk. Blue Dragon is a particularly excellent brand. If you don't shake the can before you open it, you'll find that the top third is thick cream and underneath is thin milk. Once shaken it is medium. Keeping the can in the fridge before opening makes the separation even better.

COCONUT MILK POWDER The problem with using canned coconut milk is that you are sometimes left with excess milk. This can be frozen, of course (or used in Pina Coladas to refresh the cook!), but it's a mite inconvenient. Coconut milk powder, a relatively new product, solves this. It is a thin white powder, made, like instant coffee, by freeze-drying coconut milk. It can be used by the spoonful and keeps indefinitely in an airtight container, to be used when required.

Ignore any instruction on the packet which advises you to 'mix with water' before use. Simply add it to your cooking and stir it in. It won't go lumpy. Then add water if needed.

CREAMED COCONUT This is a 200g (7 oz) block, a combination of freshly grated coconut flesh and coconut oil, which sets solid. It is the very familiar taste in restaurant Korma curries. The block must be kept refrigerated and to use, boil a little water, cut off the amount required and melt it in the hot water. If you try to fry it without water, it will burn.

DESICCATED COCONUT This is coconut flesh scrapings which are air-dried. It can be used by adding it dry to your cooking, or by simmering in water and straining it to create coconut milk.

COCONUT OIL Used in certain Indian curries particularly down south, coconut oil comes set solid in bottles with no instructions as to how to extract it. It is, however, simple. Ensure the cap is screwed on tightly then immerse the bottle in hot water for a few minutes. The oil becomes transparent and liquid as it melts. It can be used instead of sunflower or soya oils in any dish which uses coconut milk or flesh.

Dairy Products

In the main noodle lands, China, Indo China and Thailand, dairy products are not part of the main savoury diet. Nothing could be further from the case in India or Arabia, where many savoury dishes have one or more dairy products. And of course, in the West, we love to add such items to our cooking.

Herbs and Leaves

Herbs are an important flavourer, used worldwide. In India and the Orient coriander and basil are the most popular and they are used quite prolifically in cooking. Mint (spearmint) is also used. As some of my noodle recipes originate in Europe, we'll also be using parsley, oregano and fennel.

BASIL

Basil had the distinction of being nominated 'king' of herbs in ancient times. Indigenous to east Asia, it had reached Europe by the time of the Greek Empire. It was so revered that it got its name from the Greek royals (*basilikos*, meaning royal). Indeed sources state that only the sovereign (*basileus*) was permitted to eat it. And to discourage the general public from trying it, rumours abounded that this herb could turn people into scorpions.

Today there are 40 varieties of basil available worldwide. Most common in Britain is sweet basil (*ocimum basilicum*). Two varieties of purple basil (purple ruffle and dark opal) are also available. Overall a pretty beetroot in colour, the leaves of the former, are quite deeply serrated, and the latter less so, but its fragrance is more spicy, veering towards that of ginger.

Thai sweet basil (*ocimum basilicum horapha*) or *Bai Horapa* in Thai is becoming more readily available. It is slightly spicier than the Western variety, with a strong hint of fennel seed or aniseed. Its appearance is different from Western sweet basil. Its leaves are a little smaller, with a pointed tip, and sometimes have a slight purply tinge, and it is often available with small edible purple flowers.

BOTTLED MINCED BASIL This product uses the above-mentioned Thai *horapa* basil, and it encapsulates that delicious and unique aniseed flavour. A teaspoon or two is good, not only as a substitute for any recipe which calls for Thai basil, but indeed any recipe which requires any type of basil. It also works well as a good blending flavour in addition to real basil.

CORIANDER

Fresh coriander (*coriandrum sativum*) is now widely available in the West. Its musky candle waxy flavour is decidedly an acquired taste, but once acquired one cannot live without it. Incidentally like basil the word coriander also derives from a Greek word, though coriander has humbler connotations. The word is *koris*, a bug (actually said to be a bed bug, with a particularly foetid smell). Not being an expert in such matters, as I'm sure you aren't either, I can't confirm its validity.

If you want the appearance of coriander, but not its musk, use flat leaf parsley (*petro selinum sativum*). Since the two leaves look similar, the trick to identification at the greengrocer is to crush a leaf in your fingers. Only coriander has the musky smell.

BOTTLED MINCED CORIANDER This product encapsulates the flavour of coriander, albeit a little different from the real thing. A teaspoon or two is good, not only as a substitute for, but in addition to the real thing.

FENNEL

Fennel is a versatile ingredient. Its bulb is used as a vegetable, its seed as an aromatic spice, and its frond-like leaves, as a highly ornamental and decorative herb.

MINT

Mint is far too aromatic and exciting to be passed up by noodle cooks. There are numerous mint species, the best of which for noodle-cooking purposes is spearmint.

OREGANO

Particularly associated with Italian food.

PARSLEY

Used for its decorative properties as well as its flavour in many European dishes.

LEMON GRASS

FRESH LEMON GRASS Most of us are familiar with the smell of lemon grass or citronella (*cymbopogon citratus*). It is sweetish and, in my view, only vaguely lemony, but very distinctly fragrant. It is widely used in soaps.

The plant itself is indispensable to south-east Asian cooking. In Thailand it is called *takrai*, in Malaysia and Indonesia, *serai*, in Laos *sikhai*. It is a grass, but only the thin stalky bulbous end is used. Now readily available, fresh in the west, we get to purchase the bulbous end and a little of the green stalk, in pieces about 25cm (10in) long. To use, pull off any tough outer stem, cut off the bottom ½–1cm (⅓ in), and cut off the upper stalk where it changes from white to green (this should leave you with a piece between 10cm and 15cm/ 4–6 in in length).

There are two cutting methods for lemon grass referred to in the recipes in this book.

The Tassel Place the lemon grass, prepared as above, flat on the chopping board, holding the thinner upper end. Cut longways for about three quarters of their length, several times. This will create a one-piece tassel.

This method is used to infuse the lemon grass in a recipe, the tassel giving maximum surface area. It can be used as a garnish but not eaten in this form.

Cross-cut Having prepared the lemon grass, make only one cut longways, as described in the tassel. Then cross the diameter of the bulbous end towards the green end. As an option, this can be slightly diagonal. This creates thin semi-circles. Now break these apart to create half moons resembling 'finger nails'. Hopefully they are not!

Add them to the recipe as directed. They are edible in this form, the thinner the better.

Fresh lemon grass can be frozen. It is also available cross-cut dried and in powder form. Both forms need an hour or two reconstituting in water and are nothing like as good, of course, as fresh.

BOTTLED LEMON GRASS The best part of the stalks are available bottled about 7–8cm (3 in) long, preserved in sterilised lemon grass water. The Blue Dragon quality is very good, retaining the delicacy of the fragrance. In this form, they are the best substitute to fresh, and can be used in tassels or cross-cut (see above). The liquid can be used too. Please note that once opened they do not keep in the fridge for more than a few days. They can be frozen, however.

DRIED LEMON GRASS These are either dried cross-cut (see above) or whole, and must be reconstituted in water for several hours. Their disadvantage is that they do not retain as much flavour as bottled lemon grass. Their advantage is that they can be stored indefinitely in an airtight jar in the cupboard as with spices.

POWDERED LEMON GRASS The least effective of all forms, but useful if you just need a pinch or two of lemon grass flavouring now and again. As with all powdered spices, keep in the dark in an airtight jar, and replace after six months, as it will progressively lose its flavour.

Limes and Lime Leaves

WHOLE LIME There are two different types of lime found in south-east Asia. The 'regular' or common lime is a green or yellow ovate ball with a smooth skin and sharp juice (*Citrus aurantifolia*) or *Manao* in Thai.

The more commonly used Thai lime is harder to find in the West, but is worth seeking out at the Thai or oriental shop. Called the wild lime (*Citrus hytrix*), *kaffir* or *makroot* in Thai, it is about the same size and shape as the common lime, but it has a knobbly skin. Its juice is much sweeter, as is its pith and skin. Both are used in Thai cooking, whereas the common lime is rarely called for. This commonly leads to mistakes in certain Thai cookery books, which call for liberal amounts of lime juice and/or peel. This creates a sharp taste which you'd never find in Thailand. It is the *kaffir* lime you need and it is a relative of the bergamot family.

LIME LEAF Lime leaves are from the *kaffir* tree. They are another secret weapon in the south-east Asian culinary repertoire, particularly in Thailand, where they are known as *Bai-makroot*, and are used like bay leaves. They are wonderful if you can get them, but have no substitute if you can't. They are shiny, dark green, more or less circular leaves, about 4cm (1½ in) in diameter, or smaller. Their peculiarity is that they grow in pairs, one above the other, on branches with sharp thorns like rose-tree branches. They are available dried (acceptable if you can't get fresh ones, but get double the quantity), or powdered (the least useful variety). Fresh is best, of course, from the Thai and oriental shop. They can be used whole or cut into the thinnest strips (chifonade strips) after removing the stem. Whole leaves are inedible, but the shreds are delicious to eat.

Fresh lime leaves can be frozen.

Miso Mix

Miso is a Japanese flavouring paste made, like so many other food-stuffs, by fermenting soya beans and salt (brine), with a grain such as rice or barley. Its production dates back to at least the sixth century AD. It has a very intensely savoury flavour, and is used in soups and broths served with soba and udon noodles. It is available in convenient-sized sachets.

Mushrooms, dried and canned

For as long as anyone can remember, the Chinese have preserved their mushrooms by drying them in the sun to keep them more or less indefinitely. To reconstitute them, place the mushrooms in a large bowl, and pour in enough boiling water to fill the bowl. Leave to soak for 30 minutes then drain. They give a distinctive flavour, colour and texture to one's cooking. These are the principal types:

DRIED BLACK OR BROWN MUSHROOMS (*dong-gu*) These have a thick cap and strongish fragrance. The larger ones with a pale colour and cracked skins have the best flavour. These are called Shitaké mushrooms in Japan.

CLOUD EARS OR WOOD EARS (*mu-er*) These grow on trees and are used mainly for texture. They are brown and have a curly-leaf shape.

SILVER FUNGUS, SNOW EAR OR WHITE WOOD FUNGUS These are similar to cloud or wood ears, only whitish in colour. They are crunchy and pretty but rare, and so are extremely expensive. They are available dried or canned.

STRAW MUSHROOMS are small and teardrop-shaped. They are very flavourful and readily available canned.

Oils

Butter does not figure in the cooking of China, Indo-China and Thailand, nor do lard or dripping, and these latter two simply don't exist there. Their cooking always uses light, unsaturated oils, such as sunflower, soya, vegetable or corn oil. In China, but not the other countries, sesame oil is used. Butter is used in clarified form (ghee) in the curries of Malaysia, Singapore and the subcontinent, but any of the above oils can also be used. Coconut oil is used in the southern areas. None of these countries uses olive oil or nut oils. They impart too distinctive a flavour to the cooking. However, in European cooking, we can and must use these in certain recipes and I've used butter too in a few recipes in this book.

Prawn and Shrimp, and Fish Products

FISH SAUCE

Fish sauce is widely used in the cooking of south-east Asia as a salting agent. In Burma, it is called *nga-pya*, the Phillipines: *patis*; Vietnam: *nuoc mam*; Cambodia: *tuk trey*; Laos: *padek*; and Thailand: *nam pla*. This is the product you either love or hate. All these countries love it. My wife Dominique hates it, and in blind tasting sessions, she can tell if I've sneaked in even one drop.

So what is it? It is a clear brown liquid, the colour of beer. Different brands vary in darkness and in quality. Fish sauce is factory-made and is smelly. Thailand's main area for producing it is in Rayong near Pattaya, and it is here that the high-quality Blue Dragon product is made. Its main ingredient is any oily fish (but mostly small anchovies are used) mixed in large vats, with an equal volume of salt, and enough water to float the fish. The vats are left netted, but uncovered in the sun for one year. As it dries the fish ferments, and more water, salt and a little sugar is added. It is then strained and the clear brown liquid is bottled, ready for use.

If all that has put you off, you may like to know that you have almost certainly consumed and enjoyed it. Until recently it was the secret ingredient in the much copied, but never equalled Lea & Perrins Worcestershire Sauce, from its first formulation (unchanged to this day) in 1838. It is only recently that legislation compelled manufacturers to reveal their ingredients, forcing Lea & Perrins to put 'anchovies' on their list (read the label!). But in a final attempt not to reveal their key ingredient, they did not specifically call it fish sauce!

Incidentally the concept of using fermented fish and salt is far from new. The Romans used it in their mixture called *garum*. Whether that predated the East's version is not known. Of course, it came up-to-date in Britain (especially in Victorian times) in the form of anchovy essence.

As to using it, unless you are Dominique, the fish taste doesn't dominate if it is used in moderation. It does supply a lot of salt, so I have not stipulated 'salt to taste' in those recipes which call for it. If fish sauce does not suit you (and true vegetarians fall into that category) either omit it altogether and use salt or soy sauce. The taste in each case will, however, be different.

PRAWNS, DRIED

Since the original Thais settled along the waterways, they became and still are very dependent on fish and shellfish. Not only do they eat it fresh at every opportunity, they mastered the art of drying it centuries ago.

Fish are gutted and boned, spread flat, then hung up on frames to dry in the sun. Within a day of fierce Thai sunshine they are bone dry, brittle and translucent, will keep indefinitely, and can be used at any time in cooking. Take a look at the Thai shop and like as not, there will be plenty of choice. Although I've not used dried fish in the recipes in this book you can use them in any wet (not fried) fish dish by reconstituting them in water first.

PLATE THREE

CELLOPHANE AND RICE NOODLES All noodles shown full-size. See Noodle Directory (page 219) for more information.

Left to right, top row: stir-fry rice (vermicelli) noodles, rice sticks, wide – 1cm, medium-size – 6mm, shown sideways and full-on, and thin – 5mm (sen lek), Chinese fine rice sticks, and Vietnamese fine rice sticks.

Middle row: tangled rice stick, Changdou rice stick (with the red tie), below it: crispy noodles (potato flour).

Third row: fresh rice noodle sheet (with chilli in the dough), Indian gram dough sev noodles, fresh vermicelli rice noodles, and bean thread noodles.

Bottom row (after fresh rice noodle sheet with chilli): fresh rice noodles, 12mm, and 16mm, fresh silver thread needle noodles, dried Hankow broad bean noodles (with red and white tie), and baby bean thread noodles.

Likewise dried prawns. These I have specified in certain recipes. They are available in large sachets of small dried curled pink prawns. They last indefinitely, kept in an airtight jar, and are used as required.

SHRIMP PASTE

Like fish sauce, above, shrimp paste gives a fundamental flavour to many south-east Asian savoury recipes. They use a tablespoon or more (I've cut that down to a teaspoon in some recipes, and even that can be omitted – with a minor change in taste – if you don't want it).

The Burmese and Indonesian variants, *blachan* and *trasi*, are hard blocks, yellow in colour. The Thai version, *kapee*, is softer and not as strong in flavour, being a paste, often browny-pink in colour.

Most shrimp paste is made by mashing river prawns with salt and water. Factory versions come in tubs or jars with a wax seal. Once opened, it should last for months without refrigeration. A very important point should be made about factory shrimp paste. It should always be fried at a high temperature early on in the recipe. The heat will eliminate the unlikely possibility of bacteriological contamination.

Salt

Soy and fish sauce are intensely salted. One or other appears in virtually every oriental noodle recipe. Consequently I have not stated 'salt to taste' as I would normally. If you prefer to omit fish sauce then please salt to taste. Thais use rock salt

JAPANESE NOODLES All noodles are shown full-size. See Noodle Directory (page 219) for more information.

Left to right, top row: somen noodles: half-length white, full-length pink, yellow, white, pale-green, and dark-green. Soba buckwheat (longer sticks): green (cha-soba), brown and grey.

Middle row: fresh udon: white and brown.

Bottom row: Kishimen cream sticks, white udon, Kishimen white sticks, Harusame, and Ramen, Chinese-style wheat noodles, curly.

Saké and other Rice Wines

Saké is Japan's national drink. It is made by brewing fermented rice and has a high alcoholic content (up to 20 per cent). It is called a wine, and is the colour of white wine, though it tastes more like a spirit. It can be drunk warm, at room temperature or chilled, and is used in cooking. *Mirin* is also a Japanese rice wine, though it has a lower alcohol content (14 per cent) and is used only for cooking. Chinese rice wines have been continually produced since 2000 BC by fermenting glutinous rice (and to a lesser extent maize, wheat, millet or barley but never the grape) with yeast and water. The best Chinese cooking (and drinking) wine is called *Shaoxing* and comes from eastern China. It is called 'yellow' rice wine, but is in fact pale brown in colour, and is 16 per cent proof.

Seaweed (*Nori laver*)

Japanese food is often flavoured with various types of seaweed (*kaiso*). Kelp (*konbu*) is used on its own in dishes or in a stock called *dashi* (*see page* 79), with *bonito* fish flakes. A bright green powdered or flaked seaweed which is used as a sprinkler and sometimes appears in seven-spice mix (qv) is called *ao-nori*. This is made from a different species of seaweed algae from *nori* (or *nori laver*). The first *nori* was processed in Tokyo Bay in the late seventeenth century. Its main production area is now Ariake Bay in west Japan. The protein and vitamin-packed algae are drained and sun-dried to create the familiar thin sheets, which are then cut into into paper-thin sheets. The darker in colour the sheet, the better the flavour and quality. The sheets are then lightly roasted and packed in sheets of ten, with a pack of inedible silicone moisture absorber. Once the pack is opened, the *nori* will lose its crispness by taking on all the ambient moisture. This can be reversed, however, by re-roasting – a brief heat under the grill will do. *Nori's* major use is in Sushi (*see page* 95) and the Blue Dragon pack of ten 20cm (8 in) square sheets is called 'Sushi Nori'.

A further kind of seaweed is the Chinese restaurant version. Called crispy deep-fried seaweed, it isn't seaweed at all. It is deep-fried Chinese leaves, but it is supremely tasty, and a recipe for it appears on *page* 204.

Soy

Soy or soya beans are the Chinese answer to everything. As one of their main suppliers of protein, they have made this unremarkable and rather tasteless small round bean into something amazing. How exactly this came about is lost in the mists of time but many thousands of years ago the Chinese learned to use the soya bean in many forms.

In its natural state the soya bean is small and pale cream in colour. It is perfectly good cooked straightforwardly as a bean. Equally, it makes the now very familiar beansprout, which is widely available at greengrocers. The ancients learned to ferment it with salt. After some time, it turns black, brown or yellow and is then soft enough to make into thick salty flavouring pastes and thin salty runny sauces of varying strengths. The Chinese also learned to compress the bean into cheese-like blocks (tofu or bean curd – see below) which could be crumbled or cut, and cooked and into wafer-thin, pastry-like sheets (bean curd wrappers). They also learned how to make it into a cooking oil and into a milk-like drink. No wonder the Chinese revere their humble bean so much. I cannot think of another raw material or ingredient so versatile.

Soy Sauce

Soy or soya sauce is a condiment particularly essential to the Chinese and Japanese way of life. In these countries the average person consumes at least one litre (2 pints) of soy sauce per month.

It is made by fermenting soya beans, water, yeast and salt for up to six months. The resultant liquid is strained and bottled. It improves with age, but equally it is best consumed by the 'use-by' date on the bottle, after which it gradually changes in taste, and can eventually crystallise. Light soy mixture has less fermenting beans than dark soy. The latter is generally used for cooking, whilst the light is used for seasoning. Japanese soy (*shoyu*) is used for both, and is perhaps more delicate in flavour than Chinese. Indonesian soy (*ketchap manis*) is darker and more syrupy, being enhanced with sugar or molasses. Conimex is my favourite make of soy sauce and I refer to it as sweet soy in the relevant recipes. *Ketchap*, incidentally, means sauce in Indonesian, hence tomato ketchup.

Spices

Indian cuisine uses more spices than any other national style of cooking. The few Indian noodle dishes which appear in this book use common spices such as turmeric, coriander, cumin, cardamoms, cassia clove and chilli, plus a few others which are normally in everyone's store cupboard. *See also* Garam Masala and Panch Phoran on pages 83–85. Chinese dishes uses less spices, and they are more aromatic than Indian. (*See* Chinese Five-Spice and Ten-Spice on page 82.) The Japanese have a seven-spice mixture (*see page* 83). Thai dishes require the fragrance of lemon grass, lime leaves and herbs such as basil and coriander.

Sugar

Sugar is used in almost every Thai savoury recipe. The sugar they use is palm sugar (*nam taan peep*) which is processed from the Palmyra tree. Some Indian dishes require a touch of sugar, and their palm sugar is called *gur*. Indian *jaggery* (made from sugar cane) is a suitable alternative. All three are available in a soft yellow and fudge-like form from the Thai or Asian shops in packets or cans. Kept in the fridge it lasts about three months. If you have a sweet tooth, one or other is worth getting because each has a gorgeous flavour, unlike any 'ordinary' sugar. Of course 'ordinary' white or brown sugar can substitute.

I have to say that I prefer to cook my savoury dishes without sugar. Consequently, unless it is really important to the character of a particular dish (Talai Mee on page 180 is an example) I have made sugar an optional extra in the relevant recipes.

Sun Dried Tomato

Italy's secret weapon as a formidable flavourer, and now becoming widely known in the English-speaking world, this is available dried, in oil, and as a paste.

Tamarind purée

To make tamarind purée, buy a packet of tamarind (it usually comes in 300g blocks). Break it into a saucepan, cover with an ample layer of water and simmer. Work it around with the back of a spoon until husks and seeds have separated from the flesh. Strain through a sieve, working the pulp with your fingers. Return the husks and seeds to the saucepan with more water to repeat the process. Combine the two brown liquids in the saucepan. If it is thin and watery, simmer until it reduces. Use within a week or freeze.

Tofu

Tofu or (soy) bean curd has the texture of cheese. It can be either soft or firm depending on the process used to make it. It is made by soaking and puréeing white soya beans. The purée is then boiled in water which is strained to make soya milk. This is brought back to the simmer, and a curdling agent, such as lemon juice, is added. It is then restrained and the solid matter is compressed in moulds. After some time the result is a firm block of tofu. This ingenious process was first invented around 2,000 years ago by the scientists of a Chinese emperor of the Han Dynasty (206 BC to AD 221). Tofu is easily obtained in packets from delicatessens and health-food shops. It is virtually flavourless and very high in protein. It is used for its texture and can be diced, sliced, minced or mashed then boiled, baked, stir-fried or deep-fried.

TOFU OR BEAN CURD SHEETS

Following the above tofu process the soy bean curd can also be made into thin sheets. They are skin-like, pale yellow, very thin and translucent, but quite tough, though care is needed in handling them.

Available from oriental stores, in packets, the sheets are used as wrappers, following reconstitution in water. They can be substituted for wonton wrappers in any of my recipes.

Wonton Wrappers

Also known as wonton pastry, sheets or skin. Wonton is a type of very thin pastry made from wheat flour and egg. In fact, the dough for the pastry is none other than that used for egg noodles. Invented in China, the normal size of each sheet is around 8cm (3⅕ in) square. A larger version, called spring roll wrapper is about 30cm (12 in) square.

Specialist bakers make this pastry and it takes years of training to produce translucently thin pastry of even thickness. For this reason, it is convenient to buy ready-made wrappers. They are available at specialist shops, frozen, in packets containing varying numbers of sheets. If you cannot obtain them, filo pastry or samosa pads are good alternatives.

Whatever sheet you use, beware that because they are so thin, they can quickly dry out and become brittle. To prevent this, thaw the packet, before opening it. Once opened, keep the wrappers covered with a cold clean damp tea towel at all times, except when removing a sheet for use.

Making Noodles

Making noodles is easier than making bread. There is no need for a raising agent, as for bread, but there is a big need for kneading! All you have to do is make a dough. Kneading is the careful and positive mixing (strenuous to some) which yields a lovely, elastic, cohesive dough. The elasticity comes from the flour's sticky properties, the best of which is, as discussed earlier, gluten in wheat. It is for this reason that wheat flours give the best, most cohesive doughs, strong white flour used for wheat noodles (or udon) being the best. Eggs are added to wheat flour to help binding. Other doughs using rice flour, gram flour, mung bean flour and buckwheat flour are less cohesive, and the inexperienced may have to use wheat flour to help, as explained in the recipes which follow. Dough-making machines, whilst not essential, do make kneading easier. I don't think we need follow the age-old Japanese method for kneading in which they put the dough into a bag and knead it with their feet!

Egg Noodles

250g (9oz) plain flour	1 tablespoon vegetable oil
1 large egg yolk	1 teaspoon salt

1   Mix the flour with the egg yolk, oil and salt, and just enough water to form a soft, sticky dough. Knead it until it becomes elastic and cohesive.

2   Roll the dough out flat and, either cut it into strips as thinly as you
can, or use the pasta machine.

Wheat or Udon Noodles

125g (4½oz) strong white flour
125g (9oz) plain flour

1 tablespoon vegetable oil
1 teaspoon salt

1   Use the same method as for egg noodles above (omitting the egg).

Rice Noodles

250g (9oz) rice flour
1 tablespoon vegetable oil
1 teaspoon salt

1   Use the same method as for egg noodles above (omitting the egg).

NOTE: rice flour lacks the binding power of wheat flour, especially when not fresh. To overcome this use a proportion of strong
white flour. With practice in kneading it will work without. Hot
water helps too.

Soba

175g (6oz) buckwheat flour
75g (2¾oz) strong white flour

1 tablespoon vegetable oil
1 teaspoon salt

1   Use the same method as for egg noodles above (omitting the egg).

NOTE: buckwheat flour lacks the binding power (gluten) of wheat flour, especially when not fresh. To overcome this use a proportion of strong white flour. With practice in kneading it will work without. Hot water helps too.

Pasta

This is a typical pasta recipe, given for comparison with the above noodle recipes.

250g (9oz) semolina
1 egg
5g dried milk

1   Use the same method as for egg noodles above.

Cutting Noodles

The dough must be rolled out as thinly or thickly as you wish on a floured board. It is best not to work with too large a piece. To cut, simply cut the dough into parallel pieces again as large or as small as you wish. The noodles should be covered with stretch film or kitchen foil if they are not going to be cooked at once. This helps to prevent them from drying out, although it does not matter overly, if they do dry out a little. They should be boiled (see later) within a couple of days of making them.

Using a Noodle-making or Pasta machine

There are several makes, but all are much of a muchness. Choose the extrusion thickness of your desire. The dough is shaped and fed into the machine (which is either hand-cranked or electrical) and is cut into strands, the size of which is adjustable.

Dried Noodles versus Fresh Noodles

It's horses for courses, of course. There is minimal difference between the two when cooked, but note that 250g (9oz) of dried noodles is the equivalent of 500g (18oz) fresh.

Storing Noodles

Dried noodles will last indefinitely, if stored in their packets, in an airtight container, and kept in a dark place. The ultra-violet in sunlight or daylight will make them deteriorate within weeks. Fresh noodles should be kept covered in the fridge, and used within a couple of days.

Cooking Noodles

Cooking Dried Noodles by Boiling

1 Always use plenty of boiling water in a large enough pan. This allows the noodles to release their starch, and to move around and expand. And expand they will, by up to twice their dried size. Salting is quite unnecessary.

2 Once the noodles have been immersed, stir them gently to prevent them sticking together, or to the bottom of the pan, and be sure to bring the water back to the boil. Then and only then, stop stirring and turn off the heat, or keep simmering according to individual pack instructions.

3 Most packet noodles give timing instructions, but even so, it is wise to keep test-tasting until they are cooked to your liking. Noodles should always be al dente, i.e. they should have a good bite.

4 Timings will vary from one manufacturer to the next, even for a product which appears to be identical apart from the brand name. For example Blue Dragon egg noodles take 5 minutes to cook from

the moment they are immersed into boiling water. Sharwood's equivalent takes 7 minutes. The difference is probably in the flour.

5   If after the requisite time, the noodles have not softened enough, all is not lost. Simply bring the water back to the boil and simmer until ready.

6   As soon as you deem the noodles ready, drain them, shaking off all excess water, and serve them piping hot.

7   If the noodle water seems to be starchy, you may wish to rinse the cooked noodles with boiling water from a kettle, but remember it is in the nature of rice noodles to be glutinous.

8   Noodles can be chilled at once by rinsing them in cold water. They can be refrigerated and reheated (by immersing them in boiling hot water and repeating stage 6). Note: noodles treated this way will almost certainly be less 'fresh' and softer than served immediately after cooking.

9   Noodles can be frozen, although they are so quick to cook from scratch that this is only worthwhile if you have some noodles left over. Again, noodles treated this way will almost certainly be softer than served freshly cooked.

10 NOTE: the Japanese way to cook noodles is to bring the water to the boil, as in stage 1 above, but once it starts boiling, add a little cold water, enough to stop the boiling. When it reboils, repeat this process, three or four more times. Keep stirring the noodles throughout. This method takes a few minutes longer, but the Japanese believe it gives the noodles the ultimate in texture, by controlling the emission of starch. Try it and decide for yourself.

Cooking fresh noodles by soaking

Fresh noodles simply require a soak in boiling water, rather than an actual boiling. The technique is identical to the recipe for boiling given above, except that the water is brought to the boil, then the heat turned off before the noodles are immersed in the water for as long as it takes for them to become al dente.

Cooking dried noodles by soaking

Certain dried noodles are also cooked merely by soaking. These include any thin and fine dried noodles such as beancurd noodles, egg thread noodles, nest noodles and rice vermicelli. Cook by the soaking technique given for fresh noodles, above.

Noodles destined for soups or wet stews

These can be cooked by immersing them straight into the soup or stew liquid instead of pre-boiling. Time the noodles as for boiling or soaking as given above. Note that the noodles may release a little starch into the soup.

Stir-frying dried noodles

1   Follow the recipe for boiling dried noodles to stage 3, only under-cooking the noodles by about one full minute. Put another way, they should be soft right through, but more al dente than if they were boiled completely.
2   Follow stage 6 and, if necessary, stage 7 of the boiling recipe.
3   When well strained, add the noodles to the stir-fry as each relevant recipe requires. If cold, you will obviously need to give them more time to reheat, than if they are hot.

Deep-frying dried noodles

SAFETY NOTE: whatever you may have read or heard elsewhere, do not reconstitute (or soak in water) noodles intended for deep-frying. They must be absolutely dry, straight from the packet. Professional oriental chefs with suitable equipment do it, but in the home, the introduction of water to a deep-fryer can cause an almost explosive reaction, leading to a kitchen fire.

1   Heat the deep-fry oil to 190°C/375°F (chip-frying temperature).
2   Test the oil by dropping a tiny strand of noodle into the fat. It should almost jump out of the pan.
3   Have tongs and/or slotted spoon and kitchen paper ready alongside the deep-fryer.
4   Take a small quantity of noodles and place them carefully in the oil. They will whoosh up and expand rapidly, so do not do too many at once.

5   Remove the noodles at once, shaking off as much excess oil as you can, and put them on to the kitchen paper.

6   Allow the noodles to rest for a minute or two. This will enable them to 'dry out' and to become fully crispy.

CHEF'S TIP: the temperature of 190°C is critical for deep-frying. Below it, the noodles will not expand properly. Above it, they will burn, and, at worst, you risk a spontaneous oil fire. It should be pointed out that many proprietary deep-fry machines show 190°C as their highest temperature on the dial. However, their thermostats are often inaccurate, and they may never reach anywhere near the stated temperature. It is a good idea to purchase a purpose-made thermometer for the job.

Stocks

Many noodle dishes require a liquid stock base. It's worth making one or more types up in bulk and freezing them in suitable portion sizes (in large yoghurt pots, for example). Here are four types, each making enough stock for four or more dishes.

Chicken Stock

MAKES: ABOUT I LITRE (I¾ PINTS) OF STOCK

1.5 litres (2¾ pints) water
450g (1 lb) chicken bones
50g (2oz) chicken meat

50g (2oz) onion, chopped
2 cloves garlic, quartered

1   Select a pan large enough to hold both water and bones.

2   Bring the water to the boil in the pan. Add all the other ingredients.

3   Cover and simmer for 2 hours or so by which time you should have about 1 litre (1¾ pints) of stock.

4   Strain, discarding the bones and meat, and cool. Keep in the fridge and use within 2 days or freeze.

Meat Stock

MAKES: ABOUT I LITRE (I ¾ PINTS) OF STOCK

1.5 litres (2¾ pints) water
50g (2oz) onion, chopped
2 cloves garlic, quartered

2 lamb chops on the bone,
    leftover bones and cooked meat (any amount as
    available)

1   Bring the water to the boil, in a 3.5 litre (6 pint) saucepan.
2   Slash the flesh on the chops. Add them and the remaining ingredients to the saucepan.
3   Maintain a gentle simmer for at least 30 minutes, at most 45 minutes, stirring occasionally. Spoon off any scum.
4   Strain the liquid. Discard the solids.
5   Use as required. It will keep in the fridge for a few days, but should be reboiled before use. It can be frozen.

Fish Stock

Use a whole small fish, head, tail, bones and all for best results. Alternatively you can use filleted cod steaks enhanced with some prawns.

MAKES: ABOUT I LITRE (I ¾ PINTS) OF STOCK

1.5 litres (2¾ pints) water
225–300g (8–10½oz) herring or mackerel
2 tablespoons fish sauce

4 stalks lemon grass, finely cross-cut
50g (2oz) onion, chopped
2 cloves garlic, chopped

1   Bring the water to the boil in a 3.5 litre (6 pint) saucepan.
2   Roughly chop the fish, and use all of it. Add it with the remaining ingredients to the saucepan.
3   Follow the previous recipe to the end.

Vegetable Stock

A variant of the previous two stocks. True vegetarians can omit the fish sauce and replace it with light soy sauce.

MAKES: ABOUT 1 LITRE (1¾ PINTS) OF STOCK

1.5 litres (2¾ pints) water
100g (3½oz) carrot, chopped
100g (3½oz) celery, chopped
60g (2oz) dried Chinese mushrooms (optional)
60g (2oz) spring onions, chopped
60g (2oz) onion, peeled and chopped

4 stalks lemon grass, finely cross-cut
4 cloves garlic, peeled and chopped
1 tablespoon pickled ginger (see page 86)
2 tablespoons fish sauce (or light soy)
1 tablespoon spicy salt (see page 85)

1   Bring the water to the boil in a 3.5 litre (6 pint) saucepan.
2   Clean and roughly chop the vegetables and the onion. Add them and the other ingredients into the saucepan.
3   Follow the chicken stock recipe to the end.

Vintage Master Stock

The point of the vintage master stock is that once it is started, it is never allowed to run out, being topped up with any suitable bones and meat whenever available.

Vintage stocks are highly praised in China. I was told by a Chinese restaurateur that at his home in London, he had a stock which had been brought from China by his grandfather some 50 years earlier, when he first came to London as a sailor. The actual start date of this stock he did not know, but the earlier the better, he declared.

A vintage master stock will keep for ever provided that it is strained regularly and boiled at least every other day. Many international hotels run such a master stock system. Here is a traditional stock to start you off, using chicken, pork and duck.

3 litres (5 pints) water
1 cooked chicken carcass, skin removed
1 cooked duck carcass, skin removed

2 raw chicken drumsticks
2 raw pork chops, fat removed
1 tablespoon spicy salt

1   Select a large saucepan with a capacity of at least 4.5 litres (8 pints) and bring the water to the boil.

2   Break up the carcasses and drumsticks and chop up the raw meat. Put them into the boiling water with spicy salt. Put the lid on.

3   When the water comes back to the boil, reduce the heat to give a low rolling simmer.

4   Check after 1½ hours that all is well.

5   After 3 hours it will have reduced by about half. Remove from the heat. Strain, discarding the solid matter and cool.

6   Store in the fridge in a suitable lidded container.

7   Ensure that it is either reboiled every 2 days or that it is frozen.

8   Top up with any meat off cuts and sufficient water as required.

Japanese Dashi Stock

Dashi is a specialised Japanese stock which always accompanies soba (qv) noodle dishes.

As with many things Japanese, there are rigid, traditional and complicated rules about *dashi*-making. *Dashi* must always contain the seaweed *konbu* (kelp) and *bonito* (fish flakes) with *mirin* (cooking wine), sugar and *shoyu* (Japanese soy sauce). The stock goes cloudy after a day or so, so make it fresh each time. You can buy ready-made packet *dashi* mixes, though these usually contain MSG (monosodium glutamate).

MAKES: ABOUT 800ML (28 FL OZ) OF STOCK

750ml (1.3 pints) water
20g (⅔oz) bonito flakes
30g (1oz) kelp

50ml (2 fl oz) mirin
1 teaspoon sugar
shoyu to taste

1   Bring the water to the simmer, add the bonito flakes and kelp and simmer for 10 minutes.
2   Skim off any scum. Strain the keep liquid, discarding the solids.
3   Add the remaining ingredients, and serve hot, or allow it to go cold if required chilled.

Thai Magic Paste

There is a holy trinity of ingredients in Thai cooking. It comprises garlic, coriander and peppercorns, ground to a paste, and stir-fried into a dish at an early stage. It is so important to Thai cooks, that they call it their Magic Paste. Make a large batch and freeze it in your special ice cube mould (*see page 51*).

MAKES: ENOUGH FOR ABOUT 25 THAI DISHES

20 cloves garlic
200g (7oz) fresh coriander, leaves, stems and roots
50g (1¾oz) green or white peppercorns

1   Coarsely chop the garlic, coriander and peppercorns.
2   Place them in a food processor or blender, and mulch to a coarse purée, using a little water if necessary.
3   The paste will keep fresh for a few days in the fridge, or it can be frozen.

Chilli Oil

This clear red oil is frequently served in a tiny bowl as an accompaniment to the main meal. It is fiercely hot, and can only be made using fresh red chillies. It can also be used for cooking. This recipe makes a largish batch which can be bottled and kept indefinitely.

MAKES: ABOUT 350 ML (12 FL OZ) CHILLI OIL

225g (8oz) fresh red chillies
300ml (½ pint) soya or sunflower oil

1   Remove the stalks from the chillies, then slit them lengthways. Remove the seeds and any white pith.
2   Put them in a food processor and pulse into a purée. Alternatively finely chop them.
3   Heat the oil in a wok or frying pan to medium heat. Add the purée and stir-fry for 2 to 3 minutes, until the oil stops reddening.
4   Allow to cool then strain through muslin and store in an airtight bottle. Discard the chilli flesh.

Chilli and Garlic Sauce

There is the archetypal chilli sauce, which every Chinese restaurant produces on demand. Most don't actually make it – time is too pressing, they use the Blue Dragon version, which is readily available. However, if you're feeling adventurous you can make your own with relative ease. This recipe makes sufficient to bottle and, if made correctly, it can be kept indefinitely.

MAKES: ABOUT 350 ML (12 FL OZ) CHILLI OIL

450g (1lb) fresh red chillies
250ml (8 fl oz) Chinese white rice vinegar
1 teaspoon salt

4 teaspoons garlic powder
2 teaspoons sugar
2 teaspoons cornflour

1   Remove the stalks from the chillies, then slit them lengthways. Remove the seeds and any white pith.
2   Soak the chillies overnight in the vinegar and salt.
3   Next day put them into a food processor and pulse into a fine purée.

4 Add the garlic powder, sugar and cornflour and enough water to give a pourable consistency. Pulse briefly to mix.

5 Bottle and use as required.

Chinese Five-spice Powder

Also known as *ng heung fun* or *wu hsiang fen*, this wonderfully aromatic combination of spices is used regularly in Chinese cooking, so it is worth making a reasonable quantity.

It can of course be purchased, but this home-made version, being roasted, is of much better quality than anything from a factory.

MAKES: ABOUT 150G (5OZ)

30g (1oz) stick of cinnamon
30g (1oz) cloves
30g (1oz) fennel seeds

30g (1oz) star anise
30g (1oz) Szechwan peppercorns

1 Heat a wok on the stove top. It must be totally dry.
2 Mix together the whole spices and put them into the hot wok.
3 Dry stir-fry for about a minute.
4 Allow to cool completely.
5 Grind to a fine powder in a coffee grinder, electric spice mill or with a mortar and pestle.
6 Keep in an airtight jar. Use within 6 months for maximum flavour.

Chinese Ten-spice Powder

Also called Chinese Taste Powder, *wei fen* or *baa kuk tee*, this combination of flavourings is used as a sprinkler or as a dunking condiment. Use your own Five-Spice Powder (from the previous recipe). You can vary the proportions of the ingredients to suit your taste, if you wish.

MAKES: 150G (5OZ)

50g (2oz) Chinese Five-Spice Powder
50g (2oz) sea salt, finely ground
25g (1oz) caster sugar
1 teaspoon liquorice powder

20g (²⁄₃oz) Szechwan peppercorns, roasted and
  finely ground
1 teaspoon dried chives

1   Mix all the ingredients together thoroughly.
2   Store in an airtight jar. Use within 6 months for maximum flavour.

Japanese Seven-spice Powder

Called in Japanese *shichimi togarashi* and literally meaning 'seven-flavour chilli', this popular sprinkler may come in different combinations, but all must contain just seven ingredients. A typical Tokyo mix is roasted dried chilli, black sesame, noori seaweed, white poppy seeds, hemp (cannabis) seeds, Japanese sansho pepper (prickly ash seeds) and chinpi (dried citrus e.g. mandarin peel). Use it on any food, especially sushi rolls and noodle dishes.

Indian Garam Masala

Garam means 'hot' and masala means 'mixture of spices'. Whole spices are cooked by dry-frying (with no oil or liquid) or 'roasting'. They are then cooled and ground. There are almost as many recipes for the actual spice mixture as there are cooks in the Indian sub-continent!

Garam masala is used in various ways. It can be sprinkled on finished dishes, or added to yoghurt dips, or to certain curries, towards the end of cooking (to retain the aromatics), particularly those curries from north India. Or it can be used to cook with, from the beginning of the process, such as in Baltis.

The recipe I give here is for a traditional Kashmiri garam masala. Compare it with any factory-made garam masala of your choice. You will always make it fresh from now on, I guarantee! And of course, you are at liberty to vary the ingredients to your taste. The quantities are given in metric measure only, since the tiny measures do not convert easily.

MAKES: ABOUT 250G (9OZ) WHEN GROUND

60g coriander seeds
50g cumin seeds
40g fennel seeds
25g black peppercorns
15g cloves

15g brown cardamoms
3 pieces mace
25g cassia bark pieces
4 bay leaves
5g ginger powder

1 Omitting the ginger powder, mix the remaining nine whole spices together in your wok or pan. Keeping it dry, stir the mixture continuously as it heats up.

2 Very soon the mixture will give off steam, rather than smoke. The process is called 'roasting'. The volatile oils, or aromas, are now being released into the air. Stir for a few seconds more, then transfer the spices to a cold pan or bowl, to stop them cooking. They must not burn. If they do, your cooking will have a bitter, carbonised taste. If they burn, discard them and start again.

3 Allow the garam masala to cool completely for two reasons. Firstly, it will become more brittle, so will grind more easily. Secondly, if the mixture is hot when you grind it in an electric grinder, the blades could overheat the spices, and burn off the very volatile oil you are striving to capture.

4 Whether you use a mortar and pestle or an electric grinder (you can use a coffee grinder), do so in small batches. This avoids overloading the machine.

5 Grind until all the clattering noises change to a softer sound, then grind on until the mix is as fine as you want it, or as fine as the grinder will achieve.

6 Thoroughly mix all the ingredients together, including the ginger powder. Store it in an airtight jar in a dark, dry place. Like all ground spices, though it will last for many months, it will gradually lose fragrance until eventually it tastes of little or nothing. If you are unlikely to use this batch size in that time, scale the quantities down and make a smaller batch.

Indian Five-spice mixture – Panch Phoran

Panch phoran is a Bengali mixture of five (*panch*) spices. It is the equivalent of the Chinese Five-Spice (*see page 82*). Indeed one spice, fennel, is common to both mixtures. Simply mix together equal amounts of the following five spices. As a rough guide, 2 heaped teaspoons of each spice will give you a total of about 60g (2 oz) of *panch phoran*.

white cumin seeds

fennel seeds

black mustard seeds

fenugreek seeds

nigella seeds

Spicy Salt

Use this condiment as a sprinkler whenever you wish to salt oriental noodle dishes.

MAKES: ABOUT 65G (2OZ)

60g (2oz) sea salt

1 teaspoon Chinese Five-Spice powder (see page 82)

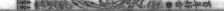

1 Mix together and grind salt and Five-Spice in a coffee grinder or with a mortar and pestle.

2 Store in an airtight jar.

85

Pickled Ginger

This is worth doing on those occasions when you have spare ginger to hand. It makes a great accompaniment to all oriental noodle dishes.

MAKES 500G (1.1 LB)

225g (8oz) fresh ginger
300ml (½ pint) Chinese white rice vinegar

1 tablespoon caster sugar
2 teaspoons spicy salt (see page 85)

1   Peel the ginger and cut into strips of about 5cm (2 in) by 6mm (¼ in). Place the vinegar in a pan and bring to the boil. Add the sugar.
2   When the sugar has dissolved, remove from the heat and allow the liquid to cool. Add the salt.
3   Place the strips of ginger in clean jars and cover with the liquid.
4   Seal with non-metallic lids and store in a cold dark place. Leave for a month before using, but check after 3 or 4 days to see if the vinegar needs topping up.

Vinegared Chillies

This is for people who like things very 'hot' indeed. Use tiny red or green chillies if you can get them for this fiery pickle.

MAKES: 1KG (2.2 LB)

450g (1lb) tiny red or green chillies
1 tablespoon spicy salt (see page 85)
600ml (1 pint) Chinese white rice vinegar

1   Cut the stalks off the chillies and discard. Spread the chillies out on a chopping board and sprinkle salt over them. Leave for a couple of hours.

2 Place the chillies in clean jars and cover with the vinegar.
3 Seal with non-metallic lids and store in a cool dark place. Leave for a month before using, but check after 3 or 4 days to see if the vinegar needs topping up.

Pickled Vegetables

This Chinese vegetable pickle is easy to make, stores indefinitely, and goes well with any oriental noodle dish

MAKES: 1KG (2.2 LB)

225g (8oz) pak-choi or spinach, coarsely shredded
225g (8oz) Chinese leaves, coarsely shredded
225g (8oz) mangetout
2 to 4 fresh green chillies

225g (8oz) carrot, coarsely chopped
110g (4oz) rhubarb, coarsely chopped
4 to 8 cloves garlic, peeled and finely chopped
50g (2oz) fresh ginger, peeled and finely chopped

FOR THE PICKLING SAUCE

1.2 litres (2 pints) water
75ml (3 fl oz) Chinese white rice vinegar
75ml (3 fl oz) Chinese yellow rice wine
2 tablespoons sugar

1 tablespoon hoisin sauce
1 tablespoon tomato ketchup
1 tablespoon salt

1 Mix all the vegetables together in a bowl.
2 Mix the pickling sauce ingredients together.
3 Pack the vegetables into jars and top up to the brim with the pickling sauce.

Leave for 2 to 3 days and then check that all is well, topping up with extra pickling sauce or vinegar if necessary. You can eat the pickle then and there or leave it to mature. The longer it is left the softer the vegetables become.

Pekingese Dipping Sauce

This dip sauce goes well with many crispy appetisers. It should be the consistency of tomato ketchup. It is, of course, a Chinese restaurant invention and it does not appear, as far as I know, in Peking. I have come across a version delightfully entitled, 'drunken dip'.

MAKES: 200G (7OZ)

6 tablespoons thick hoisin sauce

6 tablespoons Chinese yellow rice wine

1 teaspoon cornflour

2 teaspoons caster sugar

1   Mix all the ingredients together.
2   Pour into an airtight jar and use as required.

Wasabi Soy

As described on page 53, wasabi is green horseradish, much beloved by the Japanese. It is commonly mixed with Japanese soy sauce to make a dip to accompany items like tempura fritters. It can also flavour noodle dishes. You may add it to any of the noodle dishes in this book, but watch out: do not salt them as well. Here is a small portion, enough for one four-portion noodle dish.

MAKES: 30G (1OZ)

2 tablespoons Japanese soy sauce

1 teaspoon wasabi powder

1   Simply mix well in a small bowl, and serve.

CHAPTER TWO

NOODLE STARTERS AND SNACKS

We probably don't think noodles when we think starters, yet there is a wide range of opportunities. In this chapter I have brought together a number of my favourites. Some will be very familiar from the *Thai Restaurant* – satay, wontons, spring rolls, prawn toasts and crackers. Others may be new to you – golden thread pork, emerald chicken parcels, curry puffs, pastry-cloaked prawns. All sound great – and they are great.

In fact they are all so good that you may find yourself composing your whole meal of starters only. And, of course, they are great items for a large buffet party. Try them out and you'll agree.

Spicy Noodle fillings for stuffing food items

Ground Items

Ground beef, pork, chicken, prawns, or vegetables are the main ingredient(s) for stuffings or fillings for a number of recipes in this chapter. Here they are nicely spiced up.

NOTE: use the Magic Paste (*see page* 80) when you want that Thai flavour, otherwise omit it.

Ground Beef

Use only good quality steak for this. It gives better, less fatty meat.

MAKES: 250G (9OZ) GROUND BEEF

250g (9oz) frying steak (rump or fillet)
4 cloves garlic, chopped
1 tablespoon magic paste (optional – see note above)

2 tablespoons fresh coriander leaves and stems
2 teaspoons very finely chopped green chilli (cayenne)
½ teaspoon spicy salt (see page 85)

1   Roughly chop up the meat, removing any unwanted matter.
2   Place it and all the other ingredients into the food processor and pulse it until it becomes finely ground. It should be like a thick paste. The finer it is ground the silkier is the texture when cooked.

NOTE: Do not overload the food processor. Grinding meat is heavy work. It is better to do it in smaller batches, then mix them together at the end.

Ground Pork

Use pork steak (or diced lean leg) and follow the Ground Beef recipe.

Ground Chicken

Use skinned chicken breast and follow the Ground Beef recipe.

Ground Vegetables

The principle here is quite different from the previous filling recipes. We use mashed potato as the anchor.

200g (7oz) mashed potato

50g (2oz) cooked peas

50g (2oz) sweetcorn

1 tablespoon magic paste (optional – see note on page 89)

2 tablespoons fresh coriander leaves and stems

2 teaspoons very finely chopped red chilli (cayenne)

½ teaspoon spicy salt (see page 85)

I Simply mix all the ingredients together.

Pastry-cloaked Prawn

This is a fun recipe, modified from a Thai favourite called *krathak*. It's simple and very effective with a secret to tell as well! It is a king prawn, partly encased within a small wonton wrapper, as if it's a cloak. Its tail is exposed. The noodle tie is fiddly, but that's the fun bit. With or without its bow, the trick is to keep the prawn from curling up. The secret is an ancient one, as used in Japanese *tempura* (a technique using batter coating and deep-frying). Make two cuts in the prawn – see sketch – and it simply doesn't curl!

MAKES: 16

16 raw king prawns, about 7cm (2¾ in) long, measured after removing the head and shell, but keeping the tail on

2 tablespoons Worcester sauce

2 tablespoons tomato ketchup

1 teaspoon finely chopped garlic

1 tablespoon magic paste (optional)

½ teaspoon chilli powder

½ teaspoon salt

16 small wonton wrappers about 8cm (3 in) square

oil for deep-frying

I Wash the prawns, then, keeping their tails on, devein them, by carefully cutting along the top to remove the vein. Then placing one on its side, cut two slits on its inside (a) or snip with a pair of scissors, to prevent the prawn curling when cooking. Repeat with the other prawns.

2 Mix the Worcester sauce and tomato ketchup with the garlic, optional paste, chilli and salt.

3 Marinate the prawns in this mixture for 5 to 10 minutes.

4 Place a wonton wrapper on the work top. Fold over one end (b).

5 Place a prawn, slits down, on the wrapper, with the tail projecting out from the folded end (c).

6 Fold the top corner of the wrapper over the top of the prawn (d).

7 Fold one side over the prawn (e) and then fold the other side over it, to create a tightly folded roll (f).

8 Tie a noodle bow (optional) (g).

9 Repeat with the other prawns.

10 Preheat the deep-fry oil to 190°C (chip-frying temperature).

11 One at a time, put 8 prawns into the oil (too many at once will reduce the temperature too fast).

12 Fry for 8 to 10 minutes, until the prawns are cooked.

13 Remove from the fryer, shaking off the excess oil.

14 Rest on kitchen paper.

15 Repeat with the remaining prawns.

16 Serve hot with chilli sauce.

NOTE: see important deep-frying information on page 75.

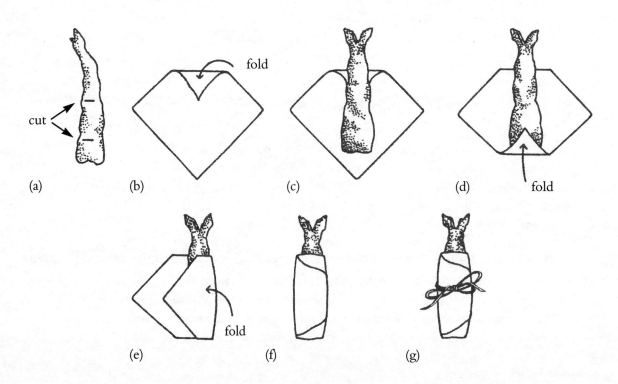

Golden Thread Pork Balls

Golden threads are of course noodles carefully wrapped around a raw filling ball, about 2cm (¾ in) in diameter, and then deep-fried. The result is a really pretty, crispy, tasty starter.

The idea is simple (again hails from Thailand), and so they are to make. Use fresh soft noodles for the wrapping and for the filling you can use ground beef, as I specify here, or pork, chicken or prawns, from any of the earlier 'fillings' recipes.

MAKES: 16 BALLS

80g (3oz) fresh egg noodles
250g (9oz) raw ground beef filling (see page 90)
oil for deep-frying

1   Soften the dried noodles and select 32 long strands.
2   Divide the ground beef into 16 portions to make balls about 2cm (¾ in) in diameter.
3   Press one end of a noodle strand on to a ball to make it stick. Carefully wind it around the ball, so that the strand doesn't overlap. Use water to help it stick. With the second strand, change direction to right angles and wind it over the original noodle. Tuck the end into the centre. The filling should be entirely covered (but if it isn't it doesn't matter).
4   Repeat with the other 15 balls (use spare noodles and/or beef for another dish).
5   Preheat the oil to 190°C (chip-frying temperature).
6   Lower the balls into the oil and fry for 3–4 minutes.
7   Remove from the fryer, shaking off the excess oil.
8   Rest the balls on kitchen paper.
9   Serve hot or cold.

NOTE: see important deep-frying information on page 75.

Sea-spicy Noodle Balls

This recipe hails from China. It is in a manner of speaking, a variation on the previous recipe, where the noodles, rather than being wrapped around the filling, are chopped into it.

They are then rolled into small balls which are then deep-fried. They can be served as they are, or added to a sauce.

MAKES: ABOUT 24 BALLS

80g (3oz) fresh noodles
2 tablespoons cornflour
250g (9oz) filling (see page 90)
1 tablespoon chopped fresh coriander leaves

2 teaspoons Chinese ten-spice powder
(see page 82)
oil for deep-frying

GARNISH
Mustard and cress

1 Steam or boil the noodles.
2 Strain the noodles and leave until cool enough to handle. Chop them finely.
3 Mix the cornflour with the filling, ten-spice powder and coriander.
4 Add the chopped noodles and if necessary loosen the mixture with a little water, to get it pliable.
5 Heat the deep-fryer to 190°C (chip-frying temperature).
6 Place a dollop of the mixture on a floured work surface and roll it into a ball about 2cm (¾ in) in diameter.
7 Repeat with the remaining mixture. Divide the balls into two batches.
8 Cook the first batch by lowering the balls, one at a time, into the hot oil. Deep-fry until golden and cooked through about 8 minutes.
9 Remove the balls from the deep-fryer and shake off excess oil. Transfer to a warmer or low oven.
10 Repeat stages 8 and 9 with the second batch.
11 Serve as they are, garnished with mustard and cress, or add them to a sauce.

NOTE: see important deep-frying information on page 75.

Noodle Sushi Nori

Sushi is unique to Japan. Basically it is the decorative preparation of sushi rice, flavoured with rice vinegar, and fish, which may or may not be raw. Other ingredients are usually added for colour and effect.

Sushi originated in ancient times, as a way to preserve fish. Over the centuries it has become an art form. The rice is a variety of glutinous rice called *mochigome*, only used for special dishes, such as sushi (most Japanese rice is non-glutinous). Ordinary rice does not work, so only buy sushi rice for this job. Its glutinous or sticky qualities enable the cook to 'glue' things in place as decoratively as possible.

Nori, as we see on page 66, is paper-thin seaweed. Its best known use is in *Sushi Nori*, or, as it is known in Japan, *Nori Maki*, or *Makisushi*. The *nori* is laid flat, on a special, readily available bamboo mat called the 'sushi mat' (or *makisu*). A layer of flavoured sushi rice is spread on the *nori*, then strips of fish and other ingredients are placed on the rice (*see* 'filling options' below). Traditional fillings include *kampyo* – a dried strip of gourd from the Japanese *yugao* (calabash) plant, which must be soaked for 30 minutes before using, and *shitaké* or Chinese (*dong-gu*) dried mushrooms (*see* page 62), which also need soaking. Both these are optional, subject to availability.

Noodles are not traditionally used in sushi, but they do work, placed longways on the rice. You don't need many, so use up some leftovers. Then the whole thing is rolled up into a sausage, the diameter of which depends on the size of your nori sheet. It is then cut into slices, which can be as thick or as thin as you wish. The result is akin to a Swiss roll. Sushi nori are always eaten cold, and make an excellent talking point at your party, as canapés or starters. They really are easier to make than they seem, and can be made early and kept in the fridge. Serve with Japanese Seven-Spice (*see* page 83) and Wasabi Soy (*see* page 88)

FILLING OPTIONS:

Choice of fish (anything goes in Japan, but here is a selection for Western tastes): smoked salmon, rollmop herring, raw tuna marinated in shoyu, anchovies in oil.

Choice of vegetables: asparagus, chives, bamboo shoots,
beansprouts, cucumber, omelette.

MAKES: 24 SUSHI NORIS

125g (4½oz) sushi rice

1 tablespoon salt

100ml (3½ fl oz) Japanese dashi stock
  (see page 79)

2 tablespoons rice vinegar

4 sheets nori, each 20cm (8 in) square

1 bamboo sushi mat

THE FILLING

16 strings of cooked egg noodles, each 20cm
  (8 in) long

2 or 3 vegetable choices (see filling options above,
  cut as above)

1 fish choice (see above) cut into strips about
  5–10mm wide x 4mm thick – enough strips to
  measure 20cm (8in) in length, four times

GARNISH

Strands of chives
Sprinklings of Japanese Seven-Spice (see page 83)
Chinese deep-fried seaweed (see page 204)

1   Bring 1 litre (1⅔ pints) water to the boil. Add the sushi rice, and stir
     continuously until it is free flowing in simmering water, and not
     sticking to the bottom of the pan.

2   Add the salt, dashi and rice vinegar, and stirring occasionally, cook
     the rice for 15 minutes minimum.

3   Drain it, and allow the rice to go cold.

4   When the rice is cold, open the nori packet, and take out four sheets.

5   Lay one sheet of nori flat, on the bamboo mat.

6   Spread a thin layer of cold sushi rice on the nori, leaving about 6–7
     cm (3 in) of the nori, rice-free (a).

7   Spread the strips of fish, vegetables and noodles across the rice end
     of the nori, and about 2cm (¾ in) in from the edge (b).

8   From the rice end, start rolling up the mat, squeezing the tube
     slightly, to compress the rice (c).

9   Once all the rice has been rolled, cut away the spare rice-free nori
     (it can be used in stock).

10   10. Remove the roll from the mat. You now have a tube 20 x 3 cm (8 x 1¼ in). Cut off each ragged end (use in stock), then cut the tube into six slices (d).

11   Repeat stages 5 to 10 with the other three rolls.

12   Place neatly on a large flat serving plate and garnish with a few long strands of chives, and some sprinklings of Japanese seven-spice and deep-fried seaweed.

NOTE: For a larger roll, spread the rice all over the nori – no need to cut as much as 7cm (2¾ in) off it, but just trim the last 1cm (½in) to tidy the nori up – then proceed with the recipe. Any spare rice can be used in stock.

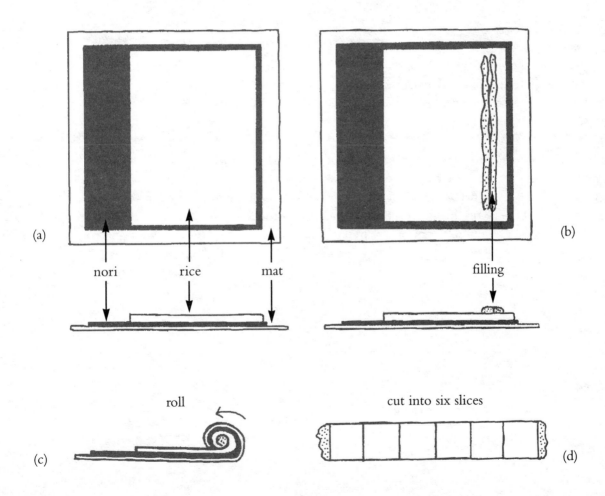

(a)

nori   rice   mat

(b)

filling

roll

(c)

cut into six slices

(d)

Spring Rolls

No wonder the celebrated Chinese Spring Roll is world-class in popularity. It is a divine piece of packaging, devised thousands of years ago. It consists of a filling encased in thin pastry, which is wrapped into a tube shape. Other countries, including Thailand, Korea and Vietnam all have their own versions, as well as the Middle East and Turkey, where they are called *Boreks*. Here, using small wonton wrappers (i.e. noodle pastry) and prawn filling, is a delightful and delicate mini prawn spring roll. Actually any of the fillings from page 90, including vegetables works well.

MAKES: 30 ROLLS

60g (2 oz) cooked noodles, chopped
about 175g (6oz) filling (see page 90)
30g (1oz) beansprouts, chopped

30 small wonton wrappers about 8cm–10cm
  (3–4 in) square
oil for deep-frying

1 Mix the filling with the noodles and beansprouts.
2 Lay one wrapper on the work surface.
3 Spread about 1½ teaspoons of filling in near the top of the sheet (a).
4 Roll the top corner of the sheet over the filling (b).
5 Fold in the outside flaps (c).
6 Roll up reasonably tightly until the last corner remains (d).

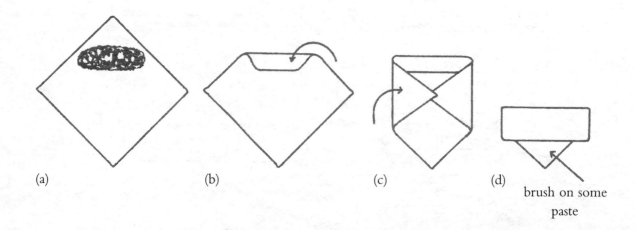

(a)   (b)   (c)   (d)

brush on some
paste

7   Press this corner down with a little water. Rest the roll with this corner underneath (it helps it to stick).

8   Make the remaining rolls. Preheat the deep-fry oil to 190°C (chip-frying temperature).

9   One by one put about 8 rolls into the oil (too many, too fast will lower the temperature too much). Fry for 5 to 6 minutes, until golden.

10 Remove from the fryer, shaking off the excess oil.

11 Rest on kitchen paper.

12 Fry the remaining rolls.

13 Serve hot or cold

NOTE: see important deep-frying information on page 75.

Steamed Rice Noodle Spring Rolls

These are like the previous spring rolls, except that the wrapping is a rice noodle sheet and the cooking is done by steaming. They are another speciality hailing from Thailand, where they are called *Kuaytiaw Lot*. The stuffing can be any of the variations on pages 90 and 91. The rice sheets can be purchased ready to use at the Thai shop, where they are called *sen yai neung*, or, as here, you can have a go and make your own.

MAKES: 4 ROLLS

1 batch rice noodle dough
4 tablespoons raw filling of choice (see pages 90–91)

1   Roll out the dough to a large thin square and cut it into 4 smaller squares which should be 12–15cm (5–6 in) per side.

2   Place one tablespoon of filling along the centre of a sheet. Fold and roll as shown in the drawing from the previous recipe.

3   Place the rolls into the steamer basket and steam for about 8 to 10 minutes.

Noodle Crisps

Everyone loves a nibble! And everyone loves nibbling at something with their aperitif, or immediately they sit down at table before the meal arrives. Whether it's prawn crackers at the Chinese and Thai restaurant, *grissini* breadsticks at the Italian, or popadams at the Indian, or just crusty rolls closer to home. The effect's the same, and the diner's attention is grabbed. Nothing could be simpler than this appetiser which I met in London's Chinatown.

SERVES: 4

2 sheets spring roll pastry or noodle dough
oil for deep-frying

1   Heat the deep-fryer to 190°C (chip frying temperature).
2   Cut the pastry or dough into thin strips about 1cm (½ in) wide. Either cut them again to create rectangles about 5cm (2 in) long or carefully tie the strips into bows.
3   Gently lower them into the deep-fryer. They will cook instantly. Remove after 5 seconds or so and place on absorbent kitchen paper to drain off excess oil and to crisp up. Serve warm.

NOTE: see important deep-frying information on page 75.

Crispy Noodle Nest

Noodle nests or baskets are a great talking point at the dinner table, and they are one of the masterpieces of Chinese food presentation. They are a wee bit fiddly, but are not difficult to master.

They look absolutely gorgeous and can be served as nibbles, used to hold starter ingredients, or as the centre-piece of the main course. They are also used to make 'mock' bird's nest soup.

Any type of noodle can be used: rice vermicelli makes white nests while egg noodles make golden nests.

The noodles must first be boiled, then allowed to dry, preferably until next day. And here's the secret: to create the nest two all-metal strainers are needed, one slightly smaller than the other. I use one with a diameter of 12.5cm (5 in) and another with a diameter of 10cm (4 in). Alternatively special bird's nest strainer sets are available.

MAKES: 4 NESTS

200g (7 oz) dried egg or other noodles
vegetable oil for deep-frying

1 Boil 1.8 litres (3 pints) water in a 3.5 litre (6 pint) saucepan. Cook the noodles as the packet directs. Strain and cool under the cold tap. Strain again.
2 Place the noodles on absorbent kitchen paper, cover and leave overnight to dry.
3 Next day, heat enough oil in the deep-fryer to 190°C to enable you to immerse the strainers.
4 Divide the noodles into four. Oil both strainers by immersing them in the oil.
5 Press one batch of noodles into the larger strainer. Press the second strainer down on to the noodles.
6 Holding both handles together, carefully lower the strainers into the hot oil. Cook for about 3 minutes.
7 Remove the strainers from the wok, shaking off excess oil. Carefully remove the smaller strainer from inside the larger one, then, using a knife if necessary, knock out the nest from the bottom strainer.
8 Repeat stages 5, 6 and 7 to make three more nests.

NOTE: see important deep-frying information on page 75.

Sev

Sev is one of a few Indian 'noodle' recipes in this book. It is an ancient and traditional Indian 'nibble', which has gained notoriety, and a new name in the modern British Indian restaurant, being an important ingredient in Bombay Mix. Actually sev is one of those squiggly crisp items you find in Bombay Mix. It is the finest noodle item, resembling fine short vermicelli. At first sight you would not think of sev as a noodle. But noodle it is, made from a gram-flour dough called *ompadi*. And as with all noodles, the dough is pressed into vermicelli-like strings. In India, they use a traditional hand press, called the *murukus*. It is a brass cylinder, which has a handle which screws the dough down on to a circular brass plate with tiny holes, called the *ompadi*. The press is held over a deep-fryer, and the sev strings are extruded straight into the hot oil and deep-fried until they are golden and crispy. You can get hold of a *murukus* press, which comes with several different *ompadi* plates, at the Asian store – that makes this recipe easy.

MAKES: ENOUGH FOR SEVERAL USES

200g (7oz) gram flour
100g (3½oz) rice flour
2 tablespoons melted ghee

salt to taste
vegetable oil for deep-frying

SPICES

1–2 teaspoons chilli powder
1–2 teaspoons lovage seeds

1 teaspoon asafoetida
1 teaspoon turmeric

1   Mix all the ingredients together with sufficient water to make a cohesive ball of dough. The easiest way to do this is to use an electric dough-maker.
2   Heat the oil in the deep-fryer to 180°C.
3   Select the *ompadi* plate with the hole size you require and place it into the *murukus* mould press.
4   Fill the press with some of the *ompadi* dough.
5   When the oil is at the required temperature, hold the press about 10cm (4 in) above the surface of the oil and press dough into the

fryer, moving the press around the surface in a slow circular motion. Do not overfill the deep fryer – allow enough space for the items to rise and not be cluttered.

6 Fry until the dough crisps up and becomes golden in colour.
7 Remove the batch from the fryer with a slotted spoon. Place on kitchen paper and allow to cool.
8 Repeat until all the dough is deep-fried.
9 When cool, break the sticks up into bite-sized pieces and store in airtight containers.

NOTE: see important deep-frying information on page 75.

Bhel Puri

Little known outside Bombay, where it is a favourite kiosk food, Bhel Puri is a tantalising cold mixture of crisp, chewy textures laced with sweet, hot and sour sauces. Crunchy squiggly savoury sev shares a bowl with diced potato, puffed rice (*mamra*) and fresh coriander. Serve it, together with separate tamarind and chilli sauces, and there you have it. Its close relative, Sev Batata Puri, is similar, but the biscuits are replaced by flakes of crisp puri. Yoghurt is incorporated and the whole dish is topped with more sev. London boasts a few successful Bhel Puri Houses, where for some decades they have served their very fresh and very cheap Bhel, whilst some of the smarter Indian restaurants charge infinitely more for the same equally delicious dishes.

SERVES: 4

25 g (1oz) sev (see above)
60 g (2oz) puffed rice (mamra)
2 large cold boiled potatoes, chopped
3 tablespoons chopped onion

2 green chillies, chopped
2 tablespoons chopped fresh coriander
1 to 2 teaspoons garam masala (see page 83)
spicy salt to taste (see page 85)

SAUCE

1 tablespoon fresh lemon juice

4 tablespoons tomato ketchup

4 tablespoons brown sauce

1 tablespoon chilli and garlic sauce (see page 81)

1 tablespoon sugar

½ teaspoon salt

1   Mix all except the sauce ingredients together and put in serving bowls.

2   Mix the sauce ingredients together.

3   Serve the sauce separately, allowing the diner to add it to taste. Serve cold.

4   Optionally, in addition serve bottled red and green chilli sauces and/or plain yoghurt.

CHAPTER THREE

NOODLE SOUPS

Soups are popular with everyone, especially in the depths of a cold winter. And they are even more nutritious when they include noodles. Indeed so nourishing are oriental noodle soups, that they can be a meal in themselves, requiring no other extras to accompany them. My selection includes three classic oriental soup dishes, known in their countries of origin as 'national dishes'.

From Burma, there is Mohinga, a fascinating combination of Indian spices, fish and noodles. From Thailand, I have chosen their celebrated mixed seafood Tom Yam, fragrant, chilli-punchy, and aromatic all at the same time, and with four further variations using chicken, prawn, beef and pork. From Malaysia comes Soto Ayam, a curry-spicy chicken and noodle soup, and there are three other lesser-known, but equally good oriental noodle soups from Singapore, Korea, and Vietnam. Of course, I could not omit China, or at least China abroad, so I have included that celebrated dish from the Chinese Restaurant – Chicken Noodle Soup, along with three of its popular variations.

Not all soups are served hot, and the Japanese Hiyamugi, with its chilli-hot broth, is, in fact, served ice-cold! But, it is not only orientals who enjoy noodles in their soup. I have included two fascinating noodle soup recipes , both from from west of Suez, and both many centuries old. Tutmaj is a venerable Middle Eastern recipe using noodles and yoghurt. And I cannot omit one more national dish, this one from the home of pasta. The celebrated Italian Minestrone soup, using not pasta, but noodles.

With such diversity I know you'll be hard-pressed to choose where to start. All I can say is, that doesn't matter providing you try them all!

Turkish Tutmaj

Noodles and Yoghurt Soup

From 100 BC when the Silk Route was established, merchants from Europe and China passed along it in both directions, accompanied by their cooks. It is entirely conceivable that noodles were a convenient food to cook when the caravan pitched tent overnight, and this may explain how isolated pockets of noodle-makers have existed in Turkey and Armenia for as long as can be remembered. Tutmaj is an example of a noodle dish found in these and other Middle Eastern countries, incorporating the much-loved ingredient of the area, yoghurt. It is normally served as a soup, but is equally delicious as a thick gravied vegetable dish.

SERVES: 4

450g (1lb) fresh egg noodles

2 tablespoons extra-virgin olive or sunflower oil

110g (4oz) onions, finely chopped

2 cloves garlic, finely chopped

750ml (1¾ pints) vegetable stock (see page 78) or water

150g (5oz) thick Greek yoghurt

1 tablespoon cornflour

1 egg

20 strands saffron (optional)

salt to taste

a sprinkling of chopped mint and parsley

1   Boil the noodles until they are al dente (*see page* 73).

2   Heat the oil in your wok. Stir-fry the onion and garlic for about 5 minutes.

3   During stage 2, whisk together the stock, yoghurt, cornflour, egg and saffron if using.

4   Remove the stir-fry from the heat and add the yoghurt mixture, stirring it in fast. Return to the heat, stirring all the time, so that the yoghurt does not curdle as it is heated.

5   Once it starts to simmer, add the noodles and mix well. Add the salt, fresh mint and parsley to taste, and serve on its own or to accompany another dish.

NOTE: You can considerably reduce the stock or water content to make a thicker dish.

Burmese Mohinga

Spicy Noodle Fish Soup

Burmese food is quite distinctive and unique, and sadly, little known. It has evolved into a combination of Indian (robust and spicy), Chinese (noodles, beansprouts, and stir-frying) and Thai (fragrance and fish sauce) cuisine. If one recipe is to be singled out to typify Burma it must be *mo-hi-nga* – literally 'noodle-spicy-fish-soup'. Indeed, it is referred to as the national dish. In Burma you buy *mohinga* from roadside stalls, or from vendors who back-pack their cooking apparatus and ingredients from house to house. It is a spicy, tart, fishy soup with a fascinating string of garnishes. The Burmese eat it as a complete main meal, but it also makes an ideal starter. The ingredients list looks a little formidable, but it is much simpler to make than it looks.

SERVES: 4

100g (4oz) egg or vermicelli noodles
2 tablespoons mustard or sesame oil
2 teaspoons finely chopped garlic
8 tablespoons finely chopped onion
1 teaspoon nga·pi (shrimp paste)
1–6 (to taste) fresh green chillies, chopped
3 tablespoons gram flour (besan)

3 tablespoons coconut milk powder
200g (7oz) canned pilchards or herrings, boned
225g (8oz) canned bamboo shoots, chopped
stock or water
juice of 2 lemons
salt to taste

GARNISH
hard-boiled egg slices
chopped spring onion leaf
chopped fresh coriander leaves
watercress or mustard and cress
peanuts
juliennes of capsicum bell peppers, red, yellow or green

1   Heat the oil, and fry the garlic for 1 minute, then add the onion and stir-fry for 3 minutes. Add the shrimp paste, mash it in and fry for 2 minutes, followed by the chillies for 2 minutes.

2 Mix the gram flour and coconut milk powder with enough water to make a thick paste. Add it to the pan and stir over heat until it will thicken no more.

3 Transfer to a saucepan. Break the fish up, and add it with its juices from the can. Add the chopped bamboo shoots with its juices.

4 Add enough stock or water to bring it to consommé consistency. Add the lemon juice and salt to taste.

5 Boil the noodles until they are al dente (*see page* 73). Drain.

6 To serve, place the noodles in a soup bowl and ladle the piping hot soup over them. Serve, allowing the diners to put their own choice of garnish items on to the soup.

Tom Yam Talay
Thai Seafood Soup

Tom Yam is Thailand's renowned soup. Literally meaning, 'boiled salad', it should be quite chilli hot, served with your choice of chicken, or meat or seafood or vegetables or any combination. This version includes noodles, and it must encapsulate all those flavours which are so essentially Thai – lemon grass, lime leaf and basil – to give a light and entrancing, fragrant, yet tongue-tinglingly sour, salty and sweet, herby and delicious soup. Tom Yam Talay is the mixed seafood version. Other versions follow.

SERVES: 4

110g (4oz) fresh or 60g (2oz) dried noodles, any type
about 250g (9oz) mixed raw seafood of your choice (e.g. king prawns, fish chunks, small prawns, crab legs, squid, mussels)
about 700ml (1¼ pints) fish stock (see page 77)

1 tablespoon magic paste (see page 80)
1 teaspoon shrimp paste (see page 64)
2 tablespoons tinned sweetcorn or baby corns
3 or 4 dried or fresh lime leaves (if available)
1 stalk lemon grass, cut to a tassel
juice of 1 lime

GARNISH
some whole coriander leaves
3 or 4 red chillies

1   Prepare the mixed seafood by divesting it of unwanted matter, and washing it, then cutting it as you wish.
2   Bring the fish stock to the boil in a 2.25 litre (4 pint) saucepan (or larger). Add the seafood and all the other ingredients except the noodles and garnish.
3   Simmer literally until the seafood becomes cooked (which will be between 5 and 12 minutes depending on the size of the seafood pieces).
4   During stage 3, add the noodles for the appropriate cooking time. (*See page* 73)
5   Place into serving bowls and garnish.

VARIATIONS

Tom Yam has many variations, which get their name from the principal ingredient.

Tom Yam Ga

Thai Chicken Soup

Use 250g (9oz) of skinned filleted chicken breast, cut into thin strips, in place of the seafood. The remaining ingredients and method remain the same.

Tom Yam Nua

Thai Beef Soup

Use 250g (9oz) of lean fillet steak, cut into thin strips, in place of the seafood. The remaining ingredients and method remain the same.

Tom Yam Moo

Thai Pork Soup

Use 250g (9oz) of lean pork, cut into thin strips, in place of the seafood. The remaining ingredients and method remain the same.

Tom Yam Gung

Thai Prawn Soup

As beef but use whole raw king prawns.

Malaysian Soto Ayam

Spicy Chicken Soup with Noodles

This soup is to be found everywhere in Malaysia and in neighbouring Indonesia. It's virtually a national dish. The basis is chicken. There they would use the best part of a whole chicken. Here I use the carcass of a roasted chicken with a reasonable amount of flesh on it.

SERVES: 4

110g (4oz) fresh or 60g (2oz) dried noodles, any type

1 litre (1¾ pints) chicken or Vintage stock (see page 78)

1 teaspoon nam pla (fish sauce)

1 stalk fresh lemon grass

2 tablespoons vegetable nut oil

2–4 garlic cloves garlic, finely chopped

2.5cm (1 in) cube ginger, chopped

1 teaspoon shrimp paste

4–5 spring onions, bulbs and leaves, chopped

175g (6oz) raw chicken breast, skinned, filleted and cut into thin slices

1 tablespoon chopped fresh coriander leaves

1 tablespoon sweet soy sauce (see page 67)

spicy salt to taste (see page 85)

SPICES

1 teaspoon coriander seeds, crushed

1 teaspoon black peppercorns

5–6 curry leaves, fresh

½ teaspoon ground turmeric

GARNISH

a few feathery fronds of fresh dill

1   Put the stock, the fish sauce, and the lemon grass into a 2.75–3.5 litre (5–6 pint) saucepan, and bring to a simmer.

2   During stage 1, heat the oil in a wok over a high heat. Add the

110

garlic and ginger, and stir-fry for 30 seconds. Add all the spices, the shrimp paste and the spring onions and stir-fry for a further 3 to 4 minutes.

3   Add the sliced raw chicken breast pieces and stir-fry these in the mixture for another 6 to 8 minutes.

4   Add this mixture to the simmering liquid. Add the fresh coriander, sweet soy sauce, spicy salt to taste, and the noodles and simmer for the appropriate noodle cooking time (*see page* 73). Providing the chicken is cooked right through, the soup is ready.

5   Garnish with the fresh dill and serve very hot.

Nonya Mee Siam

This is another noodle soup enjoyed in Malaysia and Singapore. But this one is a Nonya dish. The Nonyas are a community whose ancestry is Indian as much as Chinese, and this is reflected in their unique food which combines curry spices and tamarind and coconut redolent of south India, with the soy and noodle stir-fries from China. The name of the dish 'Mee Siam', literally means 'noodles from Siam', acknowledging the Thai flavour of lemon grass. Rice noodles are recommended for this recipe.

SERVES 4

250g (9oz) dried, or 450g (1lb) fresh rice noodles, any type

2 tablespoons black soya bean sauce

2 tablespoons tamarind purée (see page 68)

6–8 cloves garlic, chopped

6–8 spring onions, leaves and bulbs, chopped

1–4 dried red chillies, whole

3 or 4 tablespoons sesame or soya oil

1 litre (1¾ pints) vintage master, or any stock (see page 78)

2 stalks lemon grass

4 tablespoons beansprouts

110g (4oz) cooked prawns

sweet soy sauce to taste

1   Put the soya bean sauce, tamarind purée, garlic, onion bulbs and dried chillies into the blender, using, if it needs it, just enough water to mulch it down to a thick paste.

2   Boil the noodles until they are al dente, then drain and set aside for later (*see page* 73).

3   Heat the oil in your wok. Stir-fry the paste for 2 to 3 minutes.
4   Now add the stock, spring onion leaves and lemon grass, and when at a simmer, the beansprouts and the prawns.
5   Immediately add the drained noodles, and when they are at the simmer, add the soy sauce to taste. It should not need salting. Serve hot.

Korean Naeng Myon
Cold Noodle Soup

This is a popular dish in Korea, in fact it is a meal in itself. The basis is a soup in which noodles are simmered in stock, much like any other noodle soup. Two things make this dish different. One is the fact that the dish is served cold. The other is that a number of other ingredients are served on top of the soup as a substantial garnish. The choice of these ingredients is up to the cook, but here I give some typical Korean examples. The pear is typical, and the meat would be better home stir-fried and chilled, though you can buy it precooked cold. Kimchi or pickled cabbage and plentiful chilli is mandatory. Don't be put off by the long list of toppings, and feel free to omit some or add others of your fancy. Every item is cut into similar-sized strips, where possible.

SERVES: 4

450g (1lb) fresh or 225g (9oz) dried noodles, rice or egg

THE SOUP

1 litre (1¾ pints) meat or chicken stock
50ml (2 fl oz) white rice wine
1 tablespoon dark soy sauce
1 tablespoon red soya bean paste

3–6 cloves garlic, sliced
1 teaspoon sugar
1 tablespoon chilli and garlic sauce
(see page 81)

225g (9oz) cold sliced cooked beef or turkey or
    chicken
a two-egg omelette
4 spring onions, bulbs and leaves
3 or 4 fresh red chillies
1 pear
4 tablespoons rice wine vinegar
1 or 2 gherkins

1 white radish
4–6 tablespoons kimchi pickle or picked vegeta-
    bles (see page 87)
some canned anchovy fillets
2 sheets nori seaweed, heated under the grill,
    then cooled
1 tablespoon black sesame seeds

1   Bring the stock to the simmer in a 3.5 litre (6 pint) saucepan along with the rice wine, soy sauce, red soya bean paste, garlic, sugar, chilli and garlic sauce. Add the noodles and simmer until they are al dente. Remove the pan from the heat and allow it to go cold, then transfer it to a bowl, cover it, and keep it in the fridge.

2   Assemble all the topping items of your choice, and prepare them by cutting everything into thin strips in traditional Korean fashion. Immerse the pear strips in the rice wine vinegar for at least 10 minutes.

3   To serve, distribute the cold soup into four soup bowls and either place the topping on each bowl, or serve them attractively arranged on a huge platter allowing the diners to help themselves. Sprinkle the sesame seeds over the toppings. Some people like the hot taste of English mustard or Japanese wasabi served on the side.

Vietnamese Bunh Thang

Chicken and Rice Noodles with Pork and Egg

One's knowledge of Vietnamese food, it seems to me, depends on where you live. We, here in the UK, know little about it, and even cosmopolitan London has only around six Vietnamese restaurants (compared with 2,000 Indian!). Vietnam was occupied by China for a millennium and by the French for a century, and reluctantly fought over recently in a big way by the Americans and less so by the Australians for decades. I mention this because, despite all this,

Vitenam has retained its own cultural and culinary identity, although these links have led to a large post-war influx of Vietnamese immigrants, and with them, their restaurants, to those countries. Vietnam uses soy and fish sauce, lemon grass and lime, chilli and garlic. Noodles are daily fare, there, and this dish is typical. Links with France can be established by the daring, who can substitute frog's legs for chicken drumsticks!

SERVES: 4

450g (1lb) rice noodles

4 chicken drumsticks or large frog's legs

4 pork ribs (or small chops)

1 litre (1¾ pints) Vintage or chicken stock (see page 78)

2 or 3 stalks lemon grass

3 tablespoons soya oil

3 or 4 cloves garlic, finely chopped

1 teaspoon shrimp paste (see page 64)

1 teaspoon bottled minced red chilli

1 tablespoon fish sauce (see page 63)

2 eggs, beaten

1 teaspoon sugar

1 tablespoon fresh lime juice

6–8 spring onions (shallots), bulbs and leaves, chopped

fresh coriander leaves and soft stalks

bottled minced coriander

1   Keeping the meat on the bone, skin the chicken, and remove excess fat from the ribs, then cut small gashes in the meat.

2   Bring the stock to the simmer in a 3.5 litre (6 pint) saucepan. Add the chicken, the ribs and the lemon grass, and simmer for at least 15 minutes, until the meat is cooked right through. Remove any scum, should this form.

3   During stage 2, heat the oil in your wok and stir-fry the garlic, shrimp paste and chilli for a minute or so.

4   Add the stir-fry, and all the other ingredients, including the eggs which need to be quickly circulated in the soup, and the noodles, and simmer until they are al dente. Serve at once to keep the green colour of the onion and coriander.

Chicken Noodle Soup

Every city and every town in the English-speaking world has its Chinese restaurant. And every Chinese restaurant has a version of this simple soup. It is popular, quick and easy to make, and has any amount of variations, some of which I list below.

SERVES: 4

110g (4oz) fresh egg noodles

1 litre (1¾ pints) chicken stock

225g (8oz) chicken meat, off the bone, skinned and shredded

4 spring onions, leaves and bulbs, finely chopped

1 teaspoon sesame oil

2.5cm (1 in) cube fresh ginger, peeled and finely chopped

25g (1oz) ham, finely chopped

1 tablespoon chopped fresh coriander

spicy salt to taste

soy sauce to taste

GARNISH

finely chopped fresh parsley or spring onion leaves

1 Bring the stock to the boil in a 3 litre (5 pint) saucepan.

2 Add the chicken pieces, the spring onions, ginger and oil and simmer for 10 minutes.

3 Add the noodles, the ham and fresh coriander. Bring to the boil, simmer then reduce the heat for about 3 to 4 minutes. Season to taste with spicy salt and/or soy sauce.

4 Pour into individual serving bowls, garnish with the parsley and serve piping hot.

VARIATIONS

Chicken Noodle Sweetcorn Soup

In this simple variation, add 60g (2oz) fresh, canned or frozen sweetcorn at stage 3.

Chicken Noodle Mushroom Soup

In this simple variation, add 30g (1oz) dried Chinese mushrooms to the stock at stage 1.

Chicken Noodle Asparagus Soup

Since asparagus is regarded as a luxury, this soup makes a good candidate to serve at a dinner party. Use fresh, rather than canned asparagus, if possible. Add eight asparagus spears, after removing their pithy bases.

Japanese Hiyamugi

Hiyamugi is a Japanese dried noodle made from wheat flour dough, and it is a cross between somen and udon in appearance. It is available from specialist stores, and as with somen (*see page* 47), it is served chilled, with a chilli-hot, ice-cold soup. Use somen or udon if *hiyamugi* is unavailable.

Chilli (*togarashi*) is enjoyed by the brave in Japan, especially in Seven-Spice Powder (*see page* 83). Chillies of varying heat strengths are available in Japan. For example, the *santaka* chilli is a fairly hot, deep red chilli, not unlike the Mexican serraño. Whole red chillies, fresh and dried, appear in Japanese pickles. For this dish, use any amount of any type of chilli to suit your heat strength requirements (*see page* 54).

SERVES: 4

250g (9oz) dried hiyamugi noodles
800ml (28 fl oz) Japanese dashi stock
 (see page 79)

fresh red chillies, to taste (whole, if small, chopped and dressed if large)

GARNISH
spring onion leaves, chopped
a red chilli tassel

1   Boil the noodles until they are as al dente as you wish (*see page* 73). Then drain them and set aside, allowing them to go cold.

2   Make the dashi stock adding the chillies to it at stage 1, and fishing them out for use in the soup later, before discarding the solids.

3   Return the chillies to the stock. Let it go cold, then put it into the fridge.

4   When the noodles are cold, put them neatly into four serving bowls, garnish, cover and put in the fridge.

5   To serve, add some crushed ice to the stock, then put it into four small individual serving bowls.

Italian Minestrone Angel's Hair Soup

A soup from pasta land, I think, redresses the oriental balance. Minestrone is the Italian national soup, indeed *menistra* means 'soup'. It uses vermicelli pasta, which as I mentioned in the introduction means 'little worms'! Perhaps a more romantic image is one used by the Italians themselves of the finest vermicelli – they call it 'Angel's Hair'.

Minestrone is a thinnish soup, which also always contains chopped vegetables, the choice of which varies from region to region. The original minestrone, from Genoa, dates back to the fifteenth century, and was a substantial filling meal. To this day it still contains broad beans and/or red kidney beans, carrot, celery, courgettes (zucchini), basil pesto, potato and tomatoes. In Tuscany they use peas, leeks, white haricot beans, and again, celery, courgettes, and tomatoes, but no pesto. In its place is garlic sautéd in olive oil, and a garnish of fresh grated cheese. Tomatoes, of course, were not on the original ingredients list, not having arrived in Italy from the New World until later, but no modern minestrone would be correct without them. Here, in place of pasta, I am using the thinest rice vermicelli or beanthread noodles.

SERVES: 4

250g (9oz) dried or 450g (1lb) thinnest rice
   vermicelli or beanthread noodles
1 litre (1¾ pints) vegetable stock (see page 78)
4 cloves garlic, sliced
110g (4oz) canned broad beans
   or 110g (4oz) red kidney beans
85g (3oz) carrot

2 sticks celery, chopped
4 baby potatoes quartered
4 plum tomatoes chopped
2 or 3 small courgettes (zucchini), chopped
1 tablespoon basil pesto
salt to taste

GARNISH
fresh grated Parmesan or Cheddar cheese

1   Bring the stock to the simmer in a 3.5 litre (6 pint) saucepan. Add
   the garlic, beans, carrot, celery, potatoes and tomatoes.
2   Simmer for about 12 minutes, then add the courgettes, pesto and
   salt to taste, and simmer for a further three minutes.
3   During stage 2, boil the noodles until they are as al dente as you
   wish (*see page 73*). Then add them to the soup.
4   Garnish and serve at once.

CHAPTER FOUR

SALADS

Salads are wonderful things. *Larousse Gastronomique*, the great food encyclopedia, describes them as 'A dish of raw or cooked foods, usually dressed and seasoned, served as an hors d'oeuvre, side dish, etc.' This is concise and correct, but it is the 'etc.' which intrigues me. So, not wishing to undermine Larousse, let me define 'etc.'. Salads can be cold or hot. They can be savoury or sweet, containing vegetables or fruit. They can be served on a hot summer's day in the garden, or on a cold winter's night in front of the television. They can be a complete meal, or, as Larousse says, an hors d'oeuvre or side dish, to which we can add an appetiser, starter, main course, or even dessert! Their dressings can range from simple oil and vinegar to really complex mixtures.

The legendary hors d'oeuvre trolley wheeled around at posh restaurants could well be on my shortlist for the one luxury I'd take to my desert island! That, and the self-serve salad bar at some of our better restaurants, leave no stone unturned for the variety of salads they have on offer, involving so very many different ingredients. Little wonder we in the West imagine salads to be our own preserve.

But let me tell you that salads are popular in the East too. True you will not find them in India and the subcontinent. Neither are they much in evidence in China. But uniquely, one oriental nation, Thailand, has taken the salad to supreme heights. There, the fabulous combination of Thai tastes such as the fragrance of lemon grass, kaffir lime and basil, contrasting with the spice of garlic and chilli, is interwoven with cooked ingredients. When cooled are they combined with fresh herbs and salad leaves, and one, maybe two items of fresh fruit. Thai salad should maintain a good balance between salty, sweet and sour, and whilst not being obvious, it should have a slightly sweet aftertaste. At least one cold salad dish traditionally appears at every Thai meal, as one of several main course dishes. Many have noodles incorporated into them. A salad can indeed be served as part of a Thai meal, or we can serve one unaccompanied, as a dish in its own right. Try one on a hot summer's day with a glass of bubbly! I make no apology for offering you no fewer than four Thai salads out of the seven in this chapter.

Yam Mee Yaang Gub Aa-ngoon Mee
Salad of Stir-fried Beef with Grapes and Noodles

As I say, there is no salad like a Thai salad. In fact the only resemblance to most other salads, is that it is served cold. Called *Yam*, pronounced 'Yum', the Thai salad is virtually a meal in itself, and a very fragrant spicy one at that. This recipe, to my mind, gives you the ultimate in Thai salads. It tastes superb, and the colour combination of the russet-browns of the meat, the grapes and the lollo rosso leaves, with the green of the other items make this dish look so natural and outstanding.

SERVES: 4

110g (4oz) cooked egg noodles, cold and chopped

250g (9oz) lean fillet steak, weighed after stage 1

3 tablespoons sunflower or soya oil

7 tiny Thai red bird's eye chillies (optional)

1 teaspoon magic paste (see page 80)

1 teaspoon palm sugar (or brown sugar)

2 lemon grass stalks, finely cross-cut

3 or 4 lime leaves, shredded

2 teaspoons bottled minced sweet basil

10 black and 10 white seedless grapes, halved

THE SALAD BED

some curly lettuce leaves

some russet-tinged salad leaves (e.g. lollo rosso)

some whole mint leaves

some fresh basil leaves, torn

1   Divest the steak of any unwanted matter. Cut it into thin strips, about 4cm x 2cm x 4mm each.

2   Heat the oil in your wok. Add the chillies (whole) and magic paste and stir-fry for 30 seconds. Add the meat strips, sugar, most of the

lemon grass, the lime leaves and the basil, and briskly stir-fry for about 3 minutes, turning from time to time. You are trying to achieve a meat colour just browner than pink, for maximum tenderness.

3   Transfer the meat and liquid from the wok to a mixing bowl to stop the cooking.

4   When it is cold, add the grapes and noodles, and toss well.

5   On the serving plate, arrange the salad bed then place the tossed mixed items on to the salad, along with any juices.

CHEF'S TIP: To cut thin strips of meat, chill the steak in the freezer for about 45 minutes. It is then hard but not frozen and it cuts easily.

Yam Kuaytiaw Sen Lek Ped

Rice Noodles Salad with Duck and Orange

Here is our very own Western classic combination of duck and orange given a Thai twist. The Thai rice noodle is named according to it thickness. *Kuaytiaw Sen Yai* is wide at around 2–3cm (¾–1 in) per strip. *Sen Lek* (or rice sticks) is narrower at 5mm per strip, and *Sen Mee* is thinner still at 1–2mm. Another rice noodle is the very thin, wiry variety which resembles white bird's nests. Also called rice vermicelli noodles, these are known in Thai as *Kuaytiaw Jeen*.

You can use any of these in this colourful salad, although I am specifying flat medium-size rice noodles (sen lek). They should have a satisfying al dente texture, and they work exceptionally well served cold in a salad. The fruit, in this case tangerine wedges, and a few lime wedges, add to the glamour.

SERVES: 4

110g (4oz) fresh sen lek rice noodles
1 tablespoon sunflower or soya oil
2 tablespoons chopped spring onion leaves and
bulbs
2 tablespoons chopped coriander leaves
1 tablespoon chopped mint leaves

225g (8oz) cooked, thinly sliced cold duck breast
some cooked prawns (optional)
2 tablespoons freshly squeezed lime juice
1 tablespoon freshly squeezed orange juice
salt to taste

GARNISH
some tangerine and lime wedges, pith removed
red and/or green chilli tassels

1 Boil the noodles until they are as al dente as you wish (*see page* 73).
Then drain them, run cold water over them, and set them aside,
allowing them to cool.
2 Add the remaining ingredients, mixing them well in. Salt to taste.
3 Garnish and serve cold, with Thai coconut salad dressing (*see page*
128)

Yam Gai Puong

Thai Chicken and Pea Salad

This is a very pleasant salad, again from Thailand, and derived from
an excellent traditional recipe. Chicken is such a user-friendly and
popular ingredient, and it takes on all flavours used with it. With the
chicken, I am using peas, for colour and taste contrast, but it is the
accompanying flavours which give this salad its edge. As well as all
the Thai repertoire of fragrant flavours, it has coconut milk, which
makes it really creamy, and toasted peanuts, and of course noodles
for an interesting texture.

SERVES: 4

85g (3oz) cooked egg noodles, cold

200ml (7 fl oz) coconut milk

250g (9 oz) chicken breast, skinned and chopped into thin shreds

2 stalks lemon grass, cross-cut

1 teaspoon fish sauce (nam pla) (see page 63)

3 or 4 lime leaves, shredded (if available)

1 red cayenne chilli, shredded

1 teaspoon palm sugar (or brown sugar) (optional)

3 or 4 spring onions, bulbs and leaves

2 tablespoons chopped basil leaves

50g (1¾ oz) peanuts, toasted and chopped

100g (3½oz) frozen peas, thawed

GARNISH

some lettuce leaves

some green cayenne chilli, chopped

some toasted desiccated coconut (see page 57)

hard-boiled egg, crumbled

some chilli and garlic sauce (see page 81) to drizzle on

1 Bring the coconut milk to the simmer in your wok.

2 Add the chicken, lemon grass, fish sauce and lime leaves and simmer gently for 5 minutes, stirring occasionally.

3 Add the chilli and sugar and continue to stir-fry for about 5 more minutes.

4 Add the spring onions, basil leaves, and the peanuts. Stir in, and when sizzling remove the wok from the heat.

5 Allow it to cool, then mix in the noodles and the peas, put into a serving bowl on a bed of salad leaves, and garnish.

Yam Phonlamai

Savoury Fruit Salad

I mentioned the use of fruit in Thai salads, and here is an excellent example. You can choose any fruit but my personal preference, as in this recipe, is to have a mixture of citrus fruits, plus melon and strawberries or raspberries. You can optionally add cooked seafood such as crab and prawns, or shredded chicken, but whatever you do, please make sure you add the garlic and savoury-tasting ingredients, and, of course, the noodles. It makes this another Thai salad of distinction.

SERVES: 4

110 g (4 oz) cooked noodles, any type, cold
4 tablespoons sunflower or soya oil
2 teaspoons fish sauce (see page 63)
1 teaspoon palm (or brown) sugar
1 tablespoon very finely cross-cut lemon grass
    (see page 60)
1 or more green chillies, chopped
1 clove garlic, very finely chopped
4 chopped spring onion leaves only
2 tablespoons very finely chopped purple basil
    leaves

1 tablespoon very finely chopped coriander leaves
8 lime segments, all pith removed
8 orange segments, all pith removed
8 grapefruit segments, all pith removed
12 strawberries, quartered
16 raspberries, whole
1 small honeydew melon, in bite-size pieces
16 seedless black grapes, halved
200g (7oz) watermelon in bite-size pieces
some crisp salad leaves

GARNISH
some cut mint leaves
some shredded lime leaves

1   Mix the oil, fish sauce, sugar, lemon grass, chilli and garlic together and chill in the fridge.
2   Just prior to serving wash and prepare the fruit.
3   Mix with the onion, basil, coriander leaves and noodles in a large bowl.
4   Arrange the salad leaves on the serving dish and place the mixture carefully on the leaves. Garnish and serve.

NOTE: The coconut dressing on page 128 is epecially good with this salad, and a little crushed ice is gorgeous as a further garnish. Other fruits you could use include pineapple, banana, mango, apples, pears, rambutan, star fruit, longam, lychee and kiwi.

Saigon Salad

The French influence on Vietnam extends to many inheritances in that country. French baguettes are one. It also extends the other way round, and I remember once eating at a Paris restaurant called, simply Saigon. The food, as I recall was better than the average Chinese-with-fish-sauce version that so frequently masquerades as Vietnamese in European restaurants. But the Saigon had its own inventions. Two dishes I recall were Soupe Saigon and Salade Saigon. Goi is a traditional Vietnamese salad. It consists, at its most basic level, of white cabbage and carrot, shredded coleslaw-style, plus lettuce, celery, Chinese leaves, spring onions, coriander and chilli, dressed with *nuoc cham* (fish sauce). Usually seafood, meat or chicken shreds are included. The Saigon Salad took the theme further and stir-fried some tasty ingredients, which, when combined with the shredded items made for an excellent salad.

SERVES: 4

110 g (4oz) cooked noodles, any type, cold
30g (1oz) white cabbage
30g (1oz) carrot
30g (1oz) lettuce or mixed salad leaves
30g (1oz) celery

60g (2oz) cooked chicken
60g (2oz) cooked ham
60g (2oz) cooked beef
60g (2oz) cooked crabmeat, fresh or frozen
60g (2oz) cooked prawns in brine
5 tablespoons soya oil

30g (1oz) Chinese leaves
30g (1oz) spring onions
2 or 3 red fresh chillies
2 tablespoons chopped coriander

1 clove garlic, chopped
½ teaspoon shrimp paste
4–6 spring onions, bulbs and leaves, chopped
2 tablespoons nuoc cham (see page 63)
200ml (7 fl oz) Vintage master stock (see page 78)
2 tablespoons pickled vegetables (see page 87)

GARNISH
60g (2oz) chopped roasted peanuts

1 Shred the white cabbage, carrot, lettuce, celery, Chinese leaves, spring onions, and chillies, as thinly as you can. Mix them together, adding the coriander.

2   Do the same to the cooked chicken, ham and beef, crabmeat and prawns. Mix them in with the vegetables.

3   Heat the oil in your wok and stir-fry the garlic, shrimp paste and onions for about 1 minute. Take off the heat, then add the fish sauce and the stock, and allow it to cool.

4   When cool, add it, with the pickled vegetables and noodles to the original mixed items from stage 2.

5   Garnish with the peanuts and serve cold.

Japanese Somen

Only sold dried, somen are a Japanese speciality. They are very small, round, hard-wheat noodles, sold in round or flat pretty cellophane or paper packages often tied with a ribbon. They are normally served cold with a chilled broth, or with salads, and to remain al dente after cooking, they should be chilled in icy water. Here, as tradition requires, a blanched and chilled, thinly sliced leek (*sarashi negi*) is included.

SERVES: 4

250g (9oz) dried somen noodles
400ml (14 fl oz) Japanese dashi stock
  (see page 79)

shoyu sauce
leek leaves, chopped
4 cupfuls crushed ice

GARNISH
4 large cooked king prawns, peeled, but tail-on
bottled ginger pickle, shredded

1   Boil the noodles until they are al dente (*see page* 73). Then drain them and set them aside, allowing them to go cold.

2   Make the dashi stock. Add the shoyu to taste, but it should be quite concentrated and salty.

3   When the noodles are cold, cover and put in the fridge for 30 minutes.

4   Just prior to serving, chop the leek into rings, microwave or blanche to tenderise. Plunge into chilled icy water to cool.

5   To serve, put the crushed ice into four serving bowls, and neatly place the noodles on top. Garnish with one king prawn per dish, the pickled ginger and the sliced leek.

6   Put the stock into four small individual serving bowls, and serve at once.

Proscuitto Noodles Salad

And now for something completely different. Italian salads are legendary. Crisp green lettuce, fresh, tasty, plump, plum tomatoes, ivory white garlic slices, gleaming, boot-black olives and yellow peppers, speckled with black pepper, tarted up with generous squeezings of fresh lemon juice, and drenched with greeny-gold aromatic extra virgin olive oil, the real thing, not the pale odourless tasteless variety so often used. Like wine in France and ouzo in Greece, the Italian salad may well taste better in the Italian sunshine, than elsewhere but for those of us deprived of such a luxury, we must recreate our memories at home. And this salad should do just that.

I have taken all the aforementioned treasures, and added to them two other things associated with Italy – prosciutto (pronounced 'proshootoe'), the fabulous slightly hardened salty ham, available at your neighbourhood deli (get your decent olive oil there too) plus pasta – except that here I'm using curly thin egg noodles instead.

SERVES: 4

125g (4½oz) curly, thin dried egg noodles
half an iceberg or crispy lettuce
110g (4oz) prosciutto, in strips
2 fresh plum tomatoes, quartered
8 black olives, pitted and halved

1 yellow pepper, in strips
2 or 3 lemons, squeezed
freshly ground black pepper
a drizzle of extra virgin olive oil
coarse sea salt to taste

1   Boil the noodles until they are as al dente as you wish (*see page* 73). Then drain them and allow them to cool down completely.

2   Wash and chop the lettuce, and put it into a large, clean serving bowl.

3   In another bowl, mix all the other ingredients together, including the cold noodles.
4   Place the mixture over the lettuce and serve.

Yam Aus Maprao
Thai Coconut Salad Dressing

This dressing goes hand-in-glove with the Thai salads in this chapter. It requires thin coconut milk. The third pressing or the thinnest liquid from the can (*see page 55*) is what we need, otherwise the dressing becomes too rich. It will keep in the fridge for a few days (or it can freeze). Use with salad as with French dressing.

MAKES: 275ML (10 FL OZ) DRESSING

150ml (¼ pint) thin coconut milk
50ml (2 fl oz) rice vinegar
2 to 4 tablespoons chilli and garlic sauce
  (see page 81)

1 teaspoon ground white pepper
2 tablespoons freshly squeezed lime juice
2 teaspoons fish sauce
1 teaspoon palm (or brown) sugar

1   Simply mix everything together, chill and serve.

PLATE FIVE

PLATTERS OF STARTERS Kratak, Pastry-cloaked Prawns, Golden Thread Pork Balls, Noodle Sushi Nori.
  Behind right: Crispy Noodles Nests, containing Crispy Deep-fried Seaweed.
  Behind left: Thai Mee Grob, crispy noodles with a crackling caramelised topping.

CHAPTER FIVE

NOODLES WITH MEAT

Meat continues to be popular as a main ingredient all over the world, despite regularly receiving a bad press. Here is a selection of fourteen meat with noodle recipes, mostly from the Orient, but with three from Italy, and two from the USA. The peoples of China, Thailand, and Indo-China adore beef. It is number one over there, with pork and chicken. They do not eat lamb, mutton and goat, nor do they eat dairy products. The Japanese ate no meat at all, being strict adherers to Buddhism, until relatively recently.

This chapter starts with an all-time Chinese restaurant favourite, Beef with Black Bean Sauce. And still on the restaurant scene, those other two ever-popular dishes, Crispy Beef Noodles (with variations including pork, chicken and seafood) and the divine marinated fragrant pork dish, Char Siu, China's answer to Indian Tandoori. From Japan I have chosen two delightful recipes, the first is Ramen (Chinese-style noodles served here with Char Siu) and the delicate Shirataki noodles with Sukiyaki (a one-pot dish of beef and vegetables). From Indonesia comes one of their national dishes, Bhami Goreng. It literally means 'Stir-fried Noodles' which rather understates its really tasty results. From neighbouring Singapore, try the Hokkein Stir-fry Noodles. It contains pork, but is unusual in that both wheat and rice noodles appear together. From Korea comes Chap Chee, Mixed Vegetables with Beef and Vermicelli Noodles, cooked with their vegetable pickle called *kimchi*. I am pleased to be able to include one recipe from Laos – Khao Poon Moo, which literally means Rice Vermicelli with Pork.

PLATE SIX

THAI DUCK AND ORANGE SALAD Here using fresh rice noodles (sen lek), garnished with prawns.

I could not leave the meat chapter without some noodle recipes with a Western influence. I hope you will try them. The mince and celery Noodle Bolognese is no invention of mine, apart from using noodles. The sauce was developed in Bologna using finely chopped meat and vegetables back in the Middle Ages, and modified later to become mince with tomatoes. The other modification of a classic Italian recipe is Noodles Alla Carbonara, simply cooked with butter, black pepper, cheese and bacon. Staying with the Italian theme, how about Lasagne Noodle with a creamy mince filling, using flat ribboned rice noodle sheets in place of pasta? It works really well.

My final two meat with noodle dishes are offered as a tasty tribute to North America. The first is called New York Pastrami Glass Noodle. (Pastrami is a dried salted meat, and here it is cooked with a lime and honey sweet and sour sauce.) The second is one of my favourite dishes, Texan Chilli Bean Noodle. Usually the dish is eaten with garlic bread, but here I use it as a topping on egg noodles, a combination which works really well!

Black Bean and Beef Egg Noodle

This is a typical, and very popular stir-fry noodle dish, always found at the Chinese restaurant and takeaway. The beef must be best fillet steak for maximum tenderness, cut into the stir-fry cut (see method below and chef's tip on the next page). It incorporates colourful bell peppers and Chinese leaves (*pe-tsai*). The black bean is, of course, fermented soya bean, available in 120g (4½ oz) sachets. I have specified egg noodles, though any flavoured wheat noodle is equally interesting.

SERVES: 4

225g (8oz) dried egg noodles

250g (9oz) lean fillet steak, weighed after stage 1

2 tablespoons soya or light vegetable oil

2 cloves garlic, peeled and shredded

2.5cm (1 in) cube fresh ginger, peeled and sliced

1 or more red or green chilli, shredded (optional)

4 spring onions, chopped

1 tablespoon green pepper cut into diamonds

1 tablespoon red pepper cut into diamond shapes

50g (2oz) Chinese leaves, coarsely shredded

120g (4½oz) black bean sauce

1 tablespoon dark soy sauce

1 Divest the steak of any unwanted matter. Cut it into thin strips, about 4cm x 2cm x 4mm each.

2 Boil the noodles until they are as al dente as you wish (*see page* 73). Then drain them and set them aside, keeping them warm if possible, for use later.

3 Heat the oil in a wok or frying pan. Stir-fry the garlic and ginger for 20 seconds. Add the chillies and the meat strips, and briskly stir-fry for about 3 minutes, turning from time to time. You are trying to achieve a meat colour just browner than pink, for maximum tenderness.

4 Add the spring onions and continue stir-frying for a further minute.

5 Add the pepper diamonds, Chinese leaves, black bean sauce and soy sauce. Stir-fry briskly until sizzling.

6 Add the strained freshly cooked noodles. Stir until hot then serve. It should not need salt.

CHEF'S TIP: To cut thin strips of meat, chill the steak in the freezer for about 45 minutes. It will then be hard but not frozen and will cut easily. Also, cutting across the grain, not with it, gives more tender results after cooking.

Indonesian Bahmi Goreng
Stir-fried Noodles

Adjacent to Malaysia is Indonesia, the former Dutch East Indies. It consists of 13,000 islands, some of which are uninhabited. The world's fourth largest population lives on the remaining islands, which include Sumatra, Borneo, Java, New Guinea and the celebrated 'spice islands' – the Moluccas, the original home of clove, nutmeg and mace. Spices, ironically earn relatively little income for Indonesia. Most Indonesian dishes will be found in Malaysia and vice-versa. In the local languages, *Bahmi* (or *bahmee*) means 'noodles', *Go* means 'fried' and *reng* – Malay or Indonesian. You will find this national dish all over the east Indies and at the popular Indonesian restaurants all over Holland. The other celebrated national dish of the area is Nasi Go-reng, where *nasi* simply means rice.

SERVES: 4

225–350g (8–12oz) noodles

½ teaspoon ground turmeric

2 tablespoons ghee

2 cloves garlic, crushed

5cm (2 in) cube galangal or ginger, chopped

several pieces cooked sliced pork, skinned

110g (4oz) cooked prawns, shells off

1 tablespoon chopped fresh coriander

1 tablespoon chopped fresh basil

3–4 tablespoons cooked peas

PASTE

3 cloves garlic

3–4 spring onions, bulbs and leaves, chopped

1 large soft lemon grass bulb, chopped

½ teaspoon tamarind purée

½ teaspoon blachan

½ teaspoon sweet soy sauce

½ teaspoon brown sugar

1–4 teaspoons sambal manis (see glossary)

GARNISH

finely chopped fresh basil

fresh grated or desiccated coconut

chopped Macadamia or cashew nuts

1   Pulse the paste ingredients in a food processor or blender, using enough water to make a purée.

2   Adding turmeric before the noodles go in the water, boil the noodles until they are as al dente as you wish (*see page* 73). Then drain them and set them aside, keeping them warm if possible, for use later.

3   Heat the ghee in a karahi. Stir-fry the garlic for 30 seconds, add the galangal and fry for a further 30 seconds. Add the paste and briskly stir-fry for 1 or 2 more minutes.

4   Add the pork, prawns, coriander, basil, peas, and noodles. Stir carefully to mix thoroughly. Garnish with basil, coconut and chopped nuts, and serve.

Singaporean Hokkein Stir-fried Noodles

Singapore was founded in 1867 by Sir Stamford Raffles, and was used by the British as their major trading post in the area, the legacy of which is today's major business centre. Singapore's population is the most cosmopolitan of the area, with Indian, Chinese, Malay, Indonesian and European influences. The Chinese or Hokkien predominate, and little wonder, so do noodles.

Because Singapore, like Hong Kong, was created from nothing, and then populated by such a mixture of races, there has not been enough time for Singaporean cuisine to develop and for many true national dishes to evolve. But this recipe could be one of the few. It has a rare feature in that both wheat and rice noodles appear together, and the recipe works well with egg or wheat noodles and any rice noodles, fresh or dried. Select whichever type of noodle you wish to use (*see pages* 44-49).

This is one of those dishes you can watch being cooked on the streets, by the food hawkers. After a few minutes of deft wok-tossing and twisting, a few pennies change hands, and the expectant diner tucks in, just as I did some years ago. It is served with hot chilli sauces, such as bottled Sambal Oelek and Sambal Manis (see glossary).

SERVES: 4

250g (9oz) dried, or 450g (1lb) noodles, half wheat or egg, and half rice noodles

250g (9oz) lean leg of pork, weighed after stage 1

60g (2oz) mixed seafood

2 tablespoons sesame or soya oil

4–6 cloves garlic, sliced

5cm (2 in) cube ginger or galangal, shredded

300 ml (½ pint) stock, any type (see page 76)

1 egg

4–6 spring onions, leaves and bulbs, finely chopped

60g (2oz) Chinese leaves (pe-tsai or pak choi), shredded

30g (1oz) beansprouts, canned or fresh

2 tablespoons red bell pepper, shredded

1 or more green chilli, shredded

soy sauce to taste

1 tablespoon chopped fresh coriander

1 Divest the pork of any unwanted matter. Cut it into thin strips, about 4cm x 2cm x 4mm each.

2 Boil the noodles in different pans until they are as al dente as you wish (see page 73). Then drain them, mix them, and set them aside, keeping them warm if possible, for use later.

3 Heat the oil in your wok. Stir-fry the garlic and ginger or galangal for 30 seconds, add the pork and seafood, and continue to stir-fry for a further 5 to 10 minutes, adding the stock bit by bit over this time. Make sure everything is cooked right through, if not continue cooking for a while longer.

4 Immediately add the drained noodles, and the raw egg, briskly stir-fry them until they are well combined, and are hot right through, the egg coating the noodles and cooked.

5 Add the other ingredients, then transfer to a serving bowl.

Korean Chap Chee
Mixed Vegetables with Beef and Vermicelli Noodles

Koreans adore beef. It is number one there over pork and chicken. Like many south-east Asians, Koreans do not eat lamb, sheep and goat, nor do they eat dairy products. Rice and noodles are the staples. They adore home-made vegetable pickle called *kimchi*, sometimes available over here in Chinatown stores. Sesame and chilli are their predominant spices, and of course the holy trinity of garlic, ginger and spring onion are always omnipresent. Tie all that up with soy sauce, and you have Korea on a plate! And if you try this popular Korean vermicelli noodle dish, also called Jap Jee (a reference to Japan and China, I'm reliably informed) you will certainly have Korea on your plate!

SERVES: 4

110g (4oz) vermicelli noodles
250g (9oz) lean fillet steak, weighed after stage 2
3 tablespoons sesame oil

3 teaspoons white sesame seeds
4 cloves garlic, sliced
1 tablespoon sugar

4–6 spring onions, bulbs and leaves finely chopped

several (to taste) small, very hot Thai or bird's-eye chillies, chopped

2 tablespoons dark soy sauce

110g (4oz) canned straw mushrooms, halved

110g (4oz) canned bean sprouts

1 medium-sized carrot, shredded,

2 gherkins, cut into thin slices

2 tablespoons red bell pepper, cut into diamonds

4 tablespoons chopped vegetable pickle (see page 87)

GARNISH
omelette cut into strips
more soy sauce to taste
black pepper
sesame seeds, roasted

1   Boil the noodles until they are as al dente as you wish (*see page* 73). Then drain them and set them aside, keeping them warm if possible, for use later.

2   Divest the steak of any unwanted matter. Cut it into thin strips, about 4cm x 2cm x 4mm each.

3   Heat the oil in a wok or frying pan. Stir-fry the sesame seeds for about 20 seconds, then add the garlic and continue to stir-fry for 20 seconds more.

4   Add the sugar, onions and chillies and when they have softened, after a couple of minutes, add the meat strips, and briskly stir-fry for about 3 minutes, turning from time to time. You are trying to achieve a meat colour just browner than pink, for maximum tenderness. Add the soy sauce and continue stir-frying for a further 30 seconds.

5   Reserve the liquid from the mushroom and the beansprout cans. Add some 4 tablespoons of it now, along with the mushrooms and beansprouts themselves, plus the carrot, gherkins, red pepper and pickle, stir-frying until it is hot.

6   Add the noodles, and when everything is hot again, garnish and serve.

Lao Khao Poon Moo

Rice Vermicelli with Pork

It is a wretched shame that Cambodia has recently earned itself such a bad reputation for evil. Khmer Rouge is now synonymous with rouge for blood. In fact the Khmer were once a mighty people, whose empire occupied most of what is now Thailand, Vietnam and Cambodia, as well as Laos. Their remarkable city at Angkor Wat was established as capital, as early as 600 AD. Marco Polo visited there in 1290 to find it covered an area of 250 sq km, had a population of one million. It was a centre of trade, and rice in particular was mass produced, with the aid of an intricate irrigation network.

The well-preserved remains of Angkor survive to this day, beautiful, serene, ghostlike and uninhabited of course, and virtually impossible to reach, thanks to the inhospitality of today's Khmer descendants. Twelfth-century surviving bas-reliefs show a more peaceful civilisation where pigs forage in paddy fields, bees make honey and the people are hard at work fishing, at their markets, gambling and cock fighting. Polo saw all this, and his journals frequently discussed food. He told of enormous banquets for thousands of courtiers, where lacquered bowls overflowed with meats, rice, noodles and beans, soy and bamboo.

There are currently no Lao restaurants in Britain, although I did find this recipe in a Vietnamese restaurant in Sydney a while back. *Khao* means rice and *khao poon*, rice vermicelli noodles. The Lao do not eat wheat noodles, though they do eat Chinese-style mung bean cellophane noodles (*Khao Poon Chin*). In an attempt to validate my recipe, I referred to the only recent Lao cookery book that I know of, by Phia Sing, published by Prospect Books in 1995. In the nearest recipe I could find to mine, Mr Sing requires the cook to use a 'pig's lungs, a pig's head, skinned, split open, scraped clean and washed, pork, the size of a hand, scraped clean of hair and washed, and six pieces of dried pig's blood, each about three fingers by one'. Believe me, though my recipe may lose something very 'ethnic' in its simplification, it requires nothing more of the pig than some diced leg of pork, divested of all unwanted matter by the butcher, so please don't be put off!

Noodles with Meat

SERVES: 4

250g (9oz) dried rice vermicelli noodles
250g (9oz) lean leg of pork, weighed after
   stage 1
3 tablespoons soya oil
8–10 cloves garlic, sliced
5cm (2 in) cube of galangal or ginger, chopped
1 tablespoon magic paste (see page 80)
4–6 spring onions, leaves and bulbs, chopped
600 ml (1 pint) fish stock (see page 77)
2 or 3 lemon grass stalks

1–4 fresh red chillies, chopped
2 or 3 filleted fresh sardines
6–8 tinned anchovies in oil
2 tablespoons chopped coriander leaves
1 teaspoon bottled minced basil
2 teaspoons fish sauce (see page 63)
110g (4oz) Chinese leaves (pak choi) shredded
40g (1½oz) bamboo shoots, boiled and finely
   chopped

1   Divest the pork of any unwanted matter. Cut it into cubes, about
    1.5cm x 1.5 cm (¾ inch) each.
2   Boil the noodles until they are as al dente as you wish (*see page* 73).
    Then drain them and set them aside, keeping them warm if
    possible, for use later.
3   Heat the oil in your wok. Stir-fry the garlic and galangal or
    ginger for 30 seconds, add the magic paste and the spring onions,
    and 4 tablespoons of stock and continue to stir-fry for a further
    2 minutes.
4   Add the pork, and after about 2 minutes of brisk stir-frying, add
    about half of the remaining stock and the lemon grass and chilli,
    and simmer it for about 10 minutes.
5   During stage 4, chop the sardines, removing unwanted fins etc. and
    chop the anchovies, and put them, with some anchovy oil (to taste),
    into the stir-fry towards the end of the 10 minutes.
6   Add the remaining stock, the coriander, fish sauce, Chinese leaves
    and bamboo shoots and as soon as they are hot, add the drained
    noodles, and briskly stir-fry them until they are well combined with
    the other ingredients, and are hot right through.
7   Transfer to a serving bowl.

Chinese Crispy Beef Noodles
Chinese Restaurant Style

This is another of those dishes which is part and parcel of the Chinese restaurant scene. It is a recipe which makes the most of deep-fried noodles, which no book on noodles should be without. This recipe works well with any noodles – wheat, egg or rice, fresh or dried. Select the type of noodle you wish to use (*see pages* 44-49).

Crispy noodles can be served by crumbling them over the meal. Alternatively crispy noodles can be the major ingredient in a stir-fry dish such as this recipe. At the restaurant, you will get seven main variants of this dish, chicken, duck, pork, king prawn, mixed vegetable and special – which is any combination of the other six. These are detailed below.

SERVES: 4

300g (10oz) noodles, any type
250g (9oz) lean fillet steak, weighed after stage 1
2 tablespoons soya or light vegetable oil
2–4 cloves garlic, finely chopped

4–6 spring onions, leaves and bulbs, finely chopped
50g (2oz) frozen green beans, thawed
1 tablespoon dark soy sauce

1 Divest the steak of any unwanted matter. Cut it into thin shreds, about 4cm x 4mm x 4mm (2in x ⅛ in x ⅛ in) each.
2 Heat the deep-fryer to 190°C, chip-frying temperature.
3 Break up the noodles into three or four batches.
4 Place one batch into the hot oil. It will whoosh up fairly fast then settle down. Remove noodles from the oil within 30 seconds, shaking to remove excess oil, and rest them on kitchen paper.
5 Repeat stage 3 with the remaining batches of noodles.
6 Put the crispy noodles into a serving bowl and place in a warmer or low oven.
7 Heat the oil in a wok or frying pan. Stir-fry the garlic for 20 seconds. Add the spring onions and continue stir-frying for a further minute.
8 Add the shredded steak and stir fry for another 3–4 minutes.

9   Add the beans and soy sauce and bring to a sizzle. Pour the sauce over the noodles just prior to serving. Serve promptly otherwise the noodles will go soggy.

NOTE: see important deep-frying information on page 75.

VARIATIONS

Crispy Chicken Noodles

In place of the beef, substitute 250g (9oz) lean chicken breast, weighed after stage 1.

The cooking time for chicken at stage 8 may need a little longer.

Crispy Duck Noodles

In place of the beef, substitute 250g (9oz) lean duck breast, weighed after stage 1.

The cooking time for duck at stage 8 may need a little longer.

Crispy Pork Noodles

In place of the beef, substitute 250g (9oz) lean leg of pork, weighed after stage 1.

The cooking time for pork at stage 8 may need a little longer.

Crispy King Prawn Noodles

In place of the beef, substitute 250g (9oz) cooked king prawns, weighed after shelling, de-veining and washing.

The cooking time for prawns at stage 8 may need a little longer.

Crispy Mixed Vegetable Noodles

In place of the beef, substitute 250g (9oz) of any mixed vegetables of your choice, weighed after stage 1.

Crispy Special Noodles

In place of the beef, substitute 250g (9oz) of any combination of the above ingredients.

Char Siu Noodles

Red Roasted Pork with Noodles

This is to the Chinese restaurant what Tandoori is to the Indian. It is lean fillets of pork deeply steeped in a rich red marinade, then roasted. When cross-cut, into thin slices, the white meat in the centre contrasts dazzlingly with the crispy red exterior. For this dish, I chop the *char siu* further into small bite-sized pieces, and mix it well into the noodles with a little sesame oil and black pepper, making it a kind of Chinese spaghetti carbonara (*see page* 145)! It is already a meal in itself, but you can add omelette, and frozen mixed vegetables (peas, diced carrot and sweetcorn) to this dish for added colour and interest. Serve it with pickled vegetables, chilli and garlic sauce and soy sauce.

SERVES: 4

250g (9oz) dried, or 450g (1lb) fresh egg noodles
2 pork fillets, each weighing about 375g (12oz) after trimming. Their size should be around 20 x 4cm (8 x 1½ in)
some omelette, chopped (optional)

some frozen mixed vegetables (see above), thawed (optional)
1 tablespoon sesame oil
salt to taste
freshly ground black pepper to taste

THE MARINADE

50ml (2 fl oz) light or dark soy sauce

4 tablespoon hoisin sauce

1 teaspoon red food colouring (optional)

2 teaspoons Chinese ten-spice powder
  (see page 82)

2 tablespoons Chinese red rice wine

1   Trim off any excess fat and gristle from the meat, then put some small gashes into it with a sharp pointed knife.

2   Mix the marinade ingredients together in a non-metallic bowl, large enough to hold the marinade and meat comfortably.

3   Make sure the meat is thoroughly coated with the marinade. Cover the bowl with stretch film and put it into the fridge for a minimum of 12 hours, and providing the meat was fresh not frozen, a maximum of 48 hours.

4   To cook, preheat the oven to 190°C/375°F/Gas 5. Put the meat on to the oven rack above an oven tray, and place it in the centre of the oven.

5   Bake for 15 minutes. Inspect. It should be nearly done, but ovens do vary. It should need longer, so turn the meat and continue baking for the final few (probably 5) minutes.

6   Then remove the meat and rest it for a few minutes, before thinly slicing it, and cross cutting into shreds.

7   During stage 5, boil the noodles until they are as al dente as you wish (*see page 73*). Then drain them and mix them and the *char siu* in the saucepan they were boiled in, with the oil. Briskly stir-fry them until they are well combined, adding the other ingredients, until everything is hot right through.

8   Salt and pepper to taste, then transfer to a serving bowl.

Japanese Ramen Pork

The Japanese noodles in this recipe are a variation on the Chinese-style egg or wheat noodles, and they come in many dried forms, as crinkly tangles, bunches or packs. Called *chuka soba* in western Japan, they are served in a variety of ways, but usually in a bowl with a soy-based soup or broth, with slices of roast pork, pickled bamboo, fish paste and seven-spice mixture.

This Ramen dish was made famous in the late Juzo Itami's acclaimed 1986 film *Tampopo* (meaning dandelion, the young leaves of which are used in salads, or are lightly steamed). In the amusing movie the widowed Tampopo is our heroine. Desperate to learn about the vagaries of making noodles and stock, she goes to astonishing lengths. Eventually with the encouragement of a champion, the truck driver Goro, she succeeds in becoming a noodle-maker. Itami acknowledged he had parodied the western, saying it was not so much a Spaghetti Western as a Noodle Eastern! I am using the *char siu* pork from the previous recipe (not Japanese, but delicious).

SERVES: 4

250g (9oz) ramen dried or 450g (1lb) fresh egg
   noodles
2 char siu cooked pork fillets (see previous
   recipe)

500ml (16 fl oz) meat or vegetable stock
   (see pages 77–78)
50ml (2 fl oz) mirin
shoyu sauce to taste

GARNISH
deep-fried seaweed
shredded white radish

1   Boil the noodles until they are as al dente as you wish (*see page* 73). Then drain them and set them aside, keeping them warm if possible, for use later.
2   Cut the char siu into thin slices.
3   Heat up the stock. Add the mirin and the shoyu sauce for salting to taste. Put the char siu slices into the broth to heat them up.
4   Put the hot noodles into four serving bowls. Ladle the broth on top, ensuring the char siu is evenly distributed.
5   Garnish and serve.

Japanese Shirataki Sukiyaki

In the country where the pretty presentation of food is everything, Shirataki's translation, 'white waterfall', gives us a clue to this very thin noodle's delicate appearance and translucence. When cut, the root of the plant gives off a gelatinous resin. This can be formed into strings or noodles which traditionally accompany *sukiyaki* (a one-pot dish of beef and vegetables). These noodles can be bought dried or vacuum-packed with water in sachets. Alternatively use bean-thread noodles (*see page* 44).

Sukiyaki is cooked *nabemono* style, i.e. directly on the table in a copper pan above a flame. The guests help themselves to beef, vegetables, tofu, and vermicelli noodles dipped in raw egg prior to eating.

SERVES: 4

250g (9oz) dried shirataki or beanthread noodles
250g (9oz) lean fillet steak, weighed after
  stage 1
2 tablespoons soya oil
200g (7oz) pak choi (chinese spinach), chopped

6 shitake mushrooms, soaked and cut into slices
  (see page 62)
4–6 spring onions, leaves and bulbs, chopped
110g (4oz) tofu, cut into small cubes
2 raw egg yolks (optional)

THE SAUCE

100ml (3½ fl oz) shoyu sauce
200 ml (7 fl oz) mirin

1 tablespoon sugar
100 ml (3½ fl oz) water

1   Divest the steak of any unwanted matter. Cut it into thin strips, about 4cm x 2cm x 4mm each.

2   Boil the noodles until they are as al dente as you wish (*see page* 73). Then drain them and set them aside, keeping them warm if possible, for use later.

3   Heat the oil in a wok or frying pan. Add the meat strips, and briskly stir-fry for about 3 minutes, turning from time to time. You are trying to achieve a meat colour just browner than pink, for maximum tenderness.

4   If you have a table cooker, a Mongolian hot pot, or even a fondue pot, continue this recipe at the table when your guests are waiting, otherwise complete it in the wok. Mix together the sauce ingredi-

ents, then add the sauce, pak choi, spring onions and tofu into the wok or pot, and almost at once it is ready. Ideally you should add the ingredients gradually as the diners eat the food.

5 To serve, give your guests chopsticks, and let them select their sukiyaki, item by item, mouthful by mouthful. As a Japanese option, you can offer the raw eggs in a bowl as a dipping sauce, though I prefer wasabi (*see page* 88).

Mince and Celery Noodle Bolognese

Most people I have spoken to regard Spaghetti Bolognese as the world's most famous pasta dish, and since as we see in the introduction, pasta and noodles are one and the same thing, I guess that makes it the most famous noodle dish in the world. The dish is named after north Italy's ancient city of Bologna, nestling at the foot of the Apennines. Bologna did not invent pasta. That accolade went to Naples in the south. Bologna developed a thick sauce made of finely chopped vegetables back in the Middle Ages. Much later, the meat cut became mince, and tomatoes mandatory, and hey presto, we have a world-class sauce to accompany spaghetti. But can it be bettered? Maybe not, but it can be speeded up! Here is my version of this exceedingly tasty dish, made, as you might expect, with a few spices, and, as you might not expect, using egg noodles.

SERVES: 4

250g (9oz) dried, or 450g (1lb) fresh egg noodles
3 or 4 tablespoons vegetable oil
1 teaspoon white cumin seeds
1/3 teaspoon coriander seeds
4–6 cloves garlic
6–8 spring onions, leaves and bulbs, finely chopped
450g (1lb) best lean minced beef
4–6 green cardamom pods
4–6 cloves
4 bay leaves

1 teaspoon black peppercorns
1 tablespoon tomato purée
2 teaspoons mixed dried herbs
1 tablespoon tomato ketchup
4–6 tinned plum tomatoes
1 teaspoon Worcester sauce
1 teaspoon bottied green pesto
1 tablespoon chopped fresh oregano
1 tablespoon chopped fresh coriander
sea salt to taste

GARNISH
grated fresh Parmesan cheese
freshly ground black pepper
chopped fresh parsley

1   Heat the oil in your wok. Stir-fry the seeds for 30 seconds. Add the garlic and continue to stir-fry for a further 30 seconds. Add the onions, and continue to stir-fry for a further 5 minutes.

2   Add the mince, the cardamom, and cloves and stir regularly until the meat seals, i.e. it goes brown. This will take about 5 minutes.

3   Place this mixture into a suitable-sized lidded casserole dish – 2.25–2.75l (4 to 5 pint) will be enough. Add the bay leaves and peppercorns. Put the casserole, with the lid on, into the oven pre-heated to 190°C/375°F/Gas 5.

4   After some 10 minutes, or so, add the tomato purée, dried herbs, ketchup, tomatoes, Worcester sauce and the pesto, stirring well. Return to the oven.

5   After 30 more minutes, inspect. It should be sizzling nicely, but it should not be dried up. If it does look a little dry, add just enough water to ease it, stir in the fresh herbs, and return, lid on, to the oven for a final 15 minutes.

6   Boil the noodles until they are as al dente as you wish (*see page* 73).

7   Drain the noodles, then divide them between 4 suitable serving bowls.

8   Salt the mince to taste, then serve it on top of the noodles.

9   Top the noodles with the Parmesan, black pepper, and the parsley as a garnish.

Noodles Alla Carbonara

If I were to name four of your favourite tastes, would I be correct in saying they might be butter, black pepper, cheese and bacon? (Even vegetarians twitch at the smell of frying bacon!) Put those delights together with pasta, and you have one of Italy's most popular dishes. Do it with egg noodles, instead of spaghetti, and the slowest part of the cooking process is frying the bacon! Some cooks add cream at the end of stage 5.

SERVES: 4

250g (9oz) dried, or 450g (1lb) fresh egg noodles
3 or 4 tablespoons butter
110g (4oz) rindless streaky bacon, chopped into
    small pieces

freshly ground black pepper
salt to taste
2 eggs

GARNISH
some freshly grated Parmesan cheese
some sprigs of chopped parsley

1   Boil the noodles until they are as al dente as you wish (*see page* 73). Then drain them and set them aside, keeping them warm if possible, for use later.
2   Heat the butter in your wok. Stir-fry the bacon until it is crispy (about 5 minutes).
3   Immediately add the drained noodles, and briskly stir-fry them until they are well combined with the bacon, and are hot right through.
4   Pepper and salt to taste, then add the 2 eggs and briskly stir them in. Providing the noodles are hot, the egg will coat itself on the noodles, cooking as it goes.
5   Transfer to a serving bowl.
6   Top the noodles with the Parmesan, sprinkle on the parsley and serve.

Lasagne Noodle

With creamy mince filling, using flat ribboned rice noodle

Lasagne or 'lasagna' in Italian, is the name given to pasta after the dough is rolled out into wide flat sheets, i.e. before it is cut into strips. Though the classic lasagne is 'white', it is quite normal these days to use coloured sheets. Pink lasagne is flavoured with tomato, and green with spinach. Whole wheat flour gives a chewier pale brown sheet.

Lasagne also refers to a cooked dish where a number of sheets of lasagne are assembled in a flat cooking dish, with alternating layers of meat and cheese. The dish is then slowly baked in the oven, indeed the word derives from the Latin *lasanum*, a cooking pot, and there is nothing like it, when it emerges from the oven, the cheese, bubbling and sizzling. It is one of my favourite dishes, especially with the aromatic spicing, and it gives me great pleasure to offer you a noodle variation using flat rice noodle sheets.

SERVES: 4

450g (1lb) of fresh rice noodle sheet (see page 71) cut into
30 to 36 sheets about 10cm (4in) square

THE BÉCHAMEL SAUCE

500ml (18 fl oz) milk

60g (2oz) butter

60g (2oz) flour

salt, pepper and freshly grated nutmeg to taste

3 tablespoons olive oil

2–4 cloves garlic, chopped

225g (8oz) onion, finely chopped

600g (1lb 4oz) lean minced beef

200g (7oz) fresh plum tomatoes, chopped

2 tablespoons chopped red bell pepper

1–4 fresh green chillies, chopped

2 teaspoons dried mixed herbs

1 teaspoon Worcester sauce

50ml (1¾ fl oz) red wine

2 teaspoons red pesto sauce

1 tablespoon chopped fresh oregano

1 tablespoon chopped fresh coriander

spicy salt to taste (see page 85)

some grated Cheddar cheese

SPICES

4–6 whole green cardamoms

4–6 cloves

½ teaspoon cumin seeds

½ teaspoon coriander seeds

4 bay leaves

½ teaspoon black peppercorns

GARNISH
some grated Cheddar cheese
some chopped parsley

1   Make or buy the rice noodles sheets, and cut into 10cm (4in) squares, around 2mm thick.

2   Boil the noodle sheets until they are as al dente as you wish (*see page*

73). Then drain them and set them aside, keeping them warm if possible, for use later.

3   Make the béchamel sauce. Bring the milk to the simmer. In another pan, preferably a non-stick saucepan, melt the butter, then mix in the flour. Using a whisk, stir continuously, while steadily and carefully pouring in the hot milk. (If you use cold milk, you stand stirring for ages until it becomes hot). Continue whisking slowly until the sauce will not thicken further, and with luck it will be lump-free.

4   Heat the oil in your wok, then add the garlic and stir-fry for 30 seconds. Add the onions, and reduce the heat. Stir-fry for 10 minutes, until the onions become translucent and begin to brown.

5   Add the mince and spices, and stir-fry for a further 10 minutes. Mix in the tomatoes, bell pepper, chillies, mixed herbs, Worcester sauce, wine, pesto sauce, oregano, coriander and salt to taste.

6   Preheat the oven to 190°C/375°F/Gas 5, and select a suitable oven pan.

7   Pour a layer of mince mixture in, then cover the meat with a layer of noodle sheets, then a layer of béchamel sauce, then some grated cheese, and do this several times (it depends on the oven pan size) until you end with a final layer of noodle sheets, sauce then cheese.

8   Bake for 35 to 45 minutes by which time you will have a bubbling golden top with brown scorch marks.

9   Garnish and serve.

New York Pastrami Glass Noodles
With Lime and Honey Sweet and Sour Sauce

Pastrami is a traditional Yiddish ingredient which originated in biblical times. It is goat, mutton or beef meat, marinated in spices then dried, either in the sun or by smoking. The word derived from the Romanian to 'preserve'. It is found still in Israel and other eastern Mediterranean countries, for example in mezze dishes in Turkey and Greece. Its derivative, pastrami, is one of New York's specialities, and here, in this recipe is my tribute to one of my favourite cities. This dish works well with any type of noodle, fresh or dried. Select the type of noodle you wish to use (*see pages* 44-49).

SERVES: 4

250g (9oz) dried or 450g (1lb) fresh noodles, any type

2 tablespoons sesame oil

8 cloves garlic

some fresh red chilli, chopped (optional)

4–6 spring onions, leaves and bulbs, finely chopped

350g (12oz) pastrami, cut into strips

spicy salt to taste (see page 85)

THE SAUCE
4 tablespoons freshly squeezed lime juice
8 tablespoons clear honey

1   Boil the noodles until they are as al dente as you wish (see page 73). Then drain them and set aside, keeping them warm if possible, for use later.

2   Heat the oil in your wok. Stir-fry the garlic for 30 seconds, add the onions and chilli, and continue to stir-fry for a further 2 minutes.

3   Immediately add the pastrami and the drained noodles, and briskly stir-fry them until they are well combined with the other ingredients, and are hot right through.

4   Salt to taste, then transfer to a serving bowl.

5   Make the sauce in a small non-stick saucepan. Simply put the two ingredients together, and when hot pour over the noodles, then serve.

Texan Chilli Bean Noodle

In the USA the mighty chilli (spelt chile) is greatly revered, particularly in the south-western states. Every year there are numerous chilli shows and festivals at which chilli-growers, sauce-makers, trinket and clothes sellers and food stands vie with each other for the public's dollars. They even have chilli puppet shows – anything goes providing it's chilli. At some of the shows, they hold chilli eating or cooking contests and the competition gets fierce. The dish which is cooked is chilli (or as it is spelt there, chili) con carné (chilli with meat). Put another way this dish is called chilli bean. It is often assumed to be Mexican, but it's really Tex-Mex.

Usually the dish is eaten with garlic bread, but here I am using it as a topping for egg noodles, a combination which works real well!

SERVES: 4

250g (9oz) dried or 450g (1lb) fresh egg noodles
3 tablespoons vegetable oil
2–4 garlic cloves, chopped
225g (8oz) onion, finely chopped
600g (1lb 4 oz) lean minced beef
200g (7oz) fresh plum tomatoes, chopped
2 tablespoons chopped red bell pepper

1–4 fresh red chillies, chopped
1 tablespoon tomato purée
1 tablespoon tomato ketchup
1 teaspoon Worcester sauce
1 tablespoon chopped fresh coriander
4 tablespoons canned kidney beans
spicy salt to taste (see page 85)

GARNISH
some chopped parsley

1   Heat the oil in your wok, then add the garlic and stir-fry for 30 seconds. Add the onions, and reduce the heat. Stir-fry for 10 minutes, until the onions become translucent and begin to brown.
2   Add the mince, and stir-fry for a further 10 minutes.
3   Preheat the oven to 190°C/375°F/Gas 5, and select a suitable oven pan.
4   Using a suitable lidded casserole dish, combine the mince with the tomatoes, bell pepper, chillies, tomato purée, tomato ketchup, Worcester sauce and fresh coriander.
5   Cook for 30 minutes. Inspect and add the kidney beans, and little water if it needs it.
6   Cook for a further 15 minutes, then salt to taste.
7   Boil the noodles during stage 6, until they are as al dente as you wish (*see page* 73). Then drain them and divide between four serving bowls.
8   Immediately add cooked mixture on top of the noodles. Garnish and serve.

CHAPTER SIX

NOODLES WITH POULTRY

Chicken remains the Western world's most popular ingredient.

Burmese food is a bridge between Indian food with its wealth of spices, and Chinese food and the noodle culture. Burmese Kushwe Kyaw, Chicken and Shrimp Noodles is very tasty noodle dish, spiced with garam masala. Across Burma's southern border into Thailand, we find the delicious Thai Ped Soi Lampang, Curried Duck with Noodles, duck being the favourite bird in both countries. But you can substitute chicken, beef or pork for the duck. Still in Thailand, I could not resist converting Thailand's national dish to include noodles: Khaeng Keo-Wan Gai Mee, Green Curry with Chicken and Noodles. Continuing on southward into Malaya, we have Malay Ayam Panaeng, Malay-style chicken curry Here we find a dish with some similarities to Thai dishes, including the love of lemon grass, shrimp paste, sweet lime (*kaffir*) and, above all chillies. Differences include the use of tamarind to achieve a tart taste, turmeric for yellow colour and peanut to thicken. We stay in Malaysia to taste Laksa Lemak, Curried Pheasant in Coconut with Noodles, *laksa* being a major noodle dish in the area. Before leaving the orient, we visit the Chinese restaurant for two classic dishes without which my book would not be complete. There is a simple recipe for Chinese Chop Suey, with nine variations, and this is followed by Crispy Duck with Rice Noodle Pancakes.

The last three recipes in this chapter are not traditional oriental ones. They include Chilli Noodle Quail – boned chilli-marinated quail, stuffed with spicy noodles, roasted and glazed. It is an invention, based on Indian tandoori techniques, but I know from experience that it is very popular as a starter on a salad bed, or as part of the Indian main course.

151

Burmese Kaushwe Kyaw

Chicken and Shrimp Noodles

Since it was given its independence by the British in 1947, Burma has become an impoverished, virtually forgotten land, hidden away under a dictatorial regime. Even with its recent new name changes from Burma to Myanmar, and Rangoon to Yangon, it has not exactly opened the floodgates to tourism on the road to Mandalay. It is a pity, because the country has a lot to offer with its exceptionally gentle people, its amazing Buddhist pagodas and statues, and its unique food. Myanmar is perhaps the bridge between Indian food with its wealth of spices, and Chinese food and the noodle culture. This is a typically simple noodle dish, spiced with garam masala.

SERVES: 4

250g (9oz) dried or 450g (1lb) fresh egg noodles
2 tablespoons walnut or pistachio nut oil
175g (6oz) cooked minced chicken
110g (4oz) prawns in brine
2 teaspoons garam masala

1–3 fresh red chillies, chopped
1 tablespoon whole fresh coriander leaves
1 tablespoon chopped fresh mint
½ teaspoon spicy salt (see page 85)

1   Boil the noodles until they are as al dente as you wish (*see page* 73). Then drain them and set aside, keeping them warm if possible, for use later.

2   Heat the oil in your wok. Stir-fry the chicken and prawns for a couple of minutes.

3   Immediately add the drained noodles, the garam masala, chillies, coriander and mint, and briskly stir-fry them until they are well combined and hot right through.

4   Salt to taste, then transfer to a serving bowl.

NOTE: minced pork can be substituted for the chicken

Thai Ped Soi Lampang

Curried Duck with Noodles

Burma shares its south-eastern border with Thailand, and for centuries the two countries spent much time warring. Peace only came when Burma was made part of the British Empire in the nineteeth century. Indeed the only reason the British Raj colonised Burma, was to bring an end to the continual skirmishing by the Burmese in Bengal. Britain never took a territorial interest in Thailand, but the Raj opened up commercial links with northern Thailand, particularly to trade in teak, with which both countries were well endowed. A road crossing into Thailand was opened (it is sadly now long closed, the road having returned to jungle). The ancient northern Thai temple town of Lampang became a vast trading centre in teak. It still retains teak buildings and a relaxed provincial charm, complete with pony-trap taxis, curried noodles and plentiful noodle shops.

This Thai dish resembles Burma's national noodle dish, Kaushwe-Kyaw (*see opposite*), and is an excellent example of the fusion of the flavours of the subcontinent with the rather different flavours of Thailand. This version uses the favourite bird of both countries – duck, but you can substitute chicken, beef or pork for the duck. This recipe works well with any wheat, egg or rice noodles, fresh or dried. Select the type of noodle you wish to use (*see pages 44-49*).

SERVES: 4

250g (9oz) dried, or 450g (1lb) fresh egg or rice noodles

300g (10oz) duck breast fillet, weighed after stage 1

3 tablespoons soya or sunflower oil

2 or 3 cloves garlic, chopped

2 teaspoons Indian medium curry paste

1 teaspoon magic paste (see page 80)

½ teaspoon shrimp paste (optional), (see page 64)

1 stalk lemon grass, cross-cut

1 teaspoon fish sauce (see page 63)

110g (4oz) tiniest cooked baby shrimps, shell-on (optional)

2 teaspoons spring onion leaves, cross cut

2 tablespoons chopped coriander leaves

1 tablespoon chopped basil leaves

salt to taste

GARNISH
red pepper or chilli slices
freshly ground black pepper
lime wedges

1   Divest the duck breast of skin and fat, then cut it into thin slices averaging about 2–3 mm thick by 2cm long by 1cm wide.

2   Boil the noodles until they are as al dente as you wish (*see page* 73). Then drain them and set them aside, keeping them warm if possible, for use later.

3   Heat the oil in your wok. Stir-fry the garlic for 30 seconds, add the pastes and continue to stir-fry for a further 2 minutes. Add 3 tablespoons of water and stir-fry for a further minute.

4   Add the duck and lemon grass and continue to stir fry for 5 to 8 minutes, depending on the thinness of your cut, adding just enough water to keep things mobile. The duck should be just brown, but not overcooked.

5   Mix in the fish sauce and the shrimps, and stir-fry to hot.

6   Immediately add the drained noodles, and briskly stir-fry them until they are well combined with the other ingredients. Add all the leaves, salt to taste, and when everything is hot right through, transfer to a serving bowl, garnish and serve.

Thai Khaeng Keo-wan Gai Mee

Green Curry with Chicken and Noodles

Green curry is probably Thailand's most popular dish, both inside and outside the country. Cooked correctly it is a delicate blend of fragrance and flavour, of subtle colour laced together with creamy coconut milk. In fact the sauce is not and should not be green; it, and the chicken, is a buff-white colour. It is the accompanying herbs – basil and coriander – and, traditionally, pea aubergines, and huge numbers of tiny green Thai chillies that give the dish its greenness. Pea aubergines are somewhat bitter and I have omitted them here, but if they are available, you may wish to substitute them for the non-traditional green peas, green bell pepper and mangetout. Thai chillies are fiercely hot. Please don't omit chilli altogether (but remember, the green curry paste is very chilli hot). Neither should you expect this dish to resemble an Indian curry. But it is delicious. Normally it would be eaten with a number of other Thai dishes, including rice and noodles, but here the noodles are included, making it a dish in its own right.

SERVES: 4

250g (9oz) dried, or 450g (1lb) fresh
  egg noodles
400g (14oz) skinned chicken breast
3 tablespoons sunflower or soya oil
2 or 3 cloves garlic, chopped
5cm (2 in) cube galangal or ginger, chopped
2 teaspoons magic paste (see page 80)
1–3 teaspoons bottled green curry paste
400ml (14 fl oz) tinned coconut milk
2 or 3 stalks lemon grass

2 or 3 lime leaves, shredded
2 tablespoons green bell pepper, chopped
1 or more green chillies, chopped
110g (4oz) frozen peas, thawed
1 teaspoon fish sauce (optional, see page 63)
  or salt to taste
2 tablespoons chopped basil leaves
some fresh chopped coriander leaves
1 teaspoon bottled minced basil
1 teaspoon bottled minced coriander

GARNISH
whole and shredded lime leaves

1 Boil the noodles until they are as al dente as you wish (*see page* 73). Then drain them and set them aside, keeping them warm if possible, for use later.

2 Heat the oil in the wok. Add the garlic, galangal or ginger, magic paste and green curry paste, and stir-fry for about one minute.

3 Add the coconut milk, the lemon grass and lime leaves, and simmer for about 5 minutes, stirring occasionally to allow the coconut to thicken. It may look as though it is curdling, but it cannot do this so don't worry.

4 Add the chicken and cook for 10 minutes, stirring from time to time.

5 In the unlikely event it thickens too much, add water as required.

6 Add the green bell pepper, chilli and peas, fish sauce, if using, or salt, and the coriander and basil. Continue to cook for about 5 more minutes. Test that the chicken is fully cooked by cutting one piece in half which must be white right through.

7   Immediately add the drained noodles, and briskly stir-fry them until they are well combined with the other ingredients, and are hot right through.

8   Transfer to a serving bowl, garnish with the lime leaves and serve.

Malay Ayam Panaeng

Malay-style Chicken Curry

The original Malay people were known as *Orang*, and their kingdom *Malacca*. They had converted to Islam long before the British brought in immigrant Chinese and Indian workers to run the rubber plantations. North Malaya shares its border with Thailand, and it also shares many of Thailand's tastes in food. Such similarities include the love of lemon grass, shrimp paste (*belacan,* pronounced 'blachan') sweet lime (*kaffir*) and, above all chillies, the taste for really hot food diminishing as one goes southwards, away from Thailand). Differences include the use of tamarind (*asam*) to achieve a tart taste, turmeric for yellow colour and peanut to thicken. Instead of galangal, Malays use aromatic pink ginger buds with their flowers and/or zedoary (*cekur*), both hard to obtain (ginger or galangal can substitute). The paste looks tedious to assemble, but is easy to make and the results are well worth the effort. Noodles are more ubiquitous in Malaya than in Thailand, and curry with noodles is as common there as curry with rice.

SERVES: 4

THE PASTE

1 teaspoon red curry paste

2 teaspoons magic paste (see page 80)

4cm (1½ in) ginger or galangal, chopped

1 teaspoon ground coriander

½ teaspoon ground cumin

½ teaspoon turmeric

1 teaspoon shrimp paste (see page 64)

75g (2½oz) toasted peanuts or 4 tablespoons peanut butter

1 tablespoon tamarind purée

2 tablespoons tomato ketchup

150ml (5 fl oz) canned coconut milk

1 teaspoon dark brown sugar

1 teaspoon fish sauce (see page 63)

250g (9oz) dried, or 450g (1lb) fresh egg noodles

4 tablespoons vegetable oil

300g (10 oz) chicken breast, cut into bite-sized cubes

250ml (9 fl oz) chicken stock (see page 76) or water

2 star aniseed

6 green cardamoms

2 to 4 stalks lemon grass, cross-cut

2 or 3 lime leaves, shredded (if available)

4 tablespoons chopped holy (or purple) basil leaves

spicy salt to taste (see page 85)

GARNISH

whole toasted peanuts

red bell pepper slices

red chilli slices

1   Put all the paste ingredients into the blender. Pulse to achieve a thick purée using as little water as necessary.

2   Heat the oil in the wok. Stir-fry the paste for a couple of minutes, until it goes darker in colour.

3   Add the chicken cubes and briskly stir-fry for about 3 minutes to seal them and combine them with the paste.

4   Add the stock, star aniseed, cardamom, lemon grass and lime leaves, and simmer for about 10 more minutes, stirring now and again.

5   Boil the noodles until they are as al dente as you wish (*see page 73*). Then drain them and set them aside, keeping them warm if possible, for use later.

6   Check that the chicken is cooked by cutting a piece in half. It must be white right through.

7   Once it is, add the drained noodles and the fresh leaves, and briskly stir-fry them until they are well combined with the other ingredients, and are hot right through.

8   Check to see whether the dish requires further salt, then transfer to a serving bowl.

9   Garnish and serve.

Malay Laksa Lemak

Curried pheasant in coconut with noodles

Laksa is a Malaysian national dish, and is a fusion of Chinese and Indian cooking. *Laksa* is virtually a curry, in that it uses a spice paste. But as with most Malay curries, the end result is fragrant and aromatic, but not like an Indian curry. Noodles are a mandatory ingredient in *Laksa*, indeed 'Laksa' means 'noodles' in the languages of the area.

There are two distinct *Laksa* recipes. *Laksa Lemak* is from the Malacca straits of Malaya (not to be confused with the Indonesian Spice Islands, the Moluccan, or Maluku islands, original home of the nutmeg, mace and the clove). *Laksa Lemak* is an assembly of chilli, meat (in this case game bird), seafood, lemon grass, coconut and noodles. In *Laksa Penang*, fish stock and tamarind appear in the recipe, in place of the coconut, giving the dish a tart, rather than creamy taste. Since that option can easily be implemented, I have given the details of it below. Both recipes work well with any wheat, egg or rice noodles, fresh or dried. Select the type of noodle you wish to use (*see pages* 44-49).

I collected my *Laksa* recipes some years ago. They specified jungle fowl. I used to believe that our domestic chickens were descended from the guinea fowl, and had written so in my earlier books. I was delighted to be gently corrected by Richard Parsons of Brignorth, Shropshire, who tells me that the domestic chicken is descended from 'the red jungle fowl (*Gallus gallus*), found throughout Asia and Indo-China. Guinea fowl (*Numida meleagris*) belong to a quite different family of birds, which originated in Africa, and were probably not domesticated for several thousands of years after the jungle fowl'. Once, travelling on a really quiet road in Arizona, a road runner shot across the road in front of us. It was just like the cartoon version. The same happens with jungle fowl in Asia – they streak out of the jungle, across oncoming traffic. Smaller than chickens, but with beautiful plumage, they look too nice to eat. But you can use young chicken (poussins), or guinea fowl, or, as I have here a game bird, such as pheasant.

SERVES: 4

250g (9oz) dried, or 450g (1lb) fresh egg or rice
noodles
300g (10oz) pheasant leg and breast meat,
weighed after stage 1
3 tablespoons soya or sunflower oil
4 or 5 cloves garlic, finely chopped
5cm (2 in) cube of ginger or galangal, chopped
4–6 spring onions, bulbs and leaves, chopped
1–3 teaspoons (to taste) red curry paste

2 teaspoons Indian medium curry paste
200ml (7 fl oz) chicken stock (see page 76)
100ml (3½ fl oz) canned coconut milk
2–4 stalks lemon grass
150g (5oz) beansprouts
6–8 canned water chestnuts, halved
100g (3½oz) prawns in brine
1 tablespoon sugar
fish sauce to taste (see page 63)

GARNISH (USE SOME OR ALL OF THE FOLLOWING):

bottled pickled ginger, shredded (see page 86)
white radish, finely sliced into juliennes
some omelette sliced longways
fresh pineapple, cut in shreds

candlenuts (Macadamia nuts) chopped
1–4 green chillies,
4 spring onions, bulbs and leaves, sliced longways
lime wedges

1   Joint the pheasant into several pieces, then skin it and cut off all usable meat. Cut it into bite-sized pieces, then weigh it to get your 300g (10oz). Use the bones etc., to make a chicken stock.

2   Boil the noodles until they are as al dente as you wish (see page 73). Then drain them and set them aside, keeping them warm if possible, for use later.

3   Heat the oil in your wok. Stir-fry the garlic and ginger or galangal for 30 seconds, add the spring onions and curry pastes. Continue to stir-fry for a further 2 minutes.

4   Add the stock, coconut milk, lemon grass, and when simmering, add the pheasant.

5   Keep simmering until the pheasant is cooked. This is likely to be about 10 to 12 minutes, but it depends on the size of the meat.

6   Add the beansprouts, water chestnuts, prawns, and sugar. Use some of the prawn brine and fish sauce to salt to taste. Bring back to the simmer.

7   Immediately add the drained noodles, and briskly stir-fry them until they are well combined with the other ingredients, and are hot right through.

8   Transfer to a serving bowl, garnish and serve.

Laksa Penang

Omit the chicken stock and coconut milk from the Laksa Lemak recipe above. In their place, add at stage 4:

225ml (8 fl oz) fish stock (see page 77)
75ml (3 fl oz) tamarind purée (see page 68)
6 anchovies in oil, chopped, and some of the oil

Chicken Chop Suey

The well-known oriental celebrity chef, Terry Tan, recently said to me, 'Chop Suey is a lot of huey!' He made this comment to emphasise that the dish does not exist anywhere in China. We were appearing together on a television question-and-answer food programme, and the questioner was quite a stickler for authenticity. Terry wasn't upset about it, and neither was I. Terry is one of the most authentic oriental cooks around, but he is a pragmatist. And the argument about whether Chinese food, or Thai, Mexican or Indian, for that matter, is authentic at British, American and Australasian restaurants, or anywhere else outside their native countries, rages on and on. What concerns the likes of Terry and me, is that people turn on to spicy food in the first place. When, and if they become concerned about its authenticity comes later – after they are hooked! So huey or no huey, I could not omit this famous noodle dish. And yes, it comes from the Chinese restaurant, though not from China itself, and here's how.

I have found three possible explanations for the derivation of the words 'chop suey'. They all stem from the development of San Francisco's Chinatown in the nineteenth century, when the local restaurants found themselves speaking pidgin English to their non-Chinese clientele who wanted serving fast. 'Chop-chop' (or 'chop') is a pidgin Chinese word meaning 'quickly'. Alternatively, it could refer to the fact that the dish is composed of chopped mixed ingredients.

PLATE SEVEN

JAPANESE RAMEN PORK Japanese ramen (crinkly yellow wheat noodles) makes a tasty companion to Char Siu sliced pork.

Thirdly, it may derive from the Chinese *tsao sui,* meaning 'odds and ends'. Take your choice. As to the ingredients, they can indeed be more or less anything, including rice and/or noodles. Incidentally, the other archetypal Chinese restaurant dish, which is to be found nowhere in China, is Chow Mein, recipes for which are on page 174.

Below is Chicken Chop Suey. Variations for duck, beef, pork, king prawns, prawn, vegetable and a special follow.

SERVES: 4

110g (4oz) dried or 200g (7oz) fresh egg noodles
2 tablespoons soya or sunflower oil
1–2 cloves garlic, finely chopped
2.5cm (1 in) cube fresh ginger, finely chopped
6 spring onions, bulbs and leaves, sliced
60g (2oz) mangetout, sliced
125ml (4 fl oz) chicken stock (see page 76) or water
300g (10oz) cooked chicken meat

4 Chinese dried mushrooms, reconstituted and chopped
50g (2oz) canned beansprouts
25g (1oz) canned bamboo shoots, sliced
25g (1oz) red bell pepper, cut into small strips
1 tablespoon Chinese yellow rice wine or dry sherry
2 teaspoons light soy sauce
1 tablespoon potato flour (optional)

1   Boil the noodles until they are as al dente as you wish (*see page* 73). Then drain them and set them aside, keeping them warm if possible, for use later.

2   Heat the oil in your wok. Stir-fry the garlic and ginger for 30 seconds, add the spring onions, and continue to stir-fry for a further 2 minutes.

3   Add the mangetout and the stock, and when it simmers add the chicken and the mushrooms, beansprouts, bamboo shoots and red pepper. Stir-fry for a couple of minutes.

4   Add the wine and sherry and soy sauce and if you like a thicker sauce, the optional potato flour. Stir-fry until simmering,

5   Immediately add the drained noodles, and briskly stir-fry them until they are well combined with the other ingredients, and are hot right through.

6   Transfer to a serving bowl, and serve with other Chinese dishes.

PLATE EIGHT

KOREAN CHAP CHEE Mixed vegetables with beef and vermicelli (bean thread) noodles.

CHOP SUEY VARIATIONS

Duck Chop Suey

In place of the chicken, substitute 300g (10oz) cooked duck breast.

Beef Chop Suey

In place of the chicken, substitute 300g (10oz) cooked thinly sliced roast beef.

Pork Chop Suey

In place of the chicken, substitute 300g (10oz) cooked thinly sliced roast pork.

Char Siu Chop Suey

In place of the chicken, substitute 300g (10oz) cooked thinly sliced char siu (*see page* 140).

King Prawn Chop Suey

In place of the chicken, substitute 300g (10oz) cooked prawns or king prawns, weighed after shelling, deveining and washing.

Mixed Seafood Chop Suey

In place of the chicken, substitute 300g (10oz) any combination of cooked mixed seafood, or individual items – such as squid, mussels, crab, lobster, scampi, scallops, cockles – of your choice.

Vegetable Chop Suey

In place of the chicken, substitute 300g (10oz) of any cooked mixed vegetables of your choice.

Special Chop Suey

In place of, or including chicken, substitute 300g (10oz) of any combination of the above ingredients.

Rice Chop Suey

If you have some cooked rice leftovers, try adding them to this dish, keeping the noodles, of course, or reducing the noodle content to match.

Crispy Peking Duck

With noodle pancakes

The Pekingese Chinese restaurants hit the British dining scene in the early 1970s, at about the same time, and with about the same impact as the Tandoori restaurants. Suddenly curries became glamourised with clay-oven baked delights, and woe betide any restaurateur who didn't have a tandoor oven.

On the Chinese scene, the long-established Cantonese restaurants, serving their formula menu with its sometimes too bland, sometimes too sweet food, typified by such inventions as Chow Mein, Chop Suey, Chinese Curry, Sweet and Sour, and the ubiquitous Spring Roll, were eclipsed by some rather sexy upstarts. Of course, there was nothing new about Pekingese food, it had been developed centuries earlier for the tables of the dynastic emperors, whose courts were in the Forbidden Palace in Peking. It was just that their cuisine was new to the west. Such delights as wontons, drunken chicken, char sui roast pork, and fortune cookies began to become familiar Chinese restaurant offerings. But the one dish which, in my view paralleled the then new tikkas and tandoori as the menu highlight, was Peking Duck. Even the way of eating it was novel. Pancakes are served (piping hot in a bamboo steamer). On each is spread a liberal smear of hoisin sauce. Next thin strips of cucumber and spring onion are spread across the pancake, topped with shreds of duck. The pancakes are rolled up and eaten, with further dabs of hoisin sauce.

This masterpiece was devised for the Ming Emperors, China's most opulent rulers (1368–1644). Like the contemporary Indian Moghuls, they demanded the best of everything at their court. Their chefs were not exempt from such edicts, and Peking Duck, as it is now known, was, perhaps their best-loved piece of culinary craftmanship. To cook the duck the authentic way takes days and several labour-intensive cooking processes. Here is a simplified version. The recipe, by the way, qualifies for this book, because I love it. Its tenuous connection to the noodle, is simply that we can use ready made pancakes, or rice flour sheets or wonton wrappers, which we all know become noodles if cut into strands. That aside, I know you'll love it too!

SERVES: 4

2 duck breast fillets (magret de canard) about
    225g (8oz) each
4–5 tablespoons hoisin sauce
16 pancakes

ample hoisin sauce (to serve)
half a cucumber, peeled and cut into juliennes
4–6 spring onions, cut into juliennes

1   Heat the oven to 170°C/325°F/Gas 3.

2   Cover an oven tray with kitchen foil (use of foil will make subsequent washing-up easier). Place a rack over the foil. Slash the duck skin, into the fat with a sharp knife. Put the duck breasts, skin side up on the rack above the foil. Put the tray into the oven.

3   Remove after 15 to 20 minutes. Drain the oven tray of all liquid, which will be quite fatty. (See tip below.) Allow the duck to cool enough for you to be able to remove the skin and fat.

4   Coat the top and bottom of the now-skinned breasts generously with hoisin sauce. Replace on the the rack and put back into the oven.

5 Cook for a further 15 to 20 minutes then inspect and baste with more hoisin sauce.

6 Increase the oven temperature to 180°C/350°F/Gas 4 and cook for a final 10 to 15 minutes.

7 Remove the breasts, and allow to cool to handling stage, then shred as finely as you wish (using two forks and a pulling motion). The sauce should be dry enough to make this process easy. The duck should still be warm enough to serve, but if necessary return to the oven for a short reheat.

8 Serve with noodle rice pancakes, hoisin sauce, cucumber and spring onions, and eat as described above.

NOTE: stated oven temperatures and efficiency vary from oven to oven, so please use your judgement as to actual cooking time.

CHEF'S TIP: Duck fat is quite delicious, and should be kept for other cooking. The remaining liquid which comes from stage 2 above, can be used for stock. To separate the two, take a jug or bowl, and carefully add some existing stock or water to the hot liquid, then let it cool completely. Since oil and water don't mix when cold, and oil floats, the fat will now have sufficient non-fatty liquid to float on. When it cools, it can be picked easily off the top.

Chilli Noodle Quail

Boned Chilli-marinated Quail, Stuffed with Spicy Noodles, Roasted and Glazed

As a practising cook and occasional guest chef, I love 'testing' new recipes out on friends and customers. Not only does it put 'one's money where one's mouth is' you quickly find out whether a recipe works or not. Better than that you find out people's favourites.

In my line of business, spicy food, I follow traditional age-old recipes as accurately as I can, but I bring them into the modern age by incorporating time-saving methods, hopefully without sacrificing the all-important taste of the original. From time to time one can evolve a dish of one's own. It may be a just a modification of techniques, or it may combine concepts into something new. It doesn't happen often. With recipes so long-established, it is hard to come up with something truly original. But when it does, one proudly calls it one's 'signature dish'. I claim this as one of mine.

It started as tandoori quail. But the bones were irritating. So I boned the quail. Fiddly indeed, and I remember boning thirty with my great friend Dick Smith, chef-owner of the White House Hotel in Williton, Somerset, where, for years, we have held our residential cookery courses, The Curry Cook-in. It took us hours! Then I discovered specialist quail farms who sell them boned. It costs a bit more, but unless you have hours to spare, ask your game butcher. Once boned, you have a small, flat, shapeless item. Why not re-form the quail's shape, by wrapping the quail around a stuffing? I originally used cooked rice for this. Then the quails are oven- roasted. I felt the result needed a sheen, so I glazed the three-quarters baked quails with honey and Worcester sauce.

This East meets West fusion is really popular as a starter on a salad bed, or as part of the Indian main course. For a slightly larger bird, the recipe works equally well with a boned poussin (baby chicken). I have since adapted it to Thai flavours, and here is a further modification using noodles and one of the stuffings from pages 90-91. To enhance the noodles theme, the quails can be served on a bed of plain or buttered egg noodles, for example the recipe on page 70. It sounds more complicated than it is, and the results are well worth the effort.

SERVES: 4

4 boned quails

THE STUFFING

2 tablespoons chopped cooked noodles
85g (3oz) raw stuffing, any type (see pages 90–91)
2 tablespoons very finely chopped basil leaves

THE MARINADE

4 tablespoons bottled tandoori paste
4 tablespoons milk

1 tablespoon tomato ketchup
1 teaspoon chilli and garlic sauce

THE GLAZE

4 tablespoons clear honey
1 tablespoon Worcester sauce

GARNISH

red chillies, shredded
whole coriander leaves

1 Mix the marinade ingredients together in a non-metallic bowl. Work the marinade into the quail inside and out. Cover the bowl and refrigerate for 24 to 60 hours.

2 To cook, preheat the oven to 190°C/375°F/Gas 5.

3 Mix the stuffing ingredients together.

4 Carefully put one quarter of the stuffing mix into the quail, but don't overfill it, or it may spill out during cooking. Repeat with the other quails.

5 Place them on an oven tray, lined with foil (to ease the washing up), basting with any excess marinade. Roast for 10 minutes.

6 Heat the honey and Worcester sauce in a small pan. Baste it on to the quail. Bake for a final 5 to 8 minutes.

7 Garnish and serve.

Minced Chicken and Tomato Bolognese Noodle

I have already included a Spaghetti Bolognese, noodle-style recipe in the meat chaper on page 144. It uses more or less the traditional Bologna sauce, from ancient pre-Columbus, pre-tomato times. But since this is the world's favourite noodle dish, I am taking the liberty of including the world's favourite ingredient – chicken (minced chicken) – with a modern tomato-based sauce. And I am also taking the liberty of simplifying that recipe to the bare minimum. Even the 'Can't Cook Won't Cook' person CAN make this recipe in twelve minutes flat.

SERVES: 4

250g (9oz) dried or 450g (1lb) fresh egg noodles
300g (10oz) tomato passata sauce
300g (10oz) best lean minced chicken
1 teaspoon Worcester sauce

50ml (2 fl oz) red wine (optional)
1 tablespoon chopped fresh oregano
1 tablespoon chopped fresh basil
sea salt to taste

GARNISH
ready-grated fresh Cheddar or Parmesan cheese
sprigs of fresh parsley
freshly ground black pepper

1   Bring the tomato passata to the simmer in a saucepan.
2   Add the chicken, and the Worcester sauce, optional wine, oregano and basil, and cook it for 10 minutes, stirring occasionally. It should be simmering nicely, but it should not start to dry up. If, at any time, it does look a little dry, or wants to stick to the pan, add just enough water to ease it away.
3   During stage 2, boil the noodles until they are as al dente as you wish (*see page* 73). Then drain them and put them into four suitable serving bowls.
4   Salt the mince to taste, then serve it on top of the noodles in the four bowls.
5   Garnish with the cheese, black pepper, and the parsley.

NOTE: This recipe can include any of the elaborate ingredients and techniques from the recipe on page 144, by incorporating them as specified in that recipe.

Kai Jeow

Thai Omelette (various fillings)

It is my custom to put an egg dish at the end of the poultry chapter, along with the corny chicken and egg gag. (In my books the chicken recipes come first and the eggs last!) Of all the omelette recipes in my collection, none is better than the Thai omelette. As you'd expect, it is prepared attractively. No simple round disk for the

Thais. It is carefully folded into a square which contains a typically fragrant filling, into which, of course, I've wangled noodles. It makes a good light meal on its own, or it can be part of a main course. The recipe below is for a single omelette. For two or four servings make two or four omelettes individually.

MAKES: I OMELETTE

2 tablespoons sunflower or soya oil
½ teaspoon magic paste (see page 80)
½ teaspoon shrimp paste (see page 64)
85g (3oz) raw stuffing (see page 90)
½ clove garlic, finely chopped
1 teaspoon bottled minced red chilli
1 tablespoon chopped fresh basil leaves

2 cherry tomatoes, quartered
1 tablespoon chopped cooked prawns
1 tablespoon cooked sweetcorn
60g (2oz) cooked egg noodles, coarsely chopped
spicy salt to taste (see page 85)
2 large eggs
1 tablespoon salted butter

GARNISH
fresh herbs

1   Heat the oil in the wok. Add the pastes and stir-fry for 30 seconds. Add the stuffing and stir-fry for 2 or 3 minutes.
2   Add the garlic, chilli, leaves, tomatoes, prawns, sweetcorn and noodles and stir in until it is sizzling brightly. Salt to taste.
3   Strain off any liquid (reserving it for stock).
4   Beat the eggs.
5   Heat the butter in a large flat frying pan.
6   Pour the beaten egg into the pan, swirling it round to the edges and cook on medium heat until it firms up.
7   Immediately spread the filling around to a square shape in the centre of the omelette.
8   Now fold the sides in to create a square of about 12 cm (5 inch) sides.
9   Carefully turn it over, applying a little heat then remove it, garnish and serve hot.

CHAPTER SEVEN

NOODLES WITH SEAFOOD

Fish and shellfish are the most prevalent ingredients in Asian and oriental countries. There, with their abundant coastlines and tropical climates, there is no limit to the choice and quality of these ingredients, and they go particularly well with noodles.

I am starting the chapter with two recipes from the home of fish, Japan. The first is Tokyo Fish Udon. The noodles, made from soft wheat, are served with a typically flavoured Japanese stock with tuna fish. The second Japanese recipe is Soba Noodles with Tempura. Soba, buckwheat noodles, are served in a piping hot broth traditionally with tempura, a crackling crisp deep-fried fritter using king prawns, and vegetables. From China, or at any rate, the Chinese restaurant is the archetypal Chow Mein, which translates as 'stir-fried noodles', *mein*, of course, being the Chinese word for 'noodles'. I am starting with Seafood Chow Mein, and variations for beef, pork, chicken, duck, king prawns, prawn, vegetable and a special, follow. And another really interesting Chinese dish is Silver Needle Noodles with Beansprouts. The noodles resemble small beansprouts in colour, shape and size, and are served with real beansprouts, prawns and peas for taste and colour, in a simple sauce.

Moving south to Singapore, I offer you Fish Head Curry, now such a celebrated local speciality, that it is probably a Singaporean national dish. I offer it here, with dried prawns, clams and whitebait (lots of fish heads there!) but the brave can add a real fish head of their choosing. I could not omit either nearby Thailand, or lobster. Thai Talai Mee is Lobster with Thai Noodles. The dish also contains a mixture of beansprouts, water chestnuts, red bell pepper, bamboo shoots, and baby corn.

As with the previous chapters, I am taking the liberty of converting favourite pasta dishes to noodles. Try the Canelloni Creamy Noodles – big tubes stuffed with prawn and sweetcorn, topped with a creamy sauce. Here I am using rice noodle sheets, and a filling including chopped noodles, prawns and sweetcorn, topped with a cheesy creamy béchamel sauce. I have also found a way to offer you Spain's national dish made of rice, only here it is Paella Noodles. All we have to do is add some chopped cooked noodles to the rice, along with a combination of meat and seafood, and hey presto! And it's good too.

Finally, a trip to the Pacific Ocean for the two concluding seafood recipes. The first is my tribute to the adventurous cooks in Sydney, where they have no fear of fusing East with West. I hope you'll agree my Darling Harbour Crab Claws Noodle recipe is equally bold. Crab claws, obtainable from your fishmonger, nestle on top of a creamy, saucy, green noodle bed.

The last recipe takes us to the other side of the Pacific to San Francisco Bay for Crab Noodles in Pink Sauce. As its title suggests, this is a pink dish with a pink sauce, using pink noodles.

Tokyo Fish Udon

Udon noodles are made from soft wheat, and are available fresh and dried, in varying sizes. Fresh, *nama* (or raw) udon, they are long, thick or thin, round or square, narrow noodles. Dried, they come as shorter, long, flat, brittle, white sticks and are often sold in boxes. Usually udon accompanies a broth. The Japanese are rigid in the translation of their age-old recipes. This one, I admit, is a Western interpretation of a thousand traditional recipes which contain udon. However they must contain certain elements unique to Japan: miso (a soy-based flavouring), *mirin* (cooking rice-wine), Japanese soy sauce, bonito (dried fish flakes) and nori (dried seaweed sheets).

When I showed my proposed recipe title 'Tokyo Fish Udon' to my Japanese friends (whom we meet on page 29) I got an incredu-luous, 'Never heard of it...what is it?' reaction. When I explained that it was 'udon with a fish stock', they unstiffened. When I further explained that by adding the word 'Tokyo' to the recipe name, it made it clear that it was from Japan, they broke into huge smiles. Whether they were laughing at me or with me, I was not sure, but here, using tuna, is my well-intentioned udon recipe. By the way, as I was to find out, my friends enjoy drinking saké with their food, and I recommend it with this dish.

SERVES: 4

450g (1lb) fresh udon noodles or 225g (8oz) dried
250g (9oz) fresh filleted tuna steak
4–6 spring onions, leaves and bulbs, finely chopped

THE BROTH

1 litre (1¾ pints) fish stock (see page 77)
1 sachet miso mix (see page 62)
50 ml (2 fl oz) mirin

1 teaspoon Japanese soy sauce
1 tablespoon bonito flakes (optional)
some offcuts of nori (see page 66)

GARNISH
Japanese seven-spice (see page 83)
chives

1   Cut the tuna into thin slices, about 3cm x 3cm x 4mm thick.
2   Bring the stock to the simmer and add the other broth ingredients, and the tuna and simmer for about 5 minutes, or until the fish is cooked to your liking. Add the spring onions and simmer for a futher minute.
3   During stage 2, and in a separate pan, boil the noodles until they are as al dente as you wish (see page 73). Then drain them.
4   The broth should be ready at the same time. To serve, divide the noodles into four serving bowls. Carefully ladle the broth into each bowl on top of the noodles, and garnish.

Japanese Soba Noodles with Tempura

Soba (see page 71) is a very popular type of Japanese flat stick noodle made from buckwheat flour. Green soba (Cha–soba) has green powdered tea added for flavouring, and other colours, such as brown are common. We can use any soba type for this recipe. A piping hot or icy cold broth always accompanies soba. There are probably as many broth recipes as there are chefs and cooks, but this one could not be simpler. Soba is traditionally and at its best, in my view, served with tempura. Said to have been brought to Japan by the Portuguese maritime traders in the sixteenth century, tempura is a deep-fried fritter. As with all Japanese food, this is not stodgy or oily. The batter must be crackling crisp, and almost translucent, revealing the contents beneath it. To achieve the crispness and translucency, the batter flour must be correctly milled (I'm using a Blue Dragon mix here) and it must be made up within moments of being used. Furthermore, ice-cold water helps to achieve the correct texture. Here is a typically simple hot soba broth with tempura king prawns, and vegetables. You can serve wasabi and/or wasabi soy in a dipping bowl with this dish.

SERVES: 4

250g (9oz) dried soba noodles, any type
oil for deep-frying

THE BROTH

2 sachets miso mix (see page 62)
750ml (27 fl oz) water
shoyu sauce to taste

THE TEMPURA SUBJECTS

12 large cooked King prawns
8 asparagus stalks
8 baby sweet corns
8 carrot sticks
4 chillies

THE TEMPURA BATTER

150g (5oz) packet tempura mix

1   Prepare the tempura subjects. Peel, devein and wash the prawns, cut away the pithy ends of the asparagus, halve the baby corn and cut the carrot into sticks. The chilli can remain whole and washed.

2   Mix the sachets of miso stock into boiling water. Salt to taste with the shoyu if it needs it.

3   Boil the noodles until they are as al dente as you wish (*see page* 73). Then drain them and transfer to four serving bowls, into which you divide the broth, keeping them warm, for use shortly.

4   Heat the deep-fry oil to 190°C (chip-frying temperature).

5 · Prepare the tempura mix with 225 ml (750 fl oz) ice-cold water in a large cold bowl to achieve a cohesive batter.

6   At once dunk all the tempura subjects into the batter, then, with tongs, place half of them into the deep-fryer. Put the other half into the fridge in their batter bowl while the first batch deep-fries.

7   Once the frying subjects turn golden, remove them from the oil with the tongs, shaking them to discard excess and rest them on kitchen paper.

8   Repeat with the second batch, but serve the first with their soba broth, while the second batch cooks.

NOTE: see important deep-frying information on page 75.

Chinese Chow Mein

Chinese Restaurant Noodle Dish

As with 'Chop Suey', Chow Mein originated in San Francisco's Chinatown in the nineteenth century. Chow Mein translates as 'stir-fried noodles', *mein*, of course, being the Chinese word for 'noodles'. More literally 'chow' is derived from pidgin English, where *chao* or *chao chao* in Chinese means 'food' (and specifically refers to pickled vegetables, and ginger preserve, etc.). This recipe works well with any type of noodle, fresh or dried. Select the type of noodle you wish to use (*see pages* 44-49). As to the ingredients, they can indeed be more or less anything, so long as they include noodles. I am starting with Seafood Chow Mein, followed by variations for beef, pork, chicken, duck, king prawns, vegetable and a special. For Seafood Chow Mein choose one or more of the following: squid, mussels, crab, lobster, scampi, scallops, cockles, oyster, prawns, etc.

SERVES: 4

110g (4oz) dried or 200g (7oz) fresh egg noodles

2 tablespoons light vegetable oil

1–2 cloves garlic, peeled and finely chopped

2.5 cm (1 in) cube fresh ginger, peeled and finely chopped

6 spring onions, bulbs and leaves, sliced

75ml (3 fl oz) stock, any type (see pages 76–79) or water

300g (10oz) cooked mixed seafood

4 Chinese dried mushrooms, reconstituted and chopped

25g (1oz) canned bamboo shoots, sliced

25g (1oz) green pepper, cut into small strips

1 tablespoon Chinese yellow rice wine or dry sherry

2 teaspoons light soy sauce

1 tablespoon potato flour

1   Stir-fry the noodles until they are as al dente as you wish (*see page 73*).

2   Heat the oil in a wok until it starts to simmer. Throw in the garlic, ginger and spring onions and stir-fry briskly for 30 seconds.

3   Add the stock and when it simmers add the mixed seafood and the mushrooms, bamboo shoots and green pepper. Stir-fry for a couple of minutes.

4   Add the wine and sherry and soy sauce and if you like a thicker sauce, the optional potato flour. Stir-fry until simmering, then add drained noodles, and briskly stir-fry them until they are well combined with the other ingredients, and hot right through.

5   Salt if it needs it, then transfer to a serving bowl. The chow-mein is now ready to serve.

CHOW MEIN VARIATIONS

Beef Chow Mein

In place of the seafood, substitute 300g (10oz) cooked thinly sliced roast beef.

Pork Chow Mein

In place of the seafood, substitute 300g (10oz) cooked thinly sliced roast pork.

Char Siu Chow Mein

In place of the seafood, substitute 300g (10oz) cooked thinly sliced char siu (*see page* 140).

Chicken Chow Mein

In place of the seafood, substitute 300g (10oz) cooked duck breast.

Duck Chow Mein

In place of the seafood, substitute 300g (10oz) cooked duck breast.

King Prawn Chow Mein

In place of the seafood, substitute 300g (10oz) cooked prawns or king prawns, weighed after shelling, deveining and washing.

Vegetable Chow Mein

In place of the seafood, substitute 300g (10oz) any cooked mixed vegetables of your choice.

Special Chow Mein

In place of, or including seafood, substitute 300g (10oz) of any combination of the above ingredients.

Chinese Silver Needle Noodles

Silver Pin Noodles with Beansprouts

Oriental dishes often have such enchanting titles. How about Chinese Eight Treasure Rice (white rice with eight different coloured diced ingredients in it) or, from Thailand, Golden Bags (wonton wrappers enclosing a filling) and Emerald Parcels (marinated meat enclosed in a pandanus leaf knot. The 'Silver Pin' or 'Silver Needle' noodle is another such delightful name, and one can immediately picture the final effect. I have never seen silver needle noodles on sale at the Chinese store, but you can easily make them at home. A cornflour and wheat flour dough is kneaded, as described below (*see also page* 70). It is then finger-rolled into short 'needles' with pointed ends. They should resemble small beansprouts in colour, shape and size, and are served with some real beansprouts, prawns and peas for taste and colour, in a simple sauce.

SERVES: 4

THE NOODLES

110g (4oz) plain white flour
2 tablespoons cornflour
warm water

THE SAUCE

1 tablespoon soya or light vegetable oil
4 spring onions, bulbs and leaves, finely chopped
1 teaspoon white sugar
1 tablespoon Chinese yellow rice wine or dry sherry

125ml (4 fl oz) stock, any type (see pages 76–79)
110g (4oz) prawns in brine, drained
2 tablespoons frozen peas, thawed
4 tablespoons fresh beansprouts
light soy sauce to taste

THE NOODLES

1   Mix the flours together in a large mixing bowl.
2   Add enough water to make a firm pliable dough.

3   Knead until smooth then leave to stand for about 10 minutes.
4   Take one piece and roll it into a long sausage.
5   Cut this into short sausages and roll each into thin, pointed needles, each about the size of a beansprout.
6   Set up a double-deck bamboo steamer over boiling water.
7   Divide the noodles between the steamer trays and steam for 3 to 4 minutes.

THE SAUCE

8   During stage 5, heat the oil in a wok. Stir-fry the spring onions for one minute.
9   Add the sugar, and wine or sherry. When sizzling, add the stock, prawns, peas and beansprouts. When everything is hot, carefully add the steamed noodles and sprinkle on the soy sauce to taste for salting. Serve when sizzling.

Singapore Fish-head Curry

As we saw on page 133, there are relatively few true Singaporean dishes; they are usually an amalgam reflecting the multi-racial population.

One dish which *is* unique is Fish-Head Curry. Rumour has it that this dish was invented in the early 1950s, by a recently arrived south Indian chef, who, lacking funds, set up a food stall, begged fish heads from a nearby posh restaurant, and created this inexpensive dish. It became an instant success, and the chef went on to buy the restaurant! Be that as it may, Fish-Head Curry is now such a celebrated local speciality, that it is probably a Singaporean national dish. And one place to try this is at one of the many open-air Food Courts for which Singapore is famous. Years ago, with some airforce pals of mine from nearby Changi, I was taken on a 'Food Court Tour' (not far short of a pub crawl, as a very great deal of our time was spent drinking local Tiger beer in between dishes) by a Singaporean friend of mine. He spotted Fish-Head Curry which was being served with very fresh, very yellow egg (hokkein) noodles. Knowing my love for curry, he insisted I try it, which I did with some trepidation, being told by my host that I was not allowed to leave anything – I was to eat the fish head (and it was huge), bones, eyes, scales and all! (I found out just in time that he was joking, but a great deal of sucking of the head was in order). It was sensational, not least because of the crunchy texture. I offer it here, with dried prawns, clams and whitebait (lots of fish heads there!) but the brave can add a real fish head of their choosing.

SERVES: 4

450g (1lb) fresh yellow egg noodles
8 king prawns, head and shell on
12 clams
12 scallops
oil for frying
200g (7oz) whitebait
3 tablespoons vegetable oil or gheel
6–8 cloves garlic, finely chopped
2.5cm (1in) cube ginger, finely chopped
½ teaspoon turmeric

1–3 teaspoons red chilli powder
2 teaspoons bottled medium curry paste
1 teaspoon bottled red curry paste
2 tablespoons tamarind purée (see page 68)
110g (4oz) onion, finely chopped
200ml (7 fl oz) canned coconut milk
600ml (1 pint) fish stock (see page 77)
10–15 curry leaves, dried or fresh
30g (1oz) dried prawns
spicy salt to taste (see page 85)

1 Wash the king prawns, clams and scallops.
2 Heat the deep-fryer to 190°C and fry the whitebait until crispy.
3 Heat the oil in your wok. Stir-fry the garlic and ginger for 30 seconds, add the turmeric, chilli powder, and curry pastes, and continue to stir-fry for a further 2 minutes.
4 Add the tamarind purée, onion, coconut milk, stock, curry leaves and when simmering, add the king prawns, clams and scallops, and dried prawns. Simmer for about 10 minutes, adding the stock bit by bit until it is all in.
5 Add the whitebait and the fresh noodles, and briskly stir-fry them until they are well combined with the other ingredients, and are hot right through.
6 Salt to taste, then transfer to a serving bowl.

Thai Talai Mee

Lobster with Thai Noodles

Lobster is a luxury in all countries, even in Thailand, where the spiny lobster (*logsta rosea*) or rosy lobster, lives quite prolifically in the warm Asian seas. This lobster has no huge claws, unlike our own species. Confusingly, the spiny lobster is also called the 'crawfish', but in America the crawfish is what in Europe we call 'crayfish'. These are freshwater miniature lobsters, complete with pincers, known as *écrevisse* in France, which grow to a length of about 15cm (6 in). You can use any of these delicacies in this dish. As for the vegetables, use those I have specified, such as fresh celery, green bell pepper, bean sprouts and carrot. Or use any combination of your own choice. Alternatively use a 400g (14oz) can of stir-fry vegetables (which contains a convenient mixture of beansprouts, water chestnuts, red bell pepper, bamboo shoots, and baby corn).

SERVES: 4

250g (9oz) dried or 450g (1lb) fresh rice noodles
200g (7oz) lobster flesh cut into strips, 4cm x ½cm x ½cm

3 tablespoons sunflower or soya oil

4–6 cloves garlic, sliced

5cm (2 in) cube ginger, shredded

4–6 spring onions, leaves and bulbs, finely chopped

1 tablespoon cross-cut lemon grass

1 teaspoon fish sauce

1 teaspoon palm (or brown) sugar (optional)

1 or more red chillies, cross-cut

2 tablespoons rice vinegar

2 tablespoons chopped green bell pepper

Either 400g (14oz) mixture of fresh celery, baby sweetcorn, carrot (all chopped), plus beansprouts

Or 400g (14oz) canned stir-fry vegetables, and their stock (see above)

50g (1¾oz) canned straw mushrooms, halved

1 tablespoon very finely chopped coriander leaves

2 tablespoons chopped basil leaf

GARNISH
chopped chives or garlic chives

1   Boil the noodles until they are as al dente as you wish (see page 73).

Then drain them and set them aside, keeping them warm if possible, for use later.

2   Heat the oil in your wok. Stir-fry the garlic and ginger for 20 seconds. Add the onions and lemon grass and briskly stir-fry for a couple of minutes.

3   Add the fish and soy sauces, the sugar, chilli and vinegar, mixing in well, then add the green pepper, the fresh vegetables of your choice (or the canned option), the mushrooms, the leaves and the lobster strips.

4   When they are hot, add the drained noodles, and briskly stir-fry them until they are well combined with the other ingredients, and everything is hot right through.

5   Test for seasoning, adding more fish sauce if needed, then transfer to a serving bowl, garnish and serve.

Canelloni Creamy Noodles

Big tubes stuffed with prawn and sweetcorn, topped with a creamy sauce

Canneloni are pasta tubes, stuffed with sauce, and baked. The word derives from the Italian *canna*, meaning a 'reed' or 'cane', so, for example 'sugar cane' is *canna da zucchero*. Cannelloni means 'big tubes' (of pasta sheet) into which a filling of the cook's choice is stuffed. Purpose-made tubes can be bought from the deli, or you can simply wrap your own sheets around the filling in the form of cylinders. This is what I am doing here, using rice noodle sheets, and a filling including chopped noodles, prawns and sweetcorn, topped with a cheesy creamy béchamel sauce. The filling is an ideal way to use up leftovers, or, of course, you can use any other filling from this book, such as those on pages 89-91.

SERVES: 4

450g (1lb) of fresh rice noodle sheet (see page 71) cut into
12–16 sheets about 10cm x 15cm (4 x 6 in)

THE BÉCHAMEL SAUCE

500ml (18 fl oz) milk
60g (2oz) butter

60g (2oz) flour
salt, pepper and freshly grated nutmeg to taste

THE STUFFING

125g (4½oz) cooked noodles, any type
110g (4oz) grated Cheddar cheese
60g (2oz) cooked white haricot beans
3 or 4 cooked potatoes
2 tablespoons dried onion flakes
1 or more green chilli

1 tablespoon chopped fresh coriander
1 teaspoon cumin seeds
1 teaspoon red pesto sauce
1 teaspoon tomato purée
½ teaspoon spicy salt (see page 85)

½–1 teaspoon green peppercorns in brine, drained
85g (3oz) prawns in brine, drained

2 tablespoons canned sweetcorn
1 tablespoon chopped red bell pepper
110g (4oz) mozzarella cheese

GARNISH
chopped parsley

1   Make or buy the rice noodles sheets, and cut to rectangles around 10cm x15cm x 2mm thick.
2   Boil the noodle sheets until they are as al dente as you wish (*see page 73*). Then drain them and set them aside, keeping them warm if possible, for use later.
3   Make the béchamel sauce. Bring the milk to the simmer. In another pan, preferably a non-stick saucepan, melt the butter, then mix in the flour. Using a whisk, stir continuously, while steadily and carefully pouring in the hot milk. (If you use cold milk, you stand stirring for ages until it becomes hot.) Continue whisking slowly until the sauce will not thicken further, and with luck, it will be lump-free.
4   Pulse all the stuffing ingredients in the food processor, or use a mincer, to achieve a cohesive, mouldable paste. Mix in the peppercorns, prawns, sweetcorn and red pepper.
5   Select and butter a flat oven pan.
6   To make the tubes, simply place a strip of filling along one edge of a noodle sheet, then roll it up to create a plump tube, and place it seam-down, on the oven pan. Repeat with the other tubes until

they are all lined up snugly like soldiers. If you have any spare filling (and this depends on the tube size), layer it on top.

7. Preheat the oven to 190°C/375°F/ Gas 5.

8. Pour the béchamel sauce over the tubes, then top with the mozzarella cheese.

9. Bake for 35 to 45 minutes by which time you will have a bubbling golden top with brown scorch marks.

10. Garnish and serve.

Paella Noodles

Paella is Spain's national dish made of rice. In fact 'Paella' derives from Indian *Pullao*, Iranian *Pollo*, and Greek *Pilaf*, having wended its way eastwards 1,000 years ago in the hands of the Arabic Moors. Rice is the Arab staple. It was they who brought rice to Italy and Spain so how dare I convert the recipe to noodles? Easy. The dish must be cooked by 'absorption' (which is easy – just follow the recipe). Saffron is the colouring agent here, assisted by turmeric. Originally apart from the mandatory rice (and saffron), the dish included anything that had been trapped that day – rabbit, fowl, wild birds. Fishermen, of course, used 'fruits of the sea'. Here I'm using a combination of meat and seafood, par-cooked first. As for noodles, OK so it's a 'cheat' to get the dish into this book, but one that works brilliantly. But I'm just not sure about the name – maybe it should be renamed Naedella?

SERVES: 4

60g (2oz) dried egg noodles, crumbled

4 tablespoons olive oil

4 small chicken drumsticks, skin on

4 uncooked king prawns, shell-on

20–24 uncooked, peeled small prawns

4–6 large fresh mussels, shell-on

8–12 cockles, shell-on

600ml (20 fl oz) stock, any kind (see pages 76–79)

30g (1 oz) butter

½ teaspoon turmeric

4 to 6 cloves garlic, sliced

110g (4oz) onion, finely chopped

2 tablespoon chopped green bell pepper

1 or more fresh red chillies (optional)

1 tablespoon sun-dried tomato in oil, chopped (see page 68)

30–40 saffron strands

½ teaspoon sea salt

300 g (10oz) Spanish rice

60g (2oz) chorizo sausage, chopped

60g (2oz) frozen mixed vegetables, thawed (sweetcorn, beans, peas, carrot)

SPICES

4–6 green cardamom pods

4–6 cloves

5cm (2 in) piece of cassia bark

GARNISH

pitted black olives

chopped parsley

lemon wedges

1   Heat the oil in a large frying-pan or paella pan. Sear the chicken drumsticks for 5 minutes, turning frequently to achieve an even browning. Remove and set aside.

2   Using the same liquid, do the same to the king prawns. After 5 minutes, add the prawns, mussels and cockles, and stir-fry for about 3 more minutes. Strain and set aside, returning the liquid to the pan.

3   Bring the stock to the boil.

4   Preheat the oven to 190°C/375°F/ Gas 5.

5   During stage 3, heat the liquid from stage 2 in your wok with the butter. Stir-fry the turmeric and garlic for 30 seconds. Add the onion and stir-fry for 5 minutes. Add the the bell pepper, chillies, tomato, and when sizzling add the hot stock. Add the spices, saffron,

and salt and stir well. Allow this mixture to simmer for a few minutes to integrate.

6   Rinse the rice in running cold water. Run a kettle of boiling water through the rinsed rice, strain well then add it and the crumbled dried noodles to the pan. Let it come to a simmer. Do not at any time throughout its cooking, stir the rice. Doing so releases starch and can make the dish very sticky.

7   Transfer this mixture to a suitably-sized oven pan. Place the chicken, shellfish, chorizo and vegetables on top of the rice.

8   Cook for about 20 minutes. Taste test a rice grain. It should be cooked al dente, but not brittle.

9   Leave it in the oven for a few more minutes, with the heat off. It is ready to serve once the rice is tender enough for your liking.

10 To serve, leave the paella in its oven dish; garnish and serve.

Darling Harbour Crab Claws Noodle

From the Old World to the New, or as it is now known the southern hemisphere, and where is more glamourous in the world than Sydney, Australia? Few places have such a stunning natural harbour, with islands and inlets all around a major city. It is a thriving metropolis, whose tower blocks double in size every decade. At its heart, it has its funky sexy King's Cross district and its posh hotels and opal shops at the 'Rocks'. It has its bridge. It has its beaches – Bondi is legion for macho males and bronzed females – and it has its opera house. And it has that harbour. All day the harbour throbs with activity. Small snub-nosed green ferries mind their own business plying to and fro, and all night it lights up. It also has Darling Harbour, a glamorous seaboard shopping development, serviced by a monorail from adjacent downtown Sydney. At its centre, is a collection of yachts in its marina, and surrounding it are colonial houses whose pretty gardens sweep down to the sea. At one of the excellent restaurants there, I came across a dish something like this: crab claws (obtainable from your fishmonger) nestled on top of a creamy, saucy green noodle bed.

SERVES: 4

250g (9oz) dried or 450g (1lb) fresh spinach-
flavoured (green) wheat noodles
3 tablespoons vegetable oil
4 garlic cloves, finely chopped
4–6 spring onions, leaves and bulbs, chopped

175g (6oz) prawns in brine
110 g (4oz) fresh white crabmeat
60g (2oz) fresh brown crabmeat
8 cooked crab claws
salt to taste

THE BÉCHAMEL SAUCE

500ml (18 fl oz) milk
60g (2oz) butter
60g (2oz) flour
salt, pepper and freshly grated nutmeg to taste

GARNISH
deep-fried seaweed
freshly ground black pepper
long chive strands
green lime wedges

1 Boil the noodles until they are as al dente as you wish (*see page* 73). Then drain them and set them aside, keeping them warm if possible, for use later.

2 Make the béchamel sauce. Bring the milk to the simmer. In another pan, preferably a non stick saucepan, melt the butter, then mix in the flour. Using a whisk, stir continuously, while steadily and carefully pouring in the hot milk. (If you use cold milk, you stand stirring for ages until it becomes hot.) Continue whisking slowly until the sauce will not thicken further, and with luck it will be lump-free.

3 Heat the oil in your wok. Stir-fry the garlic for 30 seconds, add the onion, and continue to stir-fry for a further 2 minutes. Add all the seafood, and some of the prawn brine, to taste.

4 When everything is hot, remove the claws, keeping them warm. Add the béchamel sauce, and stir to the simmer.

5 Immediately add the drained noodles, and briskly stir-fry them until they are well combined with the other ingredients, and are hot right through.

6   Salt to taste, then transfer to four serving bowls. Place two crab
    claws on each bowl, garnish and serve.

San Francisco Crab Noodles in Pink Sauce

Talking of a beautiful harbour with a superstar bridge, there's one just an ocean away from Darling. San Francisco Bay is another stunner. View it from atop the hill, descending in a clanking hundred- year-old cable tram. View it from the bridge (and yes there are two, neither of which is 'golden' in colour; the one that counts, the suspension bridge is Indian red). View San Francisco from the Bay itself, perhaps aboard a boat en route to Alcatraz, that fearful escape-proof jail, set on a rock in the middle of the Bay, now a mere tourist spot, where for an hour or so you can chill to its horrors, before boarding the boat back to sanity.

Sanity in this case being a table at one of the seaside restaurants at the celebrated Fisherman's Wharf. Once a real working fishing dock, now a shadow of its former self in that respect, it still has great food markets, and great charisma, despite the influx of tourists. Sit in the open-air sunshine, with a glass of chilled Napa Valley Chardonnay and order a fresh seafood dish. What better indeed than this dish? And even if your own surroundings are more Frigwell than Frisco, or Naffsville than Nappa, never mind! Let your imagination roam. As its title suggests, this is a pink dish with a pink sauce. Use rosy-pale-pink Japanese somen noodles. They are very small in diameter, round, hard-wheat noodles. If these are unobtainable, use the darker pink tomato egg noodles. The star ingredients are scampi and crab, though if you're in an expensive mood, use lobster instead of or as well as the scampi and crab, and go the whole hog, and instead of pink rosé Chardonnay, use Krug vintage pink champagne!

SERVES: 4

250g (9oz) dried, pink somen noodles or Chinese tomato egg noodles

3 tablespoons vegetable oil

4 cloves garlic, finely chopped

4–6 spring onions, leaves and bulbs, chopped

110g (4oz) fresh white crabmeat

60g (2oz) fresh brown crabmeat

175g (6oz) prawns in brine

4 large cooked peeled king prawns

8 cooked scampi, shell-on

8 cooked scampi, peeled

1 tablespoon tomato ketchup

2 teaspoons tomato purée

salt to taste

THE BÉCHAMEL SAUCE

500ml (18 fl oz) milk
60g (2oz) butter
60g (2oz) flour
salt, pepper and freshly grated nutmeg to taste

GARNISH

Japanese Seven-Spice Powder (see page 83)
twists of black pepper
long chive strands
lemon wedges

1 Boil the noodles until they are as al dente as you wish (*see page* 73). Then drain them and set them aside, keeping them warm if possible, for use later.

2 Make the béchamel sauce. Bring the milk to the simmer. In another pan, preferably a non-stick saucepan, melt the butter, then mix in the flour. Using a whisk, stir continuously, while steadily and carefully pouring in the hot milk. (If you use cold milk, you stand stirring for ages until it becomes hot.) Continue whisking slowly until the sauce will not thicken further, and with luck it will be lump-free.

3 Heat the oil in your wok. Stir-fry the garlic for 30 seconds, add the onions, and continue to stir-fry for a further 2 minutes. Add all the seafood, and some of the prawn brine, to taste.

4 When everything is hot, remove the scampi, keeping them warm. Add the béchamel sauce, the ketchup and the tomato purée, and stir to the simmer.

5 Immediately add the drained noodles, and briskly stir-fry them until they are well combined with the other ingredients, and are hot right through.

6 Salt to taste, then transfer to four serving bowls. Divide the scampi equally between each bowl, garnish and serve.

CHAPTER EIGHT

NOODLES
WITH VEGETABLES

The vegetarian noodler need never be left out of noodle recipes. Most of the recipes in this book can easily become vegetarian by omitting the meat, poultry or fish/seafood ingredients. True vegetarians may even need to omit special ingredients such as fish sauce and shrimp paste; these can be present where you may not expect it, in bottled Thai curry pastes, for example. Omitting such items will result in a change in taste of the entire dish, because there is no exact substitute. In this chapter, only the Thai vegetable Pad Thai, Thailand's national dish based on a sweet and sour hot sauce, with noodles, and the Wun-sen Pad dish, Glass Noodles stir-fried with cucumber and pickled garlic, contain non-vegetarian ingredients. To compensate, I have been able to bring you a collection of curry noodle dishes – one from Japan, one from Indonesia and no fewer than three from India. The Japanese Kare Udon is merely noodles in a Japanese broth with curry paste added. I say 'merely', only because the concept is so simple. To the Japanese it is a really popular taste; to the curryholic, good though it is, it may leave you wanting. From China I have created a fusion dish – Szechuan Chilli Rice Noodles are hot and spicy. For a change, I have incorporated some rice with the noodles into the dish. The Indonesian Sayurmi Curry Noodles, with its Indian spices and soy sauce is a bridge between China and India, different, authentic and very tasty. But if it is the real curry thing you want, the three Indian dishes, again truly authentic, will, I hope delight you. But don't expect the standard curry house items. Sev Tamatar is crispy noodles in a tangy tomato curry sauce. The recipe is from Gujarat. Sev is short, crispy, golden-yellow, thread-like sticks which retain a crunchy bite. Bajra Talipeth is also from Gujarat whose noodles have chilli, spices, spinach, and coriander leaves in their dough causing it to be a fabulous green colour. The third Indian noodle recipe comes from Bengal. Bolobi Besan Noodles uses gram flour to make the dough for the noodles, which we stir-fry with spicy vegetables for a truly delicious dish, served piping hot, with mango chutney and plain greek yoghurt.

As with the other chapters, I leave the East to scour the kitchens of the West. I believe I have found some perfect noodle inter-pretations of four classic European dishes. The Italian spaghetti with olive oil and pepper translates into Noodles with Butter and Black Pepper and has no other ingredients. Nothing betters it for simplicity and effectiveness. Staying in Italy I offer you two super pasta-to-noodle conversions, ideal for everyone, vegetarian or not. The first is Noodles Napoletano, noodles in a traditional mushroom, pea, and garlic sauce developed in the 1400s in Naples, long before the tomato was brought to Europe. Still in Naples, I offer a less well-known recipe, which uses peppers, sweet bell peppers and chillies. Noodles Zappatora is not for the faint-heart-ed, and even many Italians find the real thing too hot. For the antidote, we go to France to find a classic centuries-old dish, Noodles à la Lyonnaise, au gratin. This classic Lyonnaise dish uses not potato, but noodles (*nouilles*) fried with butter and onion.

Finally, I offer you Crispy Deep-fried Seaweed as a very popu-lar appetiser or accompaniment dish, and it makes a good garnish for almost any noodle dish.

Vegetable Pad Thai

Sweet, Hot and Sour Noodles

Thailand is a beautiful country full of beautiful, smiling people, most of whom first settled in the country when they were driven from southern China in the twelfth century. As we see in the other Thai recipes in this book (*see* 'Thai' in the index), the country has long since developed a unique and fragrant cookery style of its own, though influences from its neighbours, Burma, India, Vietnam and Laos are prevalent. Also in evidence are the Chinese-inspired noodle dishes, of which Pad Thai is best known. One of Thailand's national dishes, it simply means 'Thai stir-fry', and it can contain virtually any ingredient – meat, poultry, fish or seafood, plus vegetables, in any combination (here it is with just vegetables) providing it has a backbone of noodles. Traditionally it uses small rice noodles (*sen lek*), though egg noodles (*ba mee*) are also great. In fact this recipe works well with any wheat, egg or rice noodles, fresh or dried. Select the type of noodle you wish to use (*see pages* 44-49).

SERVES: 4

250g (9oz) dried or 450g (1lb) fresh rice or egg noodles
400g (14oz) canned bean sprouts
400g (14oz) canned straw mushrooms
400g (14oz) canned stir-fry vegetables
200g (7oz) canned bamboo slices and water chestnuts
3 or 4 tablespoons sunflower oil
4–6 cloves garlic, finely chopped
5–6cm (2 in) cube galangal or ginger, finely chopped
1–2 teaspoons bottled red curry paste
120g (4½oz) sachet sweet and sour sauce
2 or 3 stalks of lemon grass
4–6 fresh or 6–8 dried lime leaves
1 red pepper, chopped into 1cm (½in) diamonds

1 yellow pepper, chopped into 1cm (½in) diamond shapes
5 or 7 red Thai extra hot chillies, whole, with stalk removed (optional, see chillies, page 54)
4–6 spring onions, leaves and bulbs, finely chopped
either 250g (9oz) fresh oriental vegetable mix
or 250g (9oz) total weight Chinese leaves, fresh carrot, fresh beansprouts, red pepper, baby sweetcorn, white radish
1 teaspoon bottled minced coriander
1 teaspoon bottled minced basil
2 tablespoons chopped fresh purple or sweet basil
soy sauce (any type) to taste

1   Open the cans. Strain off the liquid from each can into one jug, but keep the contents separate for now.
2   Divide the amounts of tinned beansprouts, straw mushrooms, mixed oriental vegetables and bamboo and water chestnuts into two. Chop any largish pieces like the sweetcorn, and the chestnuts into smaller amounts. Now the two sets can be mixed, but one set must now be frozen, with some of the tinned liquid for a future occasion.
3   Boil the noodles until they are as al dente as you wish (*see page* 73).

PLATE NINE

LASAGNE NOODLE Creamy mince filling alternating with cheese and fresh rice noodle sheet.

192

Then drain them and set them aside, keeping them warm if possible, for use later.

4   Heat the oil in your wok. Stir-fry the garlic and galangal or ginger for 30 seconds, add the red curry paste, and stir-fry for a further 30 seconds.

5   Add the sweet and sour sauce, and when this is hot, add the lemon grass, lime leaves, peppers and optional chillies, and continue to stir-fry for a further 2 minutes.

6   Add the spring onion and the canned items, and sufficient of the canned liquid to stop the sauce from burning, and to keep things literally fluid enough.

7   Add the fresh vegetables, and keep on feeding in just enough tinned liquid to keep things mobile.

8   Immediately add the drained noodles and bottled coriander and basil and the fresh basil, and briskly stir-fry them until they are well combined with the other ingredients, and are hot right through.

9   Add soy sauce to taste for salting, then transfer to a serving bowl.

VARIATIONS

Pad Thai Prawn

This dish can be considerably enhanced for the non-vegetarian by the addition of prawns. The best bet in my view are prawns in brine, which are already cooked so they only need heating up, so add them at stage 7. A little of the brine is nice too.

Pad Thai Meat or Chicken

Optionally you can also add strips of raw beef and/or pork and/or chicken and/or king prawns. Since these need cooking, add them at the end of stage 5, and stir-fry them, adding some canned liquid as required to keep things mobile until they are virtually cooked. Cutting the strips thin will make their cooking time relatively brief.

PLATE TEN

THAI GREEN CHICKEN CURRY NOODLES The classic creamy white chicken curry with green ingredients, on spinach-flavoured noodles.

Thai Wun Sen PadTaeng-kwa Kraten

Glass Noodles Stir-fried with Cucumber and Pickled Garlic

Glass noodles (*wun sen*) are made from soya beans. They are only available dried, not fresh, and resemble thinly spun fibre-glass in colour, texture and taste too, when raw.

They are hard to eat raw and hard to break. Once softened they are very palatable, becoming clear, hence their name 'glass' or 'cellophane' noodles. In Thailand they appear in salads and soups or as a spring roll stuffing. Another favourite way of cooling them is casseroled with prawns. Here they are stir-fried with optional minced pork, cucumber and pickled garlic.

SERVES: 4

85g (3oz) dried wun sen glass noodles

2 tablespoons sunflower or soya oil

1 teaspoon shrimp paste, optional (see page 64)

4 tablespoons very finely chopped onion

6 tablespoons coconut milk

250ml (9 fl oz) fish stock (see page 77) or water

1 teaspoon fish sauce (see page 63)

100g (3½oz) cooked minced pork (optional)

1 tablespoon chopped red bell peppers

10cm (4in) pieces cucumber, cut into small cubes

1 teaspoon soy sauce

3 or 4 cloves pickled garlic, chopped

GARNISH

finely chopped coriander and/or manglak basil leaves

1 Use kitchen scissors to cut off the amount of noodles you wish to use.

2 Soak them in warm water for 15 to 20 minutes, until they are translucent and soft.

3 During stage 2, heat the oil in the wok. Stir-fry the shrimp paste for 30 seconds. Add the onion and stir-fry for 30 more seconds.

4 Stir in the coconut milk, stock and fish sauce, and when simmering add the optional cooked pork and the peppers.

5 When again simmering, drain the noodles and add them to the wok. Stir until warm then add the cucumber, soy sauce and pickled garlic. Once hot, garnish and serve.

Thai Mee Grob

Crispy Noodles with a Crackling Caramelised Topping

Mee grob pronounced 'krob', means, literally 'noodles, crispy'. This typical Thai shorthand so much understates the outstanding qualities of this dish, that it is easy to pass over it on the Thai restaurant menu. But it is nearly always there – and Thais know how good it is. It's another national dish. What makes it outstanding is the syrup drizzled over it, which caramelises to cracking when it cools. It is served as a crunchy, tasty side dish, with other Thai main course dishes.

Professional Thai chefs soak the noodles then deep-fry them, claiming crispier results. This method is frankly really dangerous since adding water to the hot oil makes it potentially explosive. My method is to use the noodles dry. When deep-fried, they whoosh up quickly in the oil, but do not splutter, and if left for a while, they become perfectly crisp. But whoosh up they do, so do not put too many into the deep-fryer at once (as specified in the recipe). *See also important deep-frying information on page 75.*

SERVES: 4

125g (3½oz) dried rice vermicelli noodles
vegetable oil for deep-frying

THE SYRUP

50g (2oz) palm sugar or brown sugar
100ml (3½ fl oz) rice vinegar

GARNISH
4–6 spring onions, leaves only, finely chopped

1   Heat the sugar in a small non-stick saucepan at medium heat.
2   As soon as it starts to melt, add the vinegar. Increase the heat whilst stir-frying for about 5 minutes, or until it reduces to a reasonably thick syrup. Take off the heat.

3   Heat the deep-fryer to 190°C. Split the noodles into 3 or 4 bundles. Carefully put the first bundle into the deep-fryer. It will whoosh up and swell very fast. Once the sizzling stops, remove it with tongs and inspect it. It should have expanded to an airy, all-white, even-coloured bundle. If parts of it have not done so, the oil isn't hot enough. Try again – usually it only wastes one bundle, and there really is enough left. When satisfied, drain on kitchen paper. Repeat with the other bunches.

4   Put the warm noodles on a large, flat serving plate.

5   Make sure the syrup is still hot, then drizzle it over the noodles.

6   Allow it to go cold, and the syrup will harden and turn to caramel. Garnish and serve.

Indonesian Sayurmi Curry Noodles

Noodles with Mangetout, Green beans and Coconut

Noodles are normally associated with Chinese cooking and they do not appear in traditional Indian recipes. But go to the countries so-to-speak, between China and India, and you will find many fascinating spicy dishes featuring noodles. This Indonesian recipe typifies that culture and culinary confluence in a tasty combination.

SERVES: 4

200g (7oz) dried rice noodles

175g (6oz) green beans, fresh or frozen

half a fresh coconut and its water or 60g (2oz) coconut milk powder

4 tablespoons vegetable or coconut oil

2 teaspoons minced garlic

2 teaspoons minced ginger

2 teaspoons bottled medium curry paste

225g (8oz) onion, very finely chopped

175g (6oz) mangetout, stalks removed

6–10 fresh or dried curry leaves

2–6 dried red chillies, chopped

sweet soy sauce to taste (see page 67)

salt to taste

1   Clean, string and slice the fresh beans or thaw the frozen beans, then boil them until soft.

2   Grind the coconut flesh and its water in an electric blender or food

processor or by hand, or mix the coconut milk powder with enough water to make a paste.

3   Boil the noodles until they are as al dente as you wish (*see page* 73). Then drain them and set them aside, keeping them warm if possible, for use later.

4   Heat half the oil in a *karahi*. Stir-fry the garlic, ginger, curry paste and onion for about 5 minutes.

5   During stage 4, heat the remaining oil in a separate pan and stir-fry the mangetout, curry leaves and red chillies for about 5 minutes. Add them to the stir-fry.

6   Add the fresh coconut purée or coconut milk paste, the soy sauce and sufficient water to prevent sticking. Add salt to taste.

7   Add the green beans and when hot add the noodles and mix well. Serve immediately they are heated through.

Indian Sev Tamatar

Cripy Noodles in a Tangy Tomato Curry Sauce

This is one of the few extant Indian noodle dishes. Two more follow, and there are others in the book (*see* 'Indian' dishes in the index). The notion of curry and noodles (rather than curry and rice) may seem odd at first, but of course you only have to try these dishes to find out how great they really are, and how quick to cook too!

Given that noodles can be crispy, I think this recipe from Gujarat, the Indian state just north of Bombay, where many of the people are vegetarian, is a perfect example. Sev is made from *besan* or gram flour dough, which is pushed through a device called the *murukus* press, using the plate with the smallest holes to achieve thin noodles of vermicelli thickness. (This is described on page 102.) Sev is immediately deep-fried to obtain short crispy golden-yellow, thread-like sticks, which are at once fed into cellophane packets, and sold as ready-to-eat crispy nibbles. Sev can be made at home, but here I 'cheat' because I'm using packet sev; but not to nibble straight from the packet. Rather, I immerse them in a tangy sauce, where they will become soft, like noodles. Eaten at once though, they still retain a crunchy bite.

SERVES 4

200g (7 oz) packet sev

3 or 4 tablespoons ghee or vegetable oil

1 teaspoon white cumin seeds

½ teaspoon coriander seeds

½ teaspoon turmeric

1 teaspoon coriander powder

½ teaspoon mango powder

½ teaspoon paprika

3 or 4 cloves garlic, finely chopped

2.5 cm (1 in) piece ginger, finely chopped

4–6 spring onions, leaves and bulbs, finely chopped

1–3 green cayenne chillies, chopped

4 tinned plum tomatoes

6 tablespoons juice from the tinned tomato

2 tablespoons coconut milk powder

4 tablespoons Greek-style yoghurt

2 teaspoons garam masala

spicy salt to taste (see page 85)

2 tablespoons lemon juice

GARNISH

fresh coriander leaves

fresh red and/or green chilli rings

1   Heat the oil in your wok. Add the seeds and stir-fry them for 10 seconds. Add the turmeric, coriander, mango powder and paprika and briskly stir-fry for 20 seconds. Add the garlic and ginger and stir-fry them for 30 seconds. Now add just enough water to cool things down and create a lightly sizzling paste. Keep stirring and add the onions and chillies, and continue to stir-fry for a further 2 minutes, adding dashes of water as needed.

2   Add the tomatoes and the tomato juice, the coconut milk powder, the yoghurt and garam masala. Mix well until hot.

3   Just prior to serving, add and mix in well most of the sev. Salt to taste, then transfer to a serving bowl. Pour on the lemon juice.

4   Garnish with the remaining sev, some fresh coriander and chilli rings, and serve at once.

NOTE: This dish can be served cold. Cool it down before stage 3. Complete stages 3 and 4 just before serving.

Indian Bajra Talipeeth

There are gorgeous traditional breads from west and north India which use millet flour – bajra (*see page* 41). One is called *Debra*, and incorporates spinach and chilli into the dough. Another, *Talipeeth*, mixes spices and coriander leaves with the dough. Both produce a fabulous green-coloured dough. It is only a skip and a jump to make noodles from the dough – an innovation, the purist might say, but I encountered one such recipe at the Rama Residency hotel in Gujarat's main seaport city, Surat, years ago. I have taken the liberty of combining *Debra* and *Talipeeth* ingredients here to make my own recipe. Serve them stir-fried on their own, just with chutneys and pickles, or incorporate them into a luscious, saucy, curry gravy (for example, the one from the previous sev tamatar recipe). Simply substitute these noodles for the sev, and serve hot.

SERVES: 4

100g (3½oz) baby spinach leaves, chopped

4 tablespoons chopped coriander leaves

1 green chilli, chopped

250g (9oz) millet flour

1 large egg yolk

1 teaspoon salt

1 teaspoon chilli powder

1 teaspoon curry powder or paste

If stir-frying:

2 or 3 tablespoons butter ghee or vegetable oil

1   Purée the spinach, coriander leaves and chilli to a smooth paste in a blender.

2   Using the green paste and all its liquid and the remaining ingredients (except the ghee or oil), make the noodle dough, a detailed method for which is given on page 44. It will need some water, of course, and this is best warm, to improve the millet flour's glutinousness.

3   Roll out the dough and cut it by knife or in the pasta machine, a detailed method for which is given on page 72.

4   Boil the noodles for about 2 to 3 minutes, or until as al dente as you wish (*see page* 73). Then drain them.

5   To finish off, they can either be served straight from straining, or they can be stir-fried in a little ghee or oil, then garnished and served, with or without a curry sauce.

Indian Bolobi Besan Noodles

Travel east, far away from Surat, across the width of India, a thousand miles to Bengal: there, they love their gram flour – *besan* – so much it is even called *Bengal gram*. It is made from finely ground gram lentils – *chana dhal* – to make a gorgeous blond-coloured fine flour. This is used to make *pakoras* or, as the curry houses of the West prefer to call it – *onion bhajis*. It also appears as dumplings, to thicken curry gravy, in Bengali sweetmeats, and it makes dough for bread. One Bengali speciality bread is called *Gram Puri*. It is a small flat, circular disc, about 10cm (4 in) in diameter, which, when deep-fried, puffs up like a balloon. *Radha Bolobi* is a variation in which the puri is stuffed with spicy garlic, onion and tomato. Here, I convert the dough to noodles, which we stir-fry with spicy vegetables for a truly delicious dish. Serve piping hot, with mango chutney and plain Greek yoghurt.

SERVES: 4

THE NOODLES

250g (9oz) besan flour
1 large egg yolk
1 teaspoon salt
1 teaspoon chilli powder
1 teaspoon curry powder or paste

THE STIR FRY

3 tablespoons butter ghee
2 teaspoons panch phoran
½ teaspoon turmeric
1 teaspoon ground coriander
½ teaspoon cumin powder
3 or 4 cloves garlic, finely chopped
4–6 spring onions, bulbs and leaves, chopped
4 tablespoons juice from the can of sweetcorn
2 tablespoons chopped coriander leaves

1 green chilli, chopped
250g (9oz) baby spinach leaves, chopped
200g (7oz) canned sweetcorn
1 tablespoon chopped bottled brinjal (aubergine) pickle
2 teaspoons garam masala (see page 83)
2 or 3 tablespoons freshly squeezed lemon juice
spicy salt to taste (see page 85)

1   Using all the noodle ingredients, make the noodle dough, a detailed method for which is given on page 44. It will need some water, of course, and this is best warm, to improve the gram flour's glutinousness, although the egg will help bind it too.

2   Roll out the dough and cut it by knife or in the pasta machine, a detailed method for which is given on page 72.

3   Boil the noodles for about 2 to 3 minutes, or until as al dente as you wish (*see page* 73).

4   Drain them and set them aside whilst you make the stir fry.

5   Heat the butter ghee in your wok. Add the panch phoran and stir-fry for about 15 seconds. Add the turmeric, coriander and cumin and continue briskly stir-frying for a further 15 seconds. Add the garlic and continue briskly stir-frying for a further 30 seconds.

6   Add the spring onions, coriander leaves and the chilli, and a few splashes of water, to keep things mobile. Stir-fry for about 2 minutes, then add the spinach, the sweetcorn and its liquid. The spinach will soon soften down into the mixture. Just keep stirring gently until it does.

7   Add the brinjal pickle, garam masala, and the lemon juice, then add the noodles. Stir them around very gently until they are hot right through.

8   Salt to taste and serve pipng hot.

Japanese Kare Udon

Curry Noodles

Unexpectedly, Japan is the world's fastest growing importer of curry spices, after Britain. It is not that the Japanese have thousands of Tandoori and Curry Houses serving Tikkas, Baltis Kormas and Vindaloos. They don't, apart from a few such establishments in the major cities. But what they do have are the ubiquitous noodle shops. They are literally everywhere. Someone calculated that in Tokyo alone there are some 7,000 noodle shops, which, unlike Britain's recent influx of 8,000 curry houses, have been there for centuries. *Kare Ko*, curry powder, on the other hand, is a relatively new ingredient in Japan, introduced there by British traders in the nineteenth century. The Japanese use it or curry paste to flavour their udon and ramen noodle broths. Here is a curry vegetable ramen dish, which, nice though it is, bears no resemblance whatever to curry house flavours. Use fresh vegetables if possible, but if it's one of those days you haven't had the time to go shopping, or planned what to cook, resort to your kitchen stores and use canned vegetables and frozen beans and stock. This dish will be ready in almost no time.

SERVES: 4

250g (9oz) ramen dried or 450g (1 lb) fresh egg noodles
500ml (1.2 pints) vegetable stock (see page 78)
50ml (2 fl oz) mirin
2 teaspoons bottled medium curry paste

shoyu sauce to taste
110g (4oz) frozen green beans, thawed
85g (3oz) canned straw mushrooms
200g (7oz) canned beansprouts
85g (3oz) canned bamboo shoots, shredded

GARNISH
deep-fried seaweed (see page 204)
shredded pickled ginger (see page 86)
Japanese Seven-Spice Powder (see page 83)

1 Boil the noodles until they are as al dente as you wish (*see page* 73). Then drain them and set them aside, keeping them warm if possible, for use later.
2 Heat up the stock. Add the mirin, curry paste and the shoyu sauce for salting, to taste. Put the beans, straw mushrooms, beansprouts and bamboo shoots, with their juices into the broth to heat them up.
3 Put the hot noodles into four serving bowls. Ladle the broth on top, ensuring the vegetables are evenly distributed.
4 Garnish and serve.

Szechuan Chilli Rice Noodles

Being a lover of things chilli hot, or a 'chile-head', as the Americans prefer to call it, I have to have just one Chinese recipe from Szechuan (or Sichuan). China's western province of Szechuan shares a border with Burma. The food in the region is hot and spicy. Chilli, ginger, onion and garlic are used liberally and to great effect. The Szechuan peppercorn (*fagara*) is one heat-giving medium, though it is not as hot as regular pepper, neither is it related to it. But the real heat-givers are Szechuan chillies – small, pungent and deep crimson-red when ripe, they are so much a part of Szechuan diet, that it is hard to conceive that chillies only reached China in the sixteenth century, following their discovery in the New World, and their importation to China by Portuguese traders. Chillies never did not catch on with the rest of China in such a big way, it is said, because the contemporary ruling Ming emperors were not partial to them or the Portuguese! That's as may be, and it was their loss. But it need not be ours, as this dish shows. But, be warned it is seriously hot! To ring the changes, I have incorporated some rice into the dish. It makes for an interesting texture combination. This recipe works well with any type of noodle, fresh or dried. Select which type of noodle you wish to use (*see pages 44-49*).

SERVES: 4

175g (6oz) dried, or 350g (12 oz) fresh noodles, any type

2–4 teaspoons extra hot chilli powder

4–6 garlic cloves, sliced

5cm (2 in) cube ginger, shredded

4–6 spring onions, leaves and bulbs, finely chopped

chopped fresh red chillies to taste

tomato ketchup

85g (3oz) cooked rice

2 eggs

salt to taste

GARNISH

chopped chives

I   Boil the noodles until they are as al dente as you wish (*see page 73*). Then drain them and set them aside, keeping them warm if possible, for use later.

2   Heat the oil in your wok. Stir-fry the chilli powder, garlic and ginger for 30 seconds. Add the onions and fresh chillies, and continue to stir-fry for a further 2 minutes.

3   Add the ketchup, rice and just enough water to keep things mobile. Stir for a few minutes until hot.

4   Immediately add the drained noodles, and briskly stir-fry them until they are well combined with the other ingredients, and everything is hot right through. Add the raw eggs, which will cook into the noodles as they are stirred in.

5   Salt to taste, then transfer to a serving bowl and garnish.

Crispy Deep-fried Seaweed

Deep-fried seaweed is a very popular appetiser or accompaniment dish. It also makes a good garnish. It is easy to make, especially if you have the deep-fryer up and running. If you do not want to go to all that trouble, it is now available in vacuum packs at the deli or supermarket. Three things to say. Firstly it really is excellent. Secondly, it is not made from seaweed. Thirdly, it is to be found nowhere in China – it is yet another an invention of the clever old Chinese Restaurant. So what is it? It is finely shredded Chinese leaves – the dark green kind, *pak choi*. The finely shredded leaves are deep-fried, then sprinkled with prawn or fish powder, and served with prawn crackers and hoisin or Pekingese dip (*see page 88*).

SERVES: 4

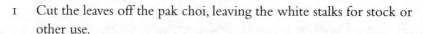

Half a pak choi (Chinese cabbage or leaves)
oil for deep-frying
prawn or fish powder for sprinkling (optional)

1   Cut the leaves off the pak choi, leaving the white stalks for stock or other use.

2   Very finely shred the green leaves.

3   Hear the deep-fryer to 190°C (chip-frying temperature). Do not use the basket.

4   Place a handful of the shreds into the deep-fryer. They will whoosh up and cook at once (within 10 seconds).

5   At once remove the shreds with a hand-strainer and strain. Shake the excess oil off, and place on kitchen paper to drain.

6   Repeat stages 5 and 6 with the remaining shreds of pak choi. When all the shreds are cooked, keep in a warm place until you are ready to serve. They will go crispy.

7   Serve warm or cold sprinkled with the powder.

NOTE: see important deep-frying information on page 75.

Noodles with Butter and Black Pepper

There is perhaps, no simpler, more effective, more elegant Italian pasta dish than spaghetti with just olive oil and black pepper. It translates equally well to wheat or egg noodles, and here I am using a combination of olive oil and butter. You can use both or either. Note the optional, but slightly exotic garnish, totally apt for noodles. Try this dish with a chilled dry rosé wine.

SERVES: 4

250g (9oz) dried or 450g (1lb) fresh egg noodles
3 tablespoons butter or extra virgin olive oil, or combination of both

salt to taste
plenty of freshly ground black pepper

GARNISH
crushed green pepper corns in brine (optional)
fresh green chilli, finely chopped (optional)

1   Boil the noodles until they are as al dente as you wish (*see page* 73). Then drain them and set them aside, keeping them warm if possible, for use later.

2   Heat the butter and/or olive oil in your wok.

3   Immediately add the drained noodles, and briskly stir-fry them

until they are well combined with the butter and/or oil, and are hot right through.

4 Salt to taste, then grind in liberal amounts of pepper.

5 Transfer to a serving bowl, garnish and serve.

Noodles à la Lyonnaise, au gratin

The classic Lyonnaise French dish uses potato, fried with butter and onion. But a lesser-known French classic uses noodles (*nouilles*) instead of the potatoes, and is an elegant starter (halve the quantities here), or main dish. And if you think this is a modern dish, we see on page 20 that Catherine de' Medici, the most celebrated member of a very powerful Tuscan family, married Henry II of France, and introduced noodles into the French court in the mid-1500s, from where they spread into other fashionable homes in Europe. It was a derivative of this dish that became Britain's macaroni cheese!

SERVES: 4

250g (9oz) dried or 450g (1lb) fresh egg noodles

4– 6 spring onions, leaves and bulbs, finely chopped

3 or 4 tablespoons butter

a fresh lemon or two, quartered

salt to taste

GARNISH

50g (1¾oz) fresh Parmesan cheese, grated

fresh grated nutmeg

sprigs of parsley

1 Boil the noodles until they are as al dente as you wish (*see page* 73). Then drain them and set them aside, keeping them warm if possible, for use later.

2 Heat the butter in your wok. Stir-fry the onions for about 2 minutes.

3 Immediately add the drained noodles, and briskly stir-fry them until they are well combined with the fried ingredients, and are hot right through.

4   Salt to taste, then transfer to a serving bowl. Squeeze on the juice of the lemon quarters.

5   Top the noodles with the Parmesan, and top that with freshly grated nutmeg. Sprinkle on the parsley and serve.

Noodles Napoletano

Noodles in a Traditional Mushroom, Peas, and Garlic Sauce

We see on page 17 that noodles were not invented in Italy, but in China around the time of the birth of Christ. The first positive record of noodles being made in mainland Italy does not appear until the 1400's. The honour goes to Naples, Italy's third largest city, founded in the sixth century BC, and incorporated into the Kingdom of Sicily in 1140. The first European reference to noodles occurred in Sicily in the Middle Ages. At that time, the island was under Arab domination, and it is probable that the noodles they mentioned were Chinese noodles, brought down the Silk Route.

Old habits die hard, as do old recipes. Here is the oldest, most traditional of all pasta sauce recipes, the Napoletano. Go into any good Naples restaurant and you will be sure to find this dish, served authentically, with exactly the ingredients used in the 1400's – ham, mushroom, peas, oregano, basil, wine and garlic. It is hard to believe that the ubiquitous Italian tomato did not come on to the Napoli scene until long after Columbus discovered it in America. But more modern interpretations of this dish do include tomato. I have included it as an option. The recipe works well with any wheat, egg or rice noodles, fresh or dried. Select the type of noodle you wish to use (*see pages* 44-49).

Incidentally, Naples is famous for inventing another world-class dish at around the same time – the pizza. One school of thought says 'pizza' derives from *pizzi*, to season. Or it could have come from the neighbouring Ottoman *Pitta* bread. Either way, the original pizza was a disc of dough, spread with garlic, ham, cheese and herbs, and baked. As with the Napoletano sauce, tomato came much later.

SERVES: 4

250g (9oz) dried or 450g (1lb) fresh egg or rice noodles

2 tablespoons sunflower oil

1 tablespoon extra virgin olive oil

3 or 4 cloves garlic, finely chopped

4–6 spring onions, leaves and bulbs, finely chopped

2 or 3 sun-dried tomatoes in oil, finely chopped (optional)

4 canned plum tomatoes, mashed (optional)

1 tablespoon tomato purée (optional)

50ml (2 fl oz) red wine

1 tablespoon finely chopped fresh oregano

1 tablespoon finely chopped basil

6–8 button mushrooms, cleaned and quartered

110g (4oz) frozen peas, thawed

salt and freshly ground black pepper to taste

2 or 3 tablespoons fresh lemon juice

GARNISH

60g (2oz) freshly grated Cheddar or Parmesan cheese

some flat-bladed parsley

1 Boil the noodles until they are as al dente as you wish (*see page* 73). Then drain them and set them aside, keeping them warm if possible, for use later.

2 Heat the oil in your wok. Stir-fry the garlic for 30 seconds, add the onion and the optional sun-dried tomatoes, and continue to stir-fry for a further 2 minutes.

3 Add the optional plum tomatoes, tomato purée, and the wine, oregano and basil, and when this is sizzling, add the mushrooms and peas.

4 Immediately add the drained noodles, and briskly stir-fry them until they are combined with the other ingredients, and are hot right through.

5 Salt and pepper to taste, then transfer to a serving bowl. Squeeze on the lemon juice.

6 Top the noodles with the grated Cheddar or Parmesan cheese, and top that with the flat-bladed parsley and serve.

PLATE ELEVEN

SAN FRANCISCO CRAB NOODLES IN PINK SAUCE Crab meat, prawns, king prawns and scampi, in a creamy pink sauce, served with somen pink noodles.

Noodles Ala Zappatora

Noodles with Sweet and Chilli Peppers and Fresh Herbs

Still in Naples, here is a lesser known, more recent recipe, which uses peppers, sweet bell peppers and chillies, lashed together with plenty of herbs. It is not for the faint-hearted, and even many Italians find the real thing too hot. Cut back on chilli content if you must, but please do not omit it! One key to success is to roast the peppers to remove their skin and sweeten them. This recipe works well with any wheat, egg or rice noodles, fresh or dried. Select the type of noodle you wish to use (*see pages* 44-49).

SERVES: 4

250g (9oz) dried, or 450g (1lb) fresh noodles
2 red bell peppers
2 green bell peppers
1 or 2 large Anaheim chillies (see page 54)
3 tablespoons butter
1 tablespoon extra virgin olive oil
4–6 cloves garlic sliced

200g (7oz) onions, chopped into 2cm x 2cm
   (¾ in) pieces
3 tablespoons chopped basil
2 tablespoons chopped flat-bladed parsley
sea salt to taste
1 lemon or 2 limes, quartered

GARNISH
freshly grated Parmesan cheese
freshly grated nutmeg

1   Roast and skin and finely chop the peppers and chillies. *See* Chef's tip, below.

2   Boil the noodles until they are as al dente as you wish (*see page* 73). Then drain them and set them aside, keeping them warm if possible, for use later.

PLATE TWELVE

HONEY NUT NOODLES Honey, almonds, walnuts, pistachio nuts, noodles and butter are stir-fried together using stir-fry dried rice noodles with 2mm strands.

3   Heat the butter and oil in your wok. Stir-fry the garlic for 30
    seconds, add the onions, and continue to stir-fry for a further 2
    minutes.
4   Add the peppers, chillies, basil and flat-bladed parsley.
5   Immediately add the drained noodles, and briskly stir-fry them until
    they are well combined with the other ingredients, and are hot right
    through.
6   Salt to taste, then transfer to a serving bowl. Squeeze on the lemon
    or lime juice.
7   Top the noodles with the Parmesan, and top that with freshly
    grated nutmeg. Sprinkle on the parsley and serve.

CHEF'S TIP

Roasting Chillies and Peppers

Any Bell Pepper, whether red, green, black, yellow or white changes
its nature when roasted, producing a pleasant sweet taste. Large
chillies can also be roasted. Here's how:

1   Keeping the peppers and chillies whole, wrap them in kitchen
    foil and place them under the grill at medium heat in the midway
    position on the rack.
2   After 8 minutes, remove the foil, and return them to the grill and
    cook until they singe irregularly a little.
3   Allow them to cool enough to handle, then peel, scrape off and
    discard the skin. If the peppers have not broken up already, cut
    them into bite-sized pieces.

NOTE: This whole operation can be done in bulk with a number
of peppers and chillies, and the finished items can be cooled then
frozen for future use, bit by bit. Freeze them on a tray, covered with
stretch film for 24 hours. Then place the frozen items together in a
labelled, airtight container, and return them to the freezer. Done
this way, the pieces will not stick together, and can be used on
demand.

CHAPTER NINE

SWEET NOODLES

Noodles as sweet dishes do not spring immediately to mind. Yet we all know of vermicelli pudding - that dish from the Victorian nursery. I am not a pudding person, myself, and there is, perhaps, a limit to the sweet noodle repertoire. Nevertheless, each of these six recipes has interesting and different characteristics.

My choice of dishes includes a more interesting version of the aforementioned nursery dish – Indian Sevian. It is a creamy, sweet vermicelli pudding topped with sugared almonds, and haunting with its subtle spicing of green cardamom. From the Old World comes Honey Nut Noodle served with Greek yoghurt.

Fruit Salad in a Bird's Nest is served cold with clotted cream, lime wedges and sprigs of mint, ideal, perhaps for a summer's day, while Noodle Fruit Compote makes a good contrast, served hot, perhaps in the depths of winter, topped with ice cream and noodle crisps. Golden Thread Sweet Balls are noodles carefully wrapped around an almond paste filling ball, then deep-fried. The result is really pretty, crispy, tasty and sweet, especially nice served with a fruit salad with ice cream. Finally try my variant of the famous savoury Chinese Spring Roll. Sweet Spring Rolls, with almond paste filling are amazing, served with crème fraîche or soured cream.

Indian Sevian

Creamy, Sweet Vermicelli Pudding

We see on page 21 that, although noodles have never featured largely in the Indian savoury diet, they have been enjoyed in sweet dishes for as long as anyone can remember. In the Punjab, sweet sev-like noodles are freshly made from wheat flour and squeezed through the murukus press (*see page* 102) to make a dish called Falooda, which is flavoured similarly to this Sevian recipe. Paloodeh originated in medieval Persia, and is still to be found there eaten with drizzlings of sour fruit syrup.

Judging by the fact that vermicelli recipes exist in various Indian regions, and the word 'vermicelli' appears in most of her languages, we can assume that vermicelli came to India in early times. In Delhi, for example, it, and the pudding it is made into, is called *Feni*. Elsewhere in India it appears under different names. In Hindi, for example, it is called *Sevian* or *Siwain*; in Tamil: *Semiya*; in Marathi: *Shevaya*, in Bengali: *Sewai*; in Kannada: *Shavige*; and in Kashmiri: *Ku'nu*. This traditional and very old recipe for Sevian uses Chinese rice vermicelli noodles, which were brought to India via Chinese and Arab traders, from the Spice Route, via Persia. Chinese noodles, they may be, but the initial treatment of the noodles, frying them raw, is uniquely Indian. And the dish is uniquely delicious.

SERVES: 4

250g (9oz) dried vermicelli rice noodles
200ml (7 fl oz) milk
200g (7oz) sweetened condensed milk
1½ teaspoons seeds from green cardamoms

4 tablespoons pure butter ghee
1 tablespoon golden sultanas
1 tablespoon molasses or brown sugar

GARNISH
sugared almonds (see Chef's tip below)

1   In a non-stick pan, bring the milk to the simmer, and add the condensed milk, and the cardamon seeds, and keep it at a rolling simmer.
2   Heat the ghee in your wok. Add the noodles, and stir-fry until the vermicelli goes golden (about 2 to 3 minutes). Add in the milk, sultanas and the molasses or sugar, and simmer the noodles until they are as al dente as you wish (*see page* 73).
3   Serve at once, garnishing with sugared almonds.

Sugared Almonds

These are delicious on their own or as a garnish for sweet dishes.

6 tablespoons butter ghee
200g (7oz) whole almonds, shelled
icing sugar

1   Heat the ghee in your wok, and stir-fry the nuts for 5 minutes.
2   Drain (keeping the ghee for another use). Sprinkle with icing sugar and store in a airtight container until needed.

Honey Nut Noodle

This is a simple dish with distinctly Old World tastes. Such ingredients were adored in biblical times, as they are today. Honey, almonds, walnuts, pistachio nuts, noodles and butter are stir-fried together. This recipe works well with any wheat, egg or rice noodles, fresh or dried. Select which type of noodle you wish to use (*see pages* 44-49).

sᴇʀᴠᴇs: 4

250g (9oz) dried, or 450g (1lb) fresh noodles
2 tablespoons unsalted butter
2 tablespoons chopped almonds
2 tablespoons chopped walnuts

2 tablespoons chopped pistachio nuts
6 green cardamom pods, cut open
6 tablespoons clear honey

1   Stir-fry the noodles until they are as al dente as you wish (*see page* 73).
2   Heat the butter in a non-stick pan. Stir-fry the nuts for about 1 minute, add the honey and continue to stir-fry for a further 30 seconds.

3   Add the nuts, with the cardamoms, to the noodles, and briskly stir-fry until they are hot right through.

4   Serve with Greek yoghurt.

Fruit Salad in a Bird's Nest

We met the Bird's Nest on *page* 100. It is, of course, a perfect food container, and need not be confined to savoury items. The nests do require some effort (although they are really easy to make), and they are a real dinner party talking point. My idea here is to make the nests well in advance, but fill them with freshly chopped chilled fruit at the last minute. That way the fruit does not make the nests soggy.

SERVES: 4

4 bird's nests (see page 100)   12 strawberries
12 bottled cherries   12 tangerine wedges
12 raspberries   1 banana, cut into 12 slices

GARNISH
thick clotted cream
icing sugar
4 lime wedges
sprigs of fresh mint

1   Make the bird's nests well in advance and let them cool to become crisp.

2   Just prior to serving, put the chilled fruit into each nest. Dollop on the cream, dust with icing sugar. Put a lime wedge on the side and a mint sprig on top.

Noodle Fruit Compote

This is a combination of hot fruit cooked in their own juices, with a little alcohol booster on a bed of hot noodles, topped with cold ice cream for a fabulous contrast of temperatures and tastes. Optionally garnish with the noodle crisps from *page* 100 for a further contrast of textures.

SERVES: 4

125g (4½oz) dried, or 225g (8oz) fresh egg
  noodles
6 peaches, stoned and sliced
6 apricots, stoned and sliced
4 Victoria plums, stoned and sliced
12 bottled cherries, pitted
2 tablespoons of the cherry juice

12 raspberries
2 tablespoons redcurrants
12 blackberries
2 tablespoons water
4 tablespoons crème de cassis
icing sugar (optional)

GARNISH
noodle crisps (see page 100)

1   Preheat the oven 190°C/ 375°F/Gas 5.
2   Place the fruit in a lidded casserole dish, and put into the oven.
3   Inspect after 20 minutes, turning the fruit over carefully. Repeat after another 20 minutes. It may need a little longer, depending on how firm you want the fruit. Add the crème de cassis and optional sugar to taste about 5 minutes before removing the fruit from the oven.
4   Towards the end of stage 3, boil the noodles until they are as al dente as you wish (*see page* 73). Then drain them and put them into four serving bowls.
5   To serve, carefully spoon the hot fruit and its liquid over the noodles. Top with ice cream and optional noodle crisps, and serve at once.

Golden Thread Sweet Balls

Golden-threads are noodles carefully wrapped around a raw filling ball, about 2cm in diameter, then deep-fried. We see on page 93 how to make these balls with a savoury filling. The result is a really pretty, crispy, tasty starter. It is equally nice to make a sweet version. Use fresh soft noodles for the wrapping and for the filling you can use the recipe below. Serve them to accompany a fruit salad with ice cream.

MAKES 16 BALLS

80g (3oz) fresh egg noodles

THE FILLING

85g (3oz) ground almonds
85g (3oz) icing sugar
whites of 2 eggs

30g (1oz) chopped raw pistachio nuts
spare egg noodles from above, finely chopped

1 Mix all the filling ingredients in a large bowl, using just enough water to create a mouldable stiff paste.
2 Soften the noodles and select 32 long strands.
3 Divide the filling into 16 to make balls about 2cm in diameter.
4 Press one end of a noodle strand on to a ball to make it stick. Carefully wind it around the ball, so that the strand doesn't overlap. Use water to help it stick. Wind the second strand over the first at right angles. Tuck the end into the centre. The filling should be entirely covered (but if it isn't it doesn't matter).
5 Repeat with the other 15 balls.
6 Preheat the oil to 190°C (chip-frying temperature).
7 Lower the balls into the oil and fry for 3 to 4 minutes.
8 Remove from the fryer, shaking off the excess oil.
9 Rest them on kitchen paper.
10 Dust with icing sugar, and serve hot or cold.

NOTE: see important deep-frying information on page 75.

Sweet Spring Rolls

We came across the celebrated Chinese Spring Roll on page 98. It consists of thin pastry – a small wonton wrapper (i.e. noodle pastry) which is wrapped into a tube shape around a filling. We normally think of them as savoury items, but they make a great surprise as a pudding item, served with crème fraîche or soured cream.

MAKES: 16 ROLLS

16 small wonton wrappers about 8–10cm (3–4 in) square
about 175g (6oz) filling (see previous recipe)

1   Mix the filling as in the previous recipe.
2   Lay one wrapper on the work surface.
3   Spread about 1½ teaspoons of filling near the top of the sheet. *See drawing (a) on page 98.*
4   Roll the top corner of the sheet over the filling (b).
5   Fold in the outside flaps (c).
6   Roll up reasonably tightly until the last corner remains (d).
7   Press this corner down with a little water. Rest the roll with this corner underneath (it helps it to stick).
8   Make the remaining spring rolls. Preheat the deep-fry oil to 190°C (chip-frying temperature).
9   One by one put about 8 rolls into the oil (too many, too fast will lower the temperature too much). Fry for 5 to 6 minutes, until golden.
10 Remove from the fryer, shaking off the excess oil.
11 Rest on kitchen paper.
12 Cook the remaining rolls.
13 Dust with icing sugar, serve hot or cold with lemon wedges and crème fraîche.

NOTE: see important deep-frying information on page 75.

THE NOODLE DIRECTORY

There are really only a basic few noodles, as described on pages 44-49, but there are many different names for them. Here is an alphabetical list, in many languages:

KEY:
(B) = Burmese; (C) = Chinese; (I) = Indian; (ID) = Indonesian; (J) = Japanese; (K) Korean; (L) = Lao; (M) = Malaysian; (N) = Nepalese; (PR) = Persian; (P) = Philippino; (S) = Singaporean; (T) = Thai; (TB) Tibetan; (V) = Vietnamese

Angel hair noodles – very thin strands (see Black angel hair noodle)

Arrowroot noodles – from Szechuan, China; dried and thread-like, yellow to amber in colour

Ba Mee (T) – egg noodles

Bahn or Bun (V) – thin-stranded rice noodles

Bahn Hoi (V) - Thinnest strand rice noodles (vermicelli)

Bahn Pho (V) – flat rice stick noodles narrow, 5mm per strip

Baifa (C) – Chinese somen

Bean-starch noodles – see bean thread noodles

Bean thread noodles, Fan-si, Fen-szu, Fun-see or Fun-sie (all C); Harusame (J); Khao poon chin (L); Mee-hoon (C); Sai fun (C); Sha-wo foon (V); Ohoon (M); So-un (ID); Tanghoon (M); Wun-sen (T) – thin and transparent, made from mung, soy and other beans. Also called bean-starch, cellophane, glass, jelly, pea-starch, shining, transparent, translucent.

Bee hun (ID) – thin dried rice stick noodles

Beijing moodles – also called Shanghai noodles

Bhamee or Bhami (ID) – Indonesian word for noodles

Black angel hair noodles – thin-stranded wheat noodles, coloured jet black using squid ink

Bihon (P) – Philippino word for noodles. See Bee hun and Pancit bihon

Bijon noodles – dried noodles made from cornflour

Bird's nest – noodles formed like a bird's nest; see index

219

Buckwheat noodles – see Soba

Cellophane noodles – See bean thread noodles

Cha-soba (J) – green powdered tea added to somen (qv) dough for flavouring and colouring

Chee-cheong-fun (M) – dried rice stick noodles

Chilli noodles – wheat noodles with chilli added for red colouring and flavouring

Chau-Chau (N) – general Nepalese word for noodles; Nepalese noodles are normally made from wheat flour, though rice, maize and millet are also used

Chau-Chau Batulo (N) – round noodles

Chau-Chau Chyapto (N) – flat noodles

Chauzhoo (C) – wheat vermicelli noodles

Chow mein (C) – stir-fried noodles

Chuka Soba (J) – see Ramen

Coloured noodles – liquid colouring is added to the dough; see black, chilli, green, green tea, pink, red and spinach in this directory

Cream noodles – wheat noodles; flat white strips

Crispy noodles – noodles made from potato flour, which when stir-fried in oil, go crispy

Curly noodles – egg noodles (qv), machine-twisted into tight twists or curls

Dan Mien (Cantonese) – round or flat egg noodles

Ee-fu (C) – egg noodles with very thin, round strands

Ee-mien (C) – Flat egg noodles

Egg noodles, Ba Mee (T); Dan Mien (Cantonese); Ee-fu (C); Ee-Mien (C); Go-nga Thukpa (TB); Hokkein Mee (C &S); Yee fu mein (C) – wheat flour dough with (duck) eggs added

Fan-si, fen-szu, fun-see or fun-sie (C) – beanthread noodles

Ghook-su (K) – general Korean word for noodles

Glass noodles – see bean thread noodles

Go-nga Thukpa (TB) – egg noodles

Green noodles – see Cha-soba and Spinach noodles

Green tea noodles – see Cha-soba

Gwaytio (T) – fresh rice noodles

Hard wheat noodles – see pasta and somen

Harusame (J) – bean thread noodles, literally, 'spring rain'

Hiyamugi (J) – dried wheat noodle, between somen and udon in size; served cold

Hokkein Mee (C & S) – thick-stranded (ribbon) egg noodles

Ho fan or Hor fun (C) – general Chinese word for rice noodles

Instant noodles – a slight overstatement, but many dry noodles are labelled 'instant'; in fact, their cooking takes just a few minutes

Jelly noodles – see Bean thread noodles

Kaushwe or Kauskee (B) – general Burmese word for noodle

Khao-Poon (L) – general Lao word for noodle, literally meaning 'rice noodle'; it is actually rice vermicelli noodle

Khao Poon Chin (L) – bean thread noodles; the only other type of noodle eaten in Laos apart from Khao-Poon

Kishimen (J) – type of udon (qv) wheat noodle, but broader and flatter

Kuaytiaw or Kwaytew or Gwaytio (T) – fresh rice noodles

Kuaytiaw Sen Yai (T) – fresh rice noodles 2–3 cm (about 1in) wide per strip

Kuaytiaw Jeen (T) – see rice noodles

Lai-fun (C) – dried rice stick noodles

Laksa (M) – Malaysian general word for noodles; also means fresh rice noodles

Longevity noodle – long noodles (supposed to give long life); also known as Mee Truong Tho (T)

Look-fun (C) – fresh rice noodles

Lo-mein or Lu mein (C) – fresh white flour wheat noodles, or noodles in a sauce

Lunchbox noodles – a brand name for a container with rapid-cooking Curly noodles (qv), and flavouring sachets

Mee (T) – general Thai word for noodles

Mee-hoon (C) – bean thread noodles

Mee-fun or Mi foon (C) – dried rice stick noodles

Mein or Mie (C) – general Chinese words for noodles

Mein-chhitshi (TB) – rice noodles

Menrui (J) – general Japanese word for noodles

Miki (C) – egg noodles to which soda and ash are added

Miswa (C) – very fine wheat noodles

Nest noodles – noodles arranged in nest-like clumps (not to be confused with Bird's nest noodles)

Ngunsi-fun (B) – dried rice stick noodles

Pan Mein (C) – tossed boiled noodles served with other ingredients

Pancit Bihon (P) – rice sticks

Pasta – the generic term for Italian noodles, which are always made from hard wheat flour, i.e. flour high in gluten content; see Wheat flour and index

Pea-starch – see Bean thread noodles

Pink noodles – somen (qv) noodles coloured stawberry ice-cream pink using food colouring; see index

Pot noodles – a product name for par-cooked, ready-flavoured noodles in a small plastic pot. Adding boiling water reconstitutes them in seconds. Not for the serious cook, perhaps, but popular none the less

Ramen (J) – Japanese version of Chinese egg or wheat noodles, they come in many dried forms, as crinkly tangles, bunches or packs; called Chuka Soba in western Japan

Red noodles – see Chilli noodles

Reshteh (PR) – literally means 'thread' in Persian, and refers to thin wheat noodles

Ribbon noodles – any dried flat, thin ribbon-like noodle (though usually rice)

Rice noodles, Bahn or Bun (V); Gwaytio (T); Khao-Poon (L); Kuaytiaw (T); Kuaytiaw Sen Yai (T); Kwaytew (T); Laksa (M); Look-fun (C); Sa hor fun (M); Sen lek (T) – noodles made of rice flour.

Rice sticks, Bahn Pho (V); Bee hun (ID); Chee-cheong-fun (M); Lai-fun (C); Mee-fun or Mi foon (C); Mein-chhitshi (TB); Ngunsi-fun (B); Pancit Bihon (P); Sen Mee (T) – dried, flat, rice flour noodles

Rice vermicelli noodles, Bahn Hoi (V); Kuaytiaw Jeen (T) – wiry, very thin, dried variety which resembles highly tangled, pure white, thin, brittle string

Sa Hor Fun (M) – flat rice flour noodles

Sai Fun (C) – Bean thread noodles; literally sia fun means 'falling rain'

Sen lek (T) – flat rice flour noodles, narrow, 5mm per strip

Sen-Mee (T) – dried rice stick noodles with thin, 1–2mm strands

Sen Yai Neung (T) – fresh rice-noodle sheet

Sevian (I) – vermicelli type noodles, see Index

Shanghai noodles – wheat flour noodles, very white in colour, ranging in size from thin somen-type rods to flat udon-type strips, made in China and Hong Kong

Sha-wo Foon (V) – see Bean thread noodles

Shiritaki (J) – very thin translucent noodle made from konnyaku, or elephant's foot or devil's tongue (amorphhopallus rivieri); always accompanies sukiyaki (see glossary)

Soba (J) – a very popular type of flat stick noodle in Japan, made from buckwheat

Soft wheat noodles – see Wheat noodles

Sohoon (M) or So-un (ID) – see Bean thread noodles

Somen (J) – round thin hard-wheat noodles, usually white but can be coloured

Spinach noodles – wheat noodles coloured a pretty shade of green, using spinach liquid

Stir-fry noodles – noodles designed to be stir-fried

Tang Mein (C) – noodles in soup

Tanghoon (M) – see Bean thread noodles

Thukpa/Thupa(TB) – general Tibetan word for noodles; Tibetan noodles are normally made from wheat flour, though rice, maize and millet are also used

Translucent or Transparent noodles – see Bean thread noodles

Udon (J) – noodles from soft-wheat, available fresh and dried, in varying sizes; the former are generally quite chunky, and square in cross-section; the latter are in flat strips. See Kishimen.

Udon Sotangon (M) – fine wheat noodles, served in Laksa dishes; see index

Vermicelli – Very fine thread-like noodles, from any dough; see Bean thread noodles

Wo Mein (C) – Noodles cooked in the pot, with their sauce

Wheat noodles – their flour is made from the endosperm component of wheat grain, i.e. white flour. Generally 'soft' white flour is used (i.e. flour with less gluten). Types include Lo-Mein (C), Ramen (J), and Pasta.

Wholewheat noodles or Yee-mein (C) – their flour is made from the bran component of whole wheat grain, i.e. brown flour, giving them a chewier texture and a pleasant brown colour

Wun-sen (T) – bean thread noodles made from soya beans; they are only available dried, not fresh, and resemble thinly spun fibre-glass in colour, texture and taste too, when raw.

Yee-mein (C) – brown wholewheat (qv) flour wheat noodles

Yee Fu Mein (C) – flavoured, pre-fried and dried egg noodles

GLOSSARY

This glossary covers items other than noodles (see pages 219-222). It is extensive, covering certain items not mentioned in the recipes. It is intended to be used as a reference work. Whether or not you find a particular word here, it is worth checking to see whether it is in the index. It may lead you to further information in the main text of the book.

KEY:

(B) = Burmese; (C) = Chinese; (I) = Indian; (ID) = Indonesian; (J) = Japanese; (K) Korean; (L) = Lao; (M) = Malaysian; (N) = Nepalese ; (P) = Philippino; (S) = Singaporean; (T) = Thai; (TB) Tibetan; (V) = Vietnamese

A

Asafoetida or Hing (I) – Indian spice made from a resin which oozes from a tree. Used in fish and lentil dishes. Rather smelly until cooked.

B

Baa Kuk Tee (C) – Chinese taste or ten-spice powder

Bay sweetcorn – tiny complete cobs of maize, cropped before they are fully grown

Bamboo shoots – soft edible tips of the bamboo plant; the canned ones are whole or sliced

Bay leaf – aromatic leaf used dried as a spice

Bean curd – see Tofu

Bean sprouts – made by causing beans (soya or mung are the most common) to sprout into crisp and pure white sprouts; highly nutritious and almost as good from the can

Bengal gram – see Gram flour

Blachan (T) – see Shrimp paste

Bonito (J) flakes – dried fish used to flavour Japanese stocks

Brown sauce – a bottled condiment, in the form of a thick smooth brown liquid, very popular on the British dining table, containing spices and tamarind

C

Candle nut, Buah keras (M), kemiri or tingkih

(ID) – round nuts from the candleberry tree native to Asia. Used to thicken Indonesian and Malaysian curries. See also Macadamia nut

Cardamom or Elaichi (I) – fragrant spice; two main pod types of which brown is a little more astringent than the smaller green

Cassia bark or Dalchini (I) – the rather coarse bark of a species of cinnamom, with a sweetish fragrance. Not as fine as Cinnamon (qv).

Cayenne – a particularly hot chilli used in Indian cookery

Cheddar – Soft white or creamy yellow English cheese

Chile – a variant spelling of Chilli

Chili – a variant spelling of a spice mixture used in the dish Chilli con Carné (see index)

Chilli – the world's hottest and most popular spice

Chinese cabbage or Pak Choi (C) – a cross between cabbage and lettuce that is white or pale green in colour and crisp in texture

Chinese leaf or spinach, Pe-tsai (C) – dark green in colour, with a white bulbous stem. Used, amongst other things, to make deep-fried 'seaweed'.

Chinpi (J) – dried citrus such as mandarin peel used in Shichimi Togarashi Japanese seven-spice powder

Cilantro – see Coriander seed

Cinnamon or Dalchini (I) – fine quills of bark from the cinnamon tree, with a sweetish fragrance. See Cassia bark

Clove – a popular, much-used, fragrant spice

Coriander seed – Dhania (I). The round seed is the spice most widely used in curry cooking. The leaf, also called Cilantro, is used as a herb

Cumin seed or Jeera (I) – a savoury spice used in curry cooking

Curry leaves, Kari Patia or Kari Phulia (I) – small fresh or dried leaves imparting a distinctive flavour to south Indian/Malaysian curries

Curry paste – refers to a bottled product containing curry spices cooked in oil

D

Dark soy sauce – see Soy

Dashi (J) – stock accompanying soba dishes containing kombu, bonito, mirin, sugar and shoyu

Dong-gu (C) – see Mushrooms, dried

F

Fennel seed – small green aromatic spice used in both Chinese and Indian cooking

Fenugreek seed or Methi (I) – savoury curry spice

Fish sauce, Nga-pya (B), tuk trey (C), padek (L), patis (P), nam pla (T), nuoc mam (V) – widely used in south-east Asian countries as a salting agent in place of soy sauce

Food colouring – refers to tartrazine (coal-based) dyes of red, yellow, green, etc. Said to have side-effects. Used unnecessarily to enhance the colour of tandoori and char siu products (see index), but not used in India and China.

G

Galangal, Lengkuas (M), kenkur, laos or isen (ID), kha (T) – a type of ginger

Garam masala (I) – a mixture of Indian spices

Gari (J) – pickled ginger, usually pink in colour, prepared by salting the ginger and then immersing it in vinegar

Ghee – clarified butter used in Indian and Middle Eastern cooking

Ginger powder – finely ground, pungent powder

Gram flour or Besan (I) – made from ground chana(I) yellow lentils

H

Hemp – cannabis seed used in shichimi togarashi (J) seven-spice powder

Hoisin (C) – thick sweet sauce, based on soya bean, also called barbecue sauce

J

Juliennes – food, particularly vegetables, cut into thin strips, 1–2mm by 3 cm

K

Kaffir (T) – sweet lime

Kampyo (J) – A dried strip of gourd from the Japanese Yugao (calabash) plant

Kaiso (J) – See seaweed

Ketchap manis (ID) – Indonesian version of soy sauce. It is sweeter and stickier than Chinese soy. The Conimex brand is available world-wide but if you can't find it, use dark soy with brown sugar added to taste

Kelp or Kaiso (J) – type of seaweed

Kimchi (K) – pickled vegetables

Kombu (J) – type of seaweed

Konnyaku (J), elephant's foot or devil's tongue (vegetable) – see Shiritaki noodles in Noodle directory

L

Lemon grass, Sereh (ID), serai (M), takrai (T) – fragrant grass stem

Light soy sauce – see Soy

Liquorice powder – used in Chinese ten-spice powder

Lovage seeds or Ajwain (I) – astringent spice used in Indian cooking

M

MSG or Monosodium glutamate – a powder unnecessarily added to Chinese restaurant food in particular, to enhance taste

Macadamia nut – Round nuts from a tree native to Australasia. Can substitute for candle nuts to thicken Indonesian and Malaysian curries

Mace – a fragrant spice, whose outer tendril surrounds the nutmeg

Magic paste – see page 80

Magret de canard – duck breast

Mamra (I) – see puffed rice

Mango powder or Am chur (I) – very sour powder made by grinding dried mangoes; used in Indian cooking

Mirin (J) – cooking wine

Miso (J) – flavouring paste

Mixed dried herbs – used in Italian cooking and typically containing chervil, parsley, sorrel and tarragon

Mu-er (C) – see Mushroom

Mushroom – Cloud ears or wood ears (mu-er) are used mainly for texture

Mushroom, dried, Dong-gu (C), Shitaké (J) – these are reconstituted in water and used in cooking

Mustard seed or Rai (I) – tiny black, brown or yellow seeds used in Indian cookery

N

Nabemono (J) – food cooked directly on the table in a copper pan above a flame

Nam Pla (T) – see Fish sauce

Ng Heung Fun (C) – Chinese five-spice powder

Nga-pi (B) – see Shrimp paste

Noori (J) – paper-thin seaweed

Nigella seed or Kalonji (I) – a tiny jet-black seed used as an aromatic spice in Indian cooking

Nyuoc Mam (V) – see Fish sauce

O

Oregano – a sweetish dried herb, also called marjoram

Oyster sauce – a condiment and cooking sauce made from soy, oyster extract, sugar and vinegar

P

Pak-choi (C) – see Chinese Cabbage

Palm sugar – fudge-like sweet sap collected from the palm tree, and popular in Thai cooking

Panch Phoran (I) – a Bengali mixture of five (panch) spices

Paprika – means pepper in Hungarian, and is a powder made by grinding bright red peppers. Usually mild, though can be hot. Also comes from Spain

Parmesan – a hard Italian cheese

Peppercorns – a most popular spice. The spherical seeds, initially green, turn black after sun-drying. White pepper is obtained by removing the black skin.

Pesto – an Italian paste from pesato (crushed) ingredients. Green pesto is made from olive oil, basil, Parmesan cheese, pine nuts and garlic. Red pesto contains the above, plus sun-dried tomato, red pepper and carrot.

Pe-tsai (C) - see Chinese Leaves or Spinach

Plum tomatoes – particularly flavourful Italian tomatoes

Poppy seed, white – a tiny white seed used as a spice to thicken Indian curries

Prawn or fish powder – made by grinding dried fish or prawn

Puffed rice or Mamra (I) – used in bhel puri. See index

R

Rice – see Sushi rice

Rice flour – made by milling rice grain

Rice vinegar (C) – made by distilling wine. Colours available as for rice wine, see below

Rice wine (C) – red white or yellow. Distinctive in flavour and good in cooking, to get an authentic taste. Sherry or any wine can be substituted, though they are different. See also Saké, Mirin, Shaoxing.

S

Saffron – the world's most expensive spice, obtained by drying the stigma of a particular crocus

Saké (J) – Japanese drinking wine

Sambal (ID) – a condiment or chutney, such as Sambal Manis (sweet chilli) and Sambal Oelek (hot chilli)

Sansho pepper (J) – prickly-ash seeds used in shichimi togarashi, Japanese seven-spice powder

Santaka (J) – a fairly hot, deep red chilli

Sarashi negi (J) – a type of leek

Seaweed or Kaiso (J) – used widely in Japanese and Chinese cooking

Sesame – black seeds used in shichimi togarashi, (J) seven-spice powder

Shaoxing (C) – best-quality Chinese yellow rice wine

Shichimi Togarashi (J) – Japanese seven-spice powder

Shitaké (J) – see Mushroom

Shoga (J) – ginger

Shoyu (J) – Japanese soy sauce

Shrimp Paste, Nga-pi (B), kapi (T), terasi or trasi (ID), petis, balchan or belecan (M), hay koh or hahm ha or hsien sha (C), mam ruoc (V) – made from salt and ground prawns. Though used in small quantities, it gives a vital, but not fishy flavour, in the cooking of many south-east Asian countries

Soy – salty, thin, dark sauce made by fermenting soya beans. See index

Soya bean sauce – available red, black or yellow

Star anise – a pretty aromatic spice used in Chinese and Indian cooking

Sukiyaki (J) – one-pot dish of beef and vegetables; see Shiritaki noodles in Noodle directory and index

Sushi mat or Makisu (J) – small bamboo mat used to form sushi nori rolls

Sushi Nori (J), Nori maki, or makisushi – rice-filled rolls. See Nori in index

Sushi rice or Mochigome (J) – a variety of glutinous rice

Szechuan chillies – small, pungent and deep crimson-red when ripe

Szechuan peppercorns (fagara) – not a real member of the peppercorn family, nor as pungent. Used in Chinese five-spice (qv)

T

Tamarind or Asam (M) – a very sour, date-like pod

Tandoori paste – refers to a bottled product containing curry spices, mixed in acetic acid

Tofu – bean curd made from soya beans

Tomato ketchup – a popular, sweet, bottled sauce made from tomatoes and sugar

Tomato passata sauce – natural Italian tomato purée, passata meaning 'passed' (through a sieve)

Tomato purée – very intense, long-life, thicker version of the above

Togarashi (J) – chilli, see Santaka

Turmeric or Huldi (I) – a yellow powder used in curry cooking

W

Wasabi (J) – green horseradish

Water Chestnut – a crunchy white vegetable, unrelated to sweet chestnuts

Wu Hsiang Fen – Chinese five-spice powder

Wei Fen – Chinese taste or ten-spice powder

White radish, Daikon (J), mooli (I) – a long white crispy vegetable

Wine – see Rice wine, Mirin, Saké, Shaoxing

Wonton – thin wheat-flour sheets used in Chinese cooking to wrap small food parcels, which are then cooked

Worcester sauce – a British invention from 1838, using a mixture of spices, chilli, tamarind and fish sauce

THE STORE CUPBOARD

This list may look a bit formidable, but it is a full list of all the specialist items you need to cook the recipes in this book. Unless you plan to work your way through each and every recipe (and I hope you do), you will not need to buy everything in one go. Of course, many of these items last for ages (most well beyond their official 'best-by' dates) in the store cupboard, the fridge or even the freezer. But, unless you enjoy stocking everything (and why not?), I suggest you photocopy this list then, putting it alongside the recipes you first wish to try, tick off all the items you need on the photocopy, and buy them. The items marked with a star ★ are Blue Dragon products (see page 233).

DRIED NOODLES

Chinese
Bean thread noodles	★100g packet
Egg noodles (wheat)	★250g packet
Mie nest noodles (wheat)	★250g packet
Thin vermicelli rice (Stir-fry) noodles	★250g packet
Thick rice noodles	★250g packet
Wholewheat noodles	★250g packet

Japanese
Ramen noodles (wheat)	
Soba noodles (buckwheat)	
Somen noodles (wheat)	
Udon noodles (wheat)	★190g packet

Flavoured noodles
Chilli noodles (wheat)	★250g packet
Crispy noodles (potato)	★125g box
Spinach egg noodles (wheat)	★250g packet

FLOURS FOR NOODLE MAKING

Buckwheat flour
Gram flour
Millet flour
Plain white flour
Rice flour
Semolina
Strong white flour
Cornflour

BOTTLED INGREDIENTS

Ginger, for sushi, pickled	*145g jar
Lemon grass whole stalks	*210g jar
Lemon grass, thinly sliced	*210g jar
Medium or mild Indian curry paste	
Minced coriander	*210g jar
Minced garlic	*210g jar
Minced ginger	*210g jar
Minced green chilli	*210g jar
Minced hot chilli, red	*210g jar
Minced sweet basil	*210g jar
Peppercorns, green, in brine	
Pesto, green and red	*163g jar
Piri Piri chillies	*100g jar
Sambal Oelek (hot chilli) Conimex	*200g jars
Sambal Manis (Sweet chilli)	*200g jars
Sun-dried tomato in oil	
Tandoori paste	
Thai curry paste, green	*210g jar
Thai curry paste, red	*210g jar
Thai 'Magic paste'	*210g jar
Tom Yum soup paste	*210g jar

CANNED FOODS

Anchovies in oil	50g can
Baby corn cobs	*410g can
Bamboo slices and water chestnuts	*225g can
Bean sprouts	*410g can
Chinese stir-fry vegetables	*410g can
Coconut milk	*400ml can
Crab & sweetcorn soup (for fish stock)	*410g can
Chicken & sweetcorn soup (for chicken stock)	*410g can
Plum tomatoes	400g can
Straw mushrooms	*410g can
Red kidney beans	*432g can

CONDIMENTS/SAUCES

Black soya bean sauce	*120g sachet
Chilli dipping sauce	*190ml bottle
Chilli sauce	*150ml bottle
Chilli and garlic sauce	*150ml bottle
Fish sauce, Thai	*190ml bottle
Hoisin sauce	*250ml jar
Oyster sauce	*150ml bottle
Red soya bean paste	
Teriyaki marinade	*150ml bottle

Cooking wine and vinegar

Chinese red, yellow rice wine	
Mirin Japanese cooking wine	*150ml bottle
Rice vinegar, Chinese white	*150ml bottle
Saké Japanese rice wine	*150ml bottle

Soya sauces

Chinese dark	*150 or 300ml bottle
Chinese light	*150 or 300 bottle
Ketchap Manis (Indonesian, sweet)	*125 or 250ml bottle
Japanese shoyu	*150ml bottle
Japanese shoyu with wasabi	*150ml bottle

DRIED FOODS

Bonito fish flakes, dried	
Chillies, hot, dried	*50g packet
Coconut, creamed	*200g packet
Desiccated coconut	
Coconut milk powder	*160g packet
Dashi stock mix	
Five-spice seasoning	*45g jar
Galangal, cut and dried	*70g packet
Kombu (kelp)	
Lemongrass, cut and dried	*60g packet
Lime leaves (Kaffir), cut and dried	*50g packet
Miso soup	*90g box
Mushrooms, dried Chinese, black	*25g packet
Palm sugar	200g tub
Prawn crackers	*100g box

APPENDIX I: THE STORE CUPBOARD

Prawn (or fish) powder		Cassia bark
Puffed rice *(mamra)*	★100g packet	Cardamom, brown
Rice-flour pancakes	★50g packet	Cardamom, green
Rice, for sushi	★500g packet	Cinnamon
Seaweed, crispy (vac packed)	★55g packet	Cloves
Sev (gram flour snack)	300g block	Coriander seeds
Seven-spice seasoning (Japanese)	★45g jar	Cummin seeds
Shrimp paste	200g tub	Curry leaves
Sushi Nori seaweed sheets	★22g packet	Fennel seeds
Tamarind block	300g block	Fenugreek seed
Tempura batter mix	★150g packet	Liquorice powder
Tofu, firm	★297g box	Lovage
Wasabi paste	★45g tube	Mace
Wasabi powder	★45g jar	Mustard, black
		Nigella
		Nutmeg
		Peppercorn, black

NUTS

Almonds	50g	Sesame, black
Peanuts		Sesame, white
Pine nut	50g	star anise
Pistachio (green)	100g	
Macadamia or cashew nuts		

Ground Spices
Chilli
Coriander
Cumin

OILS

Chilli-flavoured oil	★150ml bottle	Garlic powder
Ghee	250g pack	Ginger powder
Olive oil, extra virgin		Mango powder
Pistachio nut oil		Paprika
Sesame oil	★150ml bottle	Pepper, white
Stir-fry oil (garlic flavoured)	★300ml bottle	Turmeric
Soy oil		
Sunflower oil		
Vegetable oil		DRIED HERBS
Walnut oil		

dried chives
mixed dried herbs

SPICES

VARIOUS

Whole spices
Aniseed
Bay leaves

Chopsticks/Fortune cookies/Sushi mat/
Wok kit

BLUE DRAGON

According to Chinese lore, when Buddha called a feast in his honour, the twelve animals who attended were the rat, buffalo, tiger, rabbit, snake, horse, goat, monkey, rooster, dog, pig and dragon. To show his gratitude for their presence, Buddha honoured the animals by naming a year after each one. This symbol lasts for a full year, and it is said that people inherit the characteristics of the animal in whose year they are born. For example, 1998 is the Year of the Tiger, whose characteristics are strength and deep thinking; the rabbit (business acumen and affection) 1999; the snake (wisdom and determination) 2001; the horse (confidence and good cheer) 2002; the goat (creativity and wisdom) 2003; the monkey (skill and decisiveness) 2004; the rooster (workaholic and adventurous outlook) 2005; the dog (loyalty and industriousness) 2006; the pig (courage and kindness) 2007; the rat (charm and persistence) 2008; the buffalo (a placid nature and easy-going outlook) 2009. To calculate which is your animal, simply deduct or add in multiples of twelve years. For example, a person born in 1966 is a horse, while those born in 1940 are dragons.

To the Chinese, the dragon represents the greatest celestial power, symbolising life and growth, virtue, riches, harmony and longevity. It is apt that its sign will coincide with the start of the new millennium – the year 2000. A dragon is full of energy, sincerity and honesty. It is also a mythical figure. But its additional properties, fire-breathing and wings, make it more than a reptile, and lift it into a symbol of strength and ambition – a guardian and protector. To the Chinese, of all the twelve life symbols in their calendar, the dragon is the most exciting.

As such it is apt that it should be the symbol of Blue Dragon. As for the colour, blue is considered by Chinese philosophers to be the colour with the most depth. Red is associated with fire, energy and aggression, and green with nature, youth and truth. Blue is the clear unclouded sky, and the deep blue sea. It symbolises maturity and reflection, quality and purity.

The Blue Dragon range of Chinese products was the first of its kind to be introduced into Britain. The year was 1976, auspiciously another dragon year, and it was the time when the back-street Chinese restaurants were fast becoming popular and fashionable. As with the Indian restaurant, Chinese food (then largely Cantonese) was new, exciting, and tasty. Above all it was cheap and, not surprisingly, the number of Chinese restaurants was increasing rapidly. However, until 1976, it was not considered possible to do their cooking at home.

Blue Dragon changed all that. Its range of products, specially created to make it easy for the home cook to turn out first-rate, authentic oriental dishes thrived at once, and has subsequently grown to become, arguably, the leader in its field. No competitor has such an extensive range, and no others have introduced so many new and innovative products. Such is the quality of Blue Dragon's range that it comes as no surprise to find that many Chinese restaurants now use Blue Dragon catering products themselves.

The Blue Dragon range is widely available at delicatessens and supermarkets and now includes Japanese and Thai ingredients as well as Chinese, and as you would expect with such a popular brand, there are always new products coming on to the market. Blue Dragon experts regularly travel the Eastern world to seek out new ideas and suppliers, and also to help them maintain the quality and authenticity of existing products. Around one hundred and fifty core items have been marketed from the brand's inception, including all the perennial favourites and bestsellers. No one has a better range of delicious Chinese, Thai, Korean and Japanese cooking sauces, condiments, dips, soups, oils, oriental fruits and vegetables, accompaniments and, of course, noodles. No detail is missed, as is evidenced by such practical and fun items as wok kits, chopsticks, sushi mats and the like, not forgetting the fortune-telling Blue Dragon fortune cookie!

For a full-colour brochure of Blue Dragon noodles and other products available, please send an s.a.e. to:

Blue Dragon Noodles,
G. Costa and Co Ltd,
Unit VI. Quarry Wood Industrial Estate,
Mills Road, Aylesford, Kent, ME20 7NA

INDEX

almonds, sugared, 213
angel's hair noodles, soup, 117
arrowroot noodles, 44
asparagus, chicken noodle soup, 116
Australia:
    Darling Harbour crab claws noodles, 185

bacon, noodles alla carbonara, 145
barley, 40
basil, 58
beansprouts, spring rolls, 98
Béchamel sauce, 147
beef:
    chilli bean noodle, 149
    Chinese restaurant style, 138
    chop suey, 162
    chow mein, 175
    ground, 90
    mince and celery bolognese, 144
    salad with grapes and noodles, 120
    Thai soup, 109
    with black bean, 130
    with mixed vegetables and vermicelli noodles,
       134
bhel puri, 103
birds' nests, 100, 214
black bean and beef egg noodle, 130
black pepper and butter with noodles, 205
Blue Dragon, 233–4
broad bean noodles, 45

buckwheat, 40
buckwheat noodles, 45
Burma:
    chicken and shrimp noodles, 152
    spicy noodle fish soup, 107
butter and black pepper with noodles, 205

canneloni, 181
caramelised topping with crispy noodles, 195
carbonara, noodles alla, 145
cellophane noodles, 45
Char Siu:
    chop suey, 162
    chow mein, 176
    pork with noodles, 140
chicken:
    and shrimp noodles, 152
    and sweetcorn soup, 115
    and tomato Bolognese noodles, 167
    chop suey, 160
    chow mein, 176
    crispy noodles, 139
    green curry and noodles, 154
    ground, 90
    Malay-style curry, 156
    noodle soup, 115
    noodle asparagus soup, 116
    noodle mushroom soup, 116
    spicy soup, 110
    soup with rice noodles, 113

fish continued:
 udon, 171
Five-spice powder, 82, 85
France: noodles à la Lyonnaise, 206
freezing, 37
fruit:
 compote, 215
 salad, 123
 salad, in a bird's nest, 214
fun sie, 46

galangal, 50
Garam Masala, 83
garlic, 50
 pickled, with glass noodles and cucumber, 194
ginger, 52
 pickled, 86
glass noodles, 46
 stir-fried with cucumber and pickled garlic, 194
 with pastrami and sweet and sour sauce, 148
golden-thread noodles:
 pork balls, 93
 sweet balls, 216
gram flour, 41
Greece: honey nut noodles with Greek yoghurt, 213
green beans, with mangetout and coconut, 196

history of noodles, 16–23
hiyamugi, 116
honey:
 honey nut noodles, 213
 pastrami glass noodles with lime and honey sauce, 148
hor-fun, 46

India:
 Bajra Talipeeth, 199
 Bhel Puri, 103
 Bolobi besan noodles, 200

Garam Marsala, 83
Panch Phoran, 83
Sev, 102
Sev Tamatar, 197
Sevian, 211
Indonesia:
 Bahmi Goreng (stir-fried noodles), 131
 noodles with mangetout, green beans and coconut, 196
instant noodles, 50
Italy:
 canneloni creamy noodles, 181
 chicken bolognese, 167
 lasagne noodle, 146
 mince and celery bolognese, 144
 minestrone, 117
 Napoletano noodles, 207
 noodles alla carbonara, 145
 noodles with butter and black pepper, 205
 prosciutto salad, 127
 Zappatora, noodles ala, 209

Japan:
 Dashi stock, 79
 fish udon, 171
 hiyamugi, 116
 kare udon, 201
 ramen pork, 141
 salad, 126
 Seven-spice powder, 83
 shirataki sukiyaki, 143
 soba noodles with tempura, 172
 somen, 126
 sushi, 95
 sushi nori, 95
 wheat noodles, 46

king prawn:
 chop suey, 162
 chow mein, 176
 crispy noodles, 139